SCOTTISH COMMUNITY DRAMA ASSOCIATION EASTERN DIVISIONAL LIBRARY EDINBURGH

GALLOWS GLORIOUS
Ronald Gow

LADY PRECIOUS STREAM
S. I. Hsiung

RICHARD OF BORDEAUX
Gordon Daviot

PENGUIN BOOKS

Penguin Books Ltd, Harmondsworth, Middlesex

AUSTRALIA: Penguin Books Pty Ltd, 762 Whitehorse Road,
Mitcham, Victoria

—

Made and printed in Great Britain
by Western Printing Services Ltd
Bristol

CONTENTS

INTRODUCTION

THE qualities common to the three plays in this volume are breadth, freshness, and forthrightness. They all employ a large cast, show a series of differing scenes, and tell a story of events larger and more significant than those domestic happenings which occupy so many of our stages. For all these reasons they have proved admirable plays for schools, and they have been popular with their audiences and readers because each author has attacked his material with a penetrating eye and a vigorous pen.

Gallows Glorious is an Englishman's presentation of one of America's heroic figures. It may seem strange that John Brown should be dramatized by an author from across the Atlantic: but, as an American said to me recently, the wounds of the Civil War are still open, and the American complex of views and feelings on this matter is an intricate one – too intricate for easy dramatization. It is best expressed in Stephen Vincent Benet's great poem *John Brown's Body*, with which directors of Mr Gow's play would do well to get acquainted. Mr Gow has been content to see the story entirely through his hero's eyes, and has produced a sturdy biographical play which lifts the heart. Its directness makes it suitable to a young cast – mostly male. Mr Gow has, since 1933 when he wrote this play, made several notable adaptations for the stage, among them *Love on the Dole* (1935), *Tess of the D'Urbervilles* (1946), and *Ann Veronica* (1949).

Lady Precious Stream is one of the two most successful presentations of the customs of the Chinese theatre on the Western stage. Benrimo's *The Yellow Jacket* achieved this earlier in the century; *Lady Precious Stream* was produced in 1934 and has been constantly played since that date. Mr Hsiung has an equal knowledge of both stages; born and brought up in China, he was manager of a Shanghai theatre in 1927 before coming to England. As an author also he has worked both ways. He has written a number of novels and several other plays of Chinese life, among which *The Western Chamber* (1938) calls for mention. He has combined this with the translation into Chinese of four plays by Shaw and a dozen by Barrie. He has been a professor in Peking and a lecturer at Cambridge.

The conventions of the Chinese theatre provide in themselves a fascination for Western audiences, and Mr Hsiung has known how to exploit this without spoiling them by coyness or exaggeration. Oriental drama and dance depend for much of their effect upon symbols which the audience recognizes and accepts, sharing them with the actors; and the Western audience, meeting the symbols and the actors for the first time, has to be taught to do the same. The effect is also dependent on a good story, and here too Mr Hsiung has provided aright, using the fairy-tale pattern with its mystic trinity (of girls, this time), its journeys accomplished and its hazards surmounted to make a happy ending, yet injecting sufficient individuality into the persons to satisfy Western taste.

Richard of Bordeaux was the first great West End success made by John Gielgud, in 1932. He was already famous for his Hamlet and many other Shakespearian parts at the Old Vic; perhaps foremost among them was Richard the Second. To portray the same character in a modern play was in itself enough to arouse interest in Gordon Daviot's new reading of this piece of history. But her play won immediate esteem on its own merits, and despite the fact that it is prose to Shakespeare's poetry, will hold its place among historical dramas. It re-creates the ruthless turbulence of the times and shows us the tragic struggles of Richard and his young queen, softer and more sensitive spirits, aliens to the tough nobles of this northern isle. This is a subtler play than the other two, but is also strong enough to provide good acting material for a young company.

In saying this of the three plays here printed, I am motivated by a strong desire to see such companies do the best of drama. Shakespeare by all means; but I remember that Shakespeare's language is a big hurdle for the modern young, who lack the biblical training common to my own generation, to leap over. Besides, a change of diet is good for everyone. There is every reason why young actors should adventure into the best of adult modern drama, so long as the plays selected offer an experience which is within their range yet of a size to enlarge their understanding of God and man. This is one of the best ways of exploring the world.

E. MARTIN BROWNE

RONALD GOW

Gallows Glorious

A PLAY IN THREE ACTS

'The Saint, whose fate yet hangs in suspense,
but whose martyrdom, if it be perfected, will
make the gallows glorious like the Cross.'

Emerson, speaking about John Brown

AUTHOR'S NOTE

THE incidents in *Gallows Glorious* are unusually accurate for biographical drama. Very little transposition or condensation of events has been necessary to fit the last year of Brown's life into a three-act play.

The chief authorities have been Redpath's *Public Life of John Brown*, published a few months after the execution, *John Brown of Harper's Ferry*, by J. Newton, an Englishman, a pamphlet kindly supplied by the Storer College of Harper's Ferry, an old volume of *Harper's Magazine* containing an ex-slaveholder's views on slavery, and many of the writings and speeches by men of both sides.

The standard biography by Oswald Garrison Villard was unknown to me, but I was grateful later for his friendship and help with the American production.

R.G.

Application for professional performances to be made to Laurence Fitch Ltd, The London Play Company, 161 New Bond Street, W1

Application for amateur performances to be made to Samuel French Ltd, 26 Southampton Street, WC2

GALLOWS GLORIOUS

First produced by the Altrincham Garrick Society on 13 March 1933.
It was professionally produced by the Croydon Repertory Theatre on
24 April 1933, and afterwards at the Shaftesbury Theatre, London, on
23 May 1933, with the cast given below. It was first produced in
America by George Abbott at the Ethel Barrymore Theatre, New
York, in January 1934.

ANNIE BROWN	Nancy Hornsby
MRS JOHN BROWN	Susan Richards
ELLEN BROWN	Nova Pilbeam
OWEN BROWN	Richard Warner
UNCLE JEREMIAH	Paul Gill
SALMON BROWN	Norman Claridge
WATSON BROWN	David Steuart
BELL, *his wife*	Freda Gaye
OLIVER BROWN	James Mason
MARTHA, *his wife*	Pat Nye
JOHN BROWN	Wilfrid Lawson
SHIELDS GREEN, *a negro*	Sam Henry
A SLAVE-OWNER	George Ide
JOHN KAGI, *Brown's secretary*	Clifford Evans
STEVENS	William J. Miller, Jr
A SENTRY	John Kevan
T. W. HIGGINSON	Bryan Powley
FREDERICK DOUGLASS, *negro preacher*	David Marsh
A TELEGRAPH OPERATOR	John Kevan
A VIRGINIAN MILITIAMAN	George Ide
J. P. GALLAGHER, *of the* New York Herald	Richard Littledale
COLONEL ROBERT E. LEE	George Bishop
COLONEL LEWIS WASHINGTON	Frederic Worsley

John Brown's men, etc.

The play produced by Henry Cass
Stage settings by Ruth Keating

The action of the play takes place in America in 1859, prior to the election of Lincoln and the outbreak of the Civil War. The scenes are laid in the Adirondack Mountains of New York State in the North, and in Maryland and Virginia in the South.

ACT ONE

ACT TWO

ACT THREE

ACT ONE

SCENE I

The spring of 1859. JOHN BROWN'S *farmhouse in the Adirondack Mountains. This is the kitchen and main living-room of the house, and there is no sign of prosperity. A door and a window are in the back wall and through them can be seen the light of the setting sun on the mountains, gaunt peaks rising out of the pine-forest. There is a fireplace on the left and a door leads to the other part of the house on the right.*

MRS BROWN *and her daughter,* ANNIE, *are busily preparing a table or, rather, two tables pushed together, for a party. Cooking is in progress at the fire, and crockery is being laid on the table.* MRS BROWN *is a strong motherly woman.* ANNIE *is a bright and managing girl of sixteen, hardened by backwoods life and much older than her years.*

MRS BROWN: Don't forget spoons, Annie.

ANNIE: No, mother. There's just enough to go round. Isn't that lucky?

MRS BROWN: The sun's going down fast. I hope Oliver's through the Notch. I don't like him driving his cart in the mountains after dark.

ANNIE: Oh, he'll take special care tonight. It wouldn't do to tip *her* out, would it?

MRS BROWN [*counting*]: Five – six – seven – eight.

ANNIE: And Ellen's place here. She'll squeeze in beside me; she doesn't take much room. So you see, that's nine.

MRS BROWN: But there's only eight of us.

ANNIE: No, mother. I've counted up six times already. Nine.

MRS BROWN: There's Oliver and Martha. That's two. And Watson's bringing Bell.

ANNIE: Four.

MRS BROWN: Owen and Salmon. And you and Ellen. That's eight.

ANNIE: And one more makes nine.

MRS BROWN: Lord! Who is it? Don't tell me any more of my sons has been getting himself a wife.

ANNIE: No, mum, you've forgotten the best of all.

MRS BROWN: One, two, three . . . and two's five . . .

ANNIE [*kissing her*]: You've forgotten Mrs John Brown. Just like you!

MRS BROWN: Why, I didn't count myself! Well, I don't matter, and I never could eat at my own parties, anyway.

ANNIE: There's plenty, even if it is plain fare for a party.

MRS BROWN: Yes, it's plain fare. But we've good appetites in these parts, heaven be praised. There's naught like appetite for turning stale loaves into sugar-cakes.

ANNIE: And it isn't as though Oliver's wife were a grand lady. She'll be well used to homely food.

MRS BROWN: She'll starve in this house if she isn't. But Martha's a good girl, else my Oliver would never have chosen her. See, there's my cakes burning!

[*She runs to the fire.*]

ANNIE: It's a pity the year's too early yet for flowers. They always grace a table. I told Ellen to pull some pine-sprays in the forest.

MRS BROWN: Ellen's in the forest?

ANNIE: She's gone for sticks. Salmon's cut no wood today.

MRS BROWN: Ah, well, the poor lad's had too much on his mind. But I don't like Ellen going to the pinewoods alone. Maybe there's a bear, or a falling branch . . .

ANNIE: Mother, you're always worrying. She'll take no harm.

MRS BROWN: Maybe I should put more trust in the Lord. Your father tells me so in his letters. But I've brought up nine children, and I've no wish to strain the Lord's patience too far.

ANNIE: Shall I put the elderberry wine on the table or leave it on the dresser?

MRS BROWN: There'll be more room on the dresser. Leave it by the milk-jug.

ANNIE: I wish we could have tea and coffee the way we had at Mrs Spring's in Boston.

MRS BROWN: You know well enough your father won't have tea and coffee in the house. He says that next to wine and spirits they're the greatest evils in the land.

ANNIE: Not greater than slavery?

MRS BROWN: That's different. But he said once that just as spirits get in the system of a man and poison him, so will slavery poison our nation. And I know John's right. He always is.

ANNIE: Slavery frightens me, mother.

MRS BROWN: How can it? Slavery's in the South, and you're safe in the North.

ANNIE: It's not that way. It's a dream I have. I see slavery like a huge black monster rising up in the South, and it reaches out, and terrible big hands come clutching at father and the boys.

MRS BROWN: That's just nonsense.

ANNIE: But they got Fred. The pro-slavery men, I mean.

MRS BROWN: Yes, they got Fred. [*She is silent for a moment.*] John says they'll raise a great monument some day at Ossawatomie. It was a blow against slavery. Men are calling him 'Ossawatomie Brown' for the battle he won there. I think it's slavery should have the frightening dreams, not you, child.

ANNIE: Mother, it's strange the way you think of Fred and never cry.

MRS BROWN: He died in a great cause. John says so. Would you have me weep because a fine deed has been done?

ANNIE: I sometimes wonder what God thinks. I mean the

shooting of men, and the wars in Kansas, and the torturing of black men.

MRS BROWN: There may be times when even God must hide his face in sorrow. But his will shall be done in the end. John Brown says so.

[*Enter* ELLEN, *five years old, carrying a bundle of sticks and some pine-sprays.*]

ANNIE: Here's Ellen.

ELLEN: You see, I've brought them.

ANNIE: What beautiful pine-sprays! Why, they're better than flowers!

MRS BROWN: That's a clever girl. Weren't you frightened in the forest?

ELLEN: No. Have they come yet?

ANNIE: Good gracious, no! We're not nearly ready.

MRS BROWN: Ellen, keep an eye on those johnny-cakes, and turn 'em when they're brown. I must tidy myself for the party. [*She turns in the doorway.*] Tell Salmon to split some logs for the fire when he comes.

ANNIE: Yes, mother, I'll tell him.

[MRS BROWN *goes out.* ANNIE *decorates the room with the pine-sprays.*]

ELLEN: Why doesn't father come home for the party?

ANNIE: He's busy – down in Kansas – helping poor black slaves. You watch those cakes and don't ask questions.

[ELLEN *produces a doll and places it on the chair by the fire.*]

ELLEN [*to the doll*]: Just you sit there – and don't be getting into mischief. You ain't respeckable for a party. Your face is dirty and wants washing, and me as busy as can be.

[ELLEN *turns a cake.*]

Your wig's coming off, too. You ain't fit to be a grandchild of Captain John Brown if you can't keep your hair on.

[*Enter* OWEN BROWN, *aged about twenty-five. He is tall and handsome, and bronzed by outdoor work. At present he wears his best clothes for the party.*]

OWEN: Hello, Annie! All ready? My, what a big girl Ellen is!

ANNIE: You're here too soon, Owen. It isn't good manners to come early to a party.

OWEN: Then I reckon I'm as bad as you say I am. But I met Anderson, the postman, down the Notch, and he gave me this letter for mother. So I thought I'd best come quick.

ANNIE: That's kind of you, Owen.

OWEN: Yes. You see I met Anderson yesterday morning.

ANNIE: Yesterday?

OWEN: Um. And I thought now if that letter's urgent, mother'll be wanting it quick. So that's why I came early.

ANNIE: And you've had this letter in your pocket for two days! You ought to be ashamed of yourself. You're always doing it.

OWEN: Aw, go on, Annie. One of these days I'll bring you a letter from a nice young man. Then you'll forgive me.

ELLEN: Annie hasn't got a young man. She says she wants one badly.

OWEN: I'll see what I can do.

ANNIE: Be quiet, Ellen! You watch those cakes. That's a Boston postmark.

ELLEN: Is it from daddy?

ANNIE: No, it isn't his writing. He hasn't written for weeks, Owen. We don't even know where he is.

OWEN: That's too bad. I guess the old man's up to mischief again.

ANNIE: Shame on you! As though doing God's work was mischief. Ellen, fetch a bucket of water for Owen, he's filthy, and see that he washes his neck.

[ELLEN *goes out up* R.C.]

There's soap and towel. And, Owen, see there's some oil in the lamp, and clean your boots when you've done that. You can't come to a party in that state! [*Looks at her cakes.*] And we shall want some more wood for this fire. You'd best get some in. I'm taking this letter to mother. And don't go touching any of that food on the table. Promise!

OWEN: I promise. But I'm darned hungry, so you'd best not leave me too long. Oh, I say, Annie!

[ELLEN *returns with bucket*.]

ANNIE: What is it?

OWEN: This lamp. There's nothing on the Railroad tonight, is there?

ANNIE [*indicating* ELLEN]: Hush!

[*She goes out* R.]

ELLEN [*sternly*]: There you are. Wash! [*Puts down bucket in front of table*.]

OWEN: You know, you women are making me feel real miserable.

ELLEN: And don't forget behind your ears!

OWEN [*removes coat and washes*]: That's the worst of parties, the women lose their heads, and I don't see why they should go looking at your ears mor'n any other time!

ELLEN: Get on and don't talk so much!

[*He washes energetically*.]

OWEN [*soap in his eyes*]: Aw, where's the towel?

ELLEN [*gets towel from cupboard* R.]: Here you are. [*Pause*.] Owen, please?

OWEN: Yes, madam?

ELLEN: What is the Underground Railroad?

OWEN: Oh. It's just a name.

ELLEN: There's no railroad here.

OWEN: Of course there isn't.

ELLEN: Is it underground?

OWEN: In a kind of way, yes! [*Showing neck*.] How's that?

ELLEN [*stands on chair and inspects it*]: Turn round. Not bad, but I shouldn't sit too near the light. If there's no railroad, why do folks say there is?

OWEN [*arm round her*]: See here, little girl, when you're big and as tall as that, I'll tell you all about the Underground

Railroad. Now promise me not another word about it till then!

ELLEN: I promise! And I expect Annie will tell me anyway.

[SALMON BROWN *comes in from the fields. He is about thirty years of age.*]

SALMON: Hello, Owen, glad to see you. How's the ploughing?

OWEN: Hard ground, Salmon. Some of those stones need powder more than a plough.

SALMON: Say, do you know there's a stranger coming through the clearing?

OWEN: Oh? What do you make of him, Salmon?

SALMON: Looks as though we'll never make a horseman of him. He's nearly slipping out of the saddle.

OWEN: Some townsman.

SALMON: He's heading this way.

[*Enter* ANNIE.]

ANNIE: That letter's from Uncle Jeremiah. He's coming here.

SALMON: No! When?

ANNIE: He posted it a week ago. Owen's had the letter in his pocket two days. So likely as not he'll be here any time now.

OWEN: That'll be him on the horse.

SALMON: It is, too. I can see the cut of his beard.

ANNIE: What a man to have at a party! Why, he'll turn the milk sour.

SALMON: I wonder what brings him this way. We don't owe him money, do we?

ANNIE [*screaming*]: The cakes are burning! Ellen, you naughty girl! Oh, what a house! Get busy, all of you! Salmon, some wood for the fire. [*He goes.*] Ellen, go and wash your face. [ELLEN *runs out.*] Owen . . .

OWEN: Yes?

ANNIE: Sit where you are and keep your feet out of the way.

[*Enter* MRS BROWN *with the letter.*]

MRS BROWN: Where's that Owen Brown? You ought to be ashamed of yourself. Keeping a letter in your pocket. Your Uncle Jeremiah's coming.

OWEN: Well, I felt somehow it was bad news.

ANNIE: Mother, he's here. Uncle Jeremiah. Tying his horse to the gate.

MRS BROWN: Go and get tidied up, Annie. Leave your uncle to me.

[ANNIE *goes out.* MRS BROWN *picks up some sewing and seats herself.*]

Sit up, Owen. Straighten your hair at the back. And dust your shoes.

[OWEN *does so with his handkerchief.* UNCLE JEREMIAH *appears in the doorway. He is a tall, angular Puritan, with top hat and black clothes, rather shabby.*]

[*Rising.*] Welcome to North Elba, Jeremiah.

[JEREMIAH *sniffs, and looks at the table.*]

JEREMIAH: What's all that for?

MRS BROWN: That's just a party we're having. Oliver was married last week, and he's bringing his new wife home.

JEREMIAH: Who's Oliver?

MRS BROWN: Oliver Brown, my son. You remember.

JEREMIAH [*indicating* OWEN]: Who's that?

MRS BROWN: That's Owen Brown.

JEREMIAH: Too many children. But John never had any sense of proportion. He's a fool.

MRS BROWN: We don't think that in North Elba, Jeremiah. But sit you down. You must be tired with your journey. Can't we forget we're related, uncle, and be friends? Get up, Owen, and give your uncle the chair.

[UNCLE JEREMIAH *sits down, having removed the doll from the seat.*]

Owen, just watch on the road for Oliver's cart, and give us warning when he comes. And put your uncle's horse in the stable.

[OWEN *goes out.* MRS BROWN *sits down and resumes her sewing.*]

Is your health keeping good, Jeremiah?

JEREMIAH: No, it isn't. But I didn't travel two hundred miles to discuss my health. Did I?

MRS BROWN: You know best, Jeremiah.

JEREMIAH: It's about John.

MRS BROWN: Have you news of him?

JEREMIAH: Yes. He's mad.

MRS BROWN: But why?

JEREMIAH: Mad as a hatter. He ought to be locked up.

MRS BROWN: First you call him a fool, and then you say he's mad. He's not in trouble, is he? I hope he's not ill?

JEREMIAH: Ill? No, he's a deal too healthy. Why, at his age he ought to sit quiet by his own fireside. Instead of that he goes rampaging the country. Believe me, Mrs Brown, that husband of yours is going to run his neck into a halter if he doesn't mend his ways.

MRS BROWN: John Brown is an upright man, and an honest man. I've no doubt a man of that sort is reckoned mad in these days.

JEREMIAH: A man can have queer notions and ideas, but he's no right to drag his family into trouble.

MRS BROWN: Why, what's the matter now?

JEREMIAH [*producing a letter*]: Listen to this. He writes from Kansas. He asks me for money, and he says: 'I am satisfied that I am a chosen instrument in the hands of God to war against slavery. It is in my line of duty, and I must pursue it though it should destroy me and my family.' Well, is he mad or am I?

MRS BROWN: Tell me, Jeremiah, does he ask to borrow money?

JEREMIAH: No, not borrowing. It's the money due from the family estate he wants.

MRS BROWN: Then he merely asks for his own money.

JEREMIAH: But the man's prepared to destroy himself and his family.

MRS BROWN: I think John Brown is inspired by God, and though sometimes his words may seem strange, the fault is in our poor understanding of divine things.

JEREMIAH: Divine fiddlesticks! John Brown is raising men to march into the South.

MRS BROWN: Surely he'll never do that?

JEREMIAH: Then what about this? He's given an order to a merchant in Connecticut to make him a thousand pikes – six-foot poles with murderous blades on 'em. And now that he's broken his contract and can't pay up he wants me to find the money for them. Why should I be drawn into his villainy? What d'ye think the Federal Government will say to its citizens making arms in secret?

MRS BROWN: Is it your own neck you're afraid for, Jeremiah, or John Brown's?

JEREMIAH: I believe you're as mad as your husband, Mrs Brown. D'ye know what he means to do?

MRS BROWN: You must remember he hasn't been home to North Elba for nearly a year.

JEREMIAH: He calls it a blow for Freedom. It's nothing more nor less than an armed raid into the slave States, Missouri or Virginia, and all I can say is, God help him! And his family too, for that matter.

MRS BROWN: Slavery is a wicked thing, Jeremiah.

JEREMIAH: There's a heap of wickedness in the American Constitution, but that's no good reason for every zealous Christian taking his Bible and sword, like as if he's the Archangel Michael himself.

MRS BROWN: If God be with John Brown, who can be against him?

JEREMIAH: D'ye know he's travelling up and down the States, making speeches in every big town, and raising money where he can find fools to believe him?

MRS BROWN: Nothing on earth will stop John once he gets an idea.

JEREMIAH: And there's another thing. This Underground Railroad. Is that a lawful game for a god-fearing man to play?

MRS BROWN: What is it but Christian charity? We do no more than give shelter for the night to those who pass this way.

JEREMIAH: Shelter for the night! You take in escaping slaves and hide them from the law, and your sons aid and abet them in escaping and pass them over into Canada. Do you know the penalty for this Underground Railroad, as you call it?

MRS BROWN: We do not speak of that, Jeremiah. There's hundreds of poor black souls passed along it, but there's as many thousands in chains and misery in the South, and it's a poor righteousness to kill their hope of salvation with idle words.

JEREMIAH: Well, John Brown's mad, and he'll get neither money nor support for his schemes out of me. Is it a righteous thing for a man to sacrifice his wife and family the way he does?

MRS BROWN: I sometimes think that's what we came into the world for – to make sacrifices.

JEREMIAH [*rising*]: I don't rightly know the name of John Brown's disease, but I'll say that it's catching, and you seem to have got it as bad yourself. [*He inspects some books on a shelf.*] See that. *The Life of Oliver Cromwell*. And there – *Napoleon Bonaparte*. Rare books for a godly man.

MRS BROWN: I've no great faith in the books myself, but John is a studious man. And if your eyes were sharper and kinder you'd see a Bible there, and *Pilgrim's Progress*, and a book of Dr Watts's hymns, which John loves.

JEREMIAH: It's my opinion these wars in Kansas have unhinged his mind. And, like all who go that way, they get set on one thing, and one thing only, till in their madness they destroy themselves. He tells me he's a chosen instrument to war against slavery. When a man talks like that, I know he's mad. This slavery business has turned his brain.

MRS BROWN: Then his brain was turned long ago. He's talked of it for twenty years.

JEREMIAH: Very well, if my words won't put the light of reason in you, perhaps my money will.

MRS BROWN: Your money?

JEREMIAH: I've a fair pile laid by, and I'd a mind to let some of it come to John's children when I die. But there's none of it comes here if this goes on.

MRS BROWN: The things we do here, Jeremiah, are not done for the hope of riches.

JEREMIAH: That's what *you* say. I wonder what your children think. Are they to be sacrificed for an old man's tomfoolery; aye, and an old woman's vanity, too? Slavery! Sentimental rubbish. Let the South settle its own hash. Who cares about slavery?

MRS BROWN: John Brown does – very strongly.

JEREMIAH: Bah! I'm tired. Where am I sleeping?

MRS BROWN: But you'll have some food with us?

JEREMIAH: No, I don't want any.

MRS BROWN: You're worn out, Jeremiah, that's what's wrong with you. We thought, if you wouldn't take it ill, we'd make up a bed in the wool-shed for you. It's clean and dry, and there's been no fleeces there for two years.

JEREMIAH: Anywhere, so long as I don't hear the noise of your infernal party.

[ANNIE *comes in with a bundle of bedding in her arms.*]
Who's that girl?

MRS BROWN: That's Annie. You remember her?

JEREMIAH: Is she one of yours?

MRS BROWN: Why, Jeremiah, can't you see that look of her father in her face?

JEREMIAH: No, I can't. And it's God help a woman with John Brown's devilment in her. Where's my horse?

ANNIE: Owen's stabled it for you. He's feeding it, too.

JEREMIAH: Come on, then. Let's see this wool-shed.

MRS BROWN: Put three blankets below the sheets, Annie. The nights are still cold.

ANNIE: Yes, mother.

[ANNIE *goes out with* UNCLE JEREMIAH. MRS BROWN *attends to the fire.* SALMON *enters hurriedly with the wood.*]

SALMON: Mother!

MRS BROWN: What is it, Salmon?

SALMON: The signal!

MRS BROWN: Not tonight?

SALMON: Sure enough. Out on the hillside by Jackson's Farm.

MRS BROWN: They say troubles never come singly.

SALMON: What are we going to do?

MRS BROWN: There's only one thing we can do, Salmon. We must carry on your father's work.

SALMON: I'm glad you said that.

MRS BROWN: Put the lamp in the window, Salmon.

[SALMON *prepares an oil-lamp.*]

SALMON: I guess father's been at it again. I'd a kind of feeling working in the fields today we were about due for a load of trouble. Things have been marvellous quiet on the Railroad these last months.

[OWEN *comes in.*]

Say, Owen, you'll be busy before the night's out. They've given the signal at the Farm.

OWEN: We can't do it with all the family here.

SALMON: All the better. Throw them off the scent, if there's any trouble.

OWEN: This means another trip over to Canada.

MRS BROWN: It's God's work, Owen.

OWEN: Aw, that's all right, mother. I was thinking of my ploughing.

SALMON: We'll see to that.

> [SALMON *puts the lamp in the window. Then he takes down a gun and loads it.*]

Got a gun, Owen?

> [OWEN *draws back his jacket and pats the holster of a revolver.*]

Good. What's Uncle Jerry wanting, mother?

MRS BROWN: I'd like a word with you, boys. Your uncle's upset. I think he's afraid he may get drawn into the service. I know it's a queer thing for a man to be afraid of helping God's work, but Jeremiah doesn't see things the way we do. He's the sort with little thought beyond the making of money. I've no ill-will against him. There are many of his sort in America these days. But he can't understand John Brown.

SALMON: I'll be bound you gave him the rough edge of your tongue, mother.

MRS BROWN: He's not so mighty pleased with what I told him. But I'm afraid of a thing he said. He spoke of his money, and how he had a mind to let some of it come here when he died.

OWEN: I hope you told him to keep it.

MRS BROWN: It's foolish of me to think it – but suppose he offered you money to leave John Brown's service?

SALMON: Mother! You can't think that.

MRS BROWN: I'm sorry, boys. I should have trusted you. But an old woman gets doubts and fears in her mind. I knew all the time in my heart that my sons were not to be bought with money.

> [OWEN *is standing by the door. It is almost dark outside.*]

OWEN: Hello, I can hear a cart on the road.

SALMON: They're coming, mother.

OWEN: There it is, on the edge of the clearing.

MRS BROWN: They're on us, and the food not dished. [*Calling*] Annie! Call Annie, one of you. Light the stable lantern to show them the way.

[*She carries dishes to the table.* SALMON *and* OWEN *go out.* ELLEN *comes in.*]

ELLEN: They're coming, mum, they're coming!

MRS BROWN: Put the johnny-cakes on the table, Ellen, and mind you don't drop them.

[ANNIE *comes in from outside.*]

ANNIE: Oliver and Watson, mother, and Bell and Martha. And Martha's wearing a silk gown with little pink ribbons ...

MRS BROWN: Never mind what she's wearing. Light the candles, girl. Run to meet them, Ellen. And mind Oliver's horse; he bites.

[ELLEN *runs out.*]

ANNIE: We've forgotten the maple-syrup, mother.

MRS BROWN: There, in the cupboard.

[*They put the finishing touches to the table, while the voices outside grow louder.* ELLEN *dances joyfully in the doorway.*]

ELLEN: They're coming! They're coming! Oo, look at Oliver with a wife!

MRS BROWN: Hush! Don't make the boy nervous.

[*Enter* OLIVER *with his bride. They kiss* MRS BROWN. WATSON *follows with his wife.* MARTHA *and* BELL *are not yet out of their teens. Their husbands are finely built young men of twenty-two and twenty-three.* OWEN *and* SALMON *bring up the rear.*]

Welcome home, Oliver. And you, Martha dear, how pretty you look. Welcome to North Elba.

WATSON: Hello, mother. Here's Bell.

MRS BROWN: Good evening, Bell. Is Watson behaving?

BELL: He gets better and better.

WATSON: What's for supper, mother?

MRS BROWN: I thought as much. Bell's been starving you.

BELL: Oh, I haven't starved him. He eats like a horse.

OLIVER: You're a greedy fellow, Watson.

WATSON: You wait. You haven't been married as long as I have.

MRS BROWN: Well, there's johnny-cakes, and roast mutton, and porridge.

WATSON: Ah!

ELLEN: With maple-syrup specially because of the wedding. Oliver hasn't kissed me yet.

[OLIVER *does so.*]

MRS BROWN: Annie, take the girls along to your room, where they can tidy up after the ride.

WATSON: I reckon Martha needs a bit of tidying up. Oliver got kind of enthusiastic in the cart.

ANNIE: Come along with me, Martha. Watson's always like that.

[ANNIE *leads out the girl, accompanied by* ELLEN.]

ELLEN: Do you think Oliver will make a nice husband, Martha?

ANNIE: Come along, Ellen. Don't ask so many questions.

[*They have gone.*]

MRS BROWN: Now, Salmon, you start carving the meat. I'll hurry the girls along. They'll take hours if I don't.

[MRS BROWN *goes out. As soon as she has gone* OLIVER *seizes* WATSON'S *arm.*]

OLIVER: You young blackguard! So you'd tell on me, would you?

SALMON: Say, Oliver, guess who's here?

OLIVER: I dunno.

SALMON: Uncle Jerry.

OLIVER: Not old dough-face? What's he after?

OWEN: Just upset about things, that's all.

WATSON [*pointing to the window*]: Hello! Look at that, Oliver.

OLIVER: Why, the lamp's in the window! Have you had the signal?

OWEN: Yes, there'll be work on the Railroad tonight.

OLIVER: Then Martha's going to start learning young.

OWEN: Does she know about – what we do here?

WATSON: There's an innocent young bachelor for you!

OLIVER: What's been happening on the Railroad lately?

SALMON: There's been nothing since Christmas. I'm glad of that with the snow in the passes, because niggers don't take kindly to the cold.

OLIVER: Poor devils!

OWEN: Two of them died in the Notch last fall.

SALMON: Yes, Owen had a bad journey through the mountains.

OWEN: I learned more about negroes that trip than I ever knew before. God, how they're treated – they use the women for breeding slaves. I wish father could get the money for his plans – we'd clear the whole South of its slaves.

OLIVER: What route does the Railroad take these days?

SALMON: When they lift the slaves from Missouri, they bring them by way of Kansas and Iowa.

OWEN: They show a light at Jackson's Farm, and Jackson gets the signal across the lake. Oh, there's a regular chain of farms and cabins now.

SALMON: There's other ways to the east as well, but this is handy for the crossing into Canada.

OWEN: Under the paw of the British Lion, as father calls it. They're safe in Canada.

OLIVER: Hell! Britain abolished her slavery; why can't we?

WATSON: Maybe we aren't civilized yet.

SALMON: Britain's been through the fire – we haven't; and that's the difference. Just you read their history. They've had to fight for the things they got. We're young and we've a long way to go.

OLIVER: You mean there'll be fighting in America?

SALMON: I think the wars in Kansas were just the beginning of something great. Something that may take us all.

OWEN: God give me a chance to be in it.

SALMON: Fighting's a terrible thing.

WATSON: Father says his way will avoid the fighting.

OLIVER: What is this plan of father's?

SALMON: I reckon it's to do with Virginia, but more I can't find out.

OLIVER: I'm with him, whatever it is.

WATSON: Listen! Wants to desert his wife already.

OLIVER: Oh, Martha's all right on the slavery question.

WATSON: I bet he asked her that before he married her.

[*Enter* MRS BROWN, *followed by the others.*]

MRS BROWN: Come along now, the food will be spoiling. Oliver and Martha, you sit here beside me. We haven't enough chairs, so some of you will have to make do with boxes.

WATSON: Oh, that's all right, mother.

[*They take their seats, all talking together.*]

OWEN: Let Bell have a chair, then, Watson. You sit there.

ANNIE: Sit here, Ellen, and don't ask questions.

WATSON: Hooray! There's nothing beats mother's johnny-cakes!

ANNIE: Hush, Watson! Manners at a party.

OLIVER: Look at the candles. Reminds me of New York.

MRS BROWN: Children! Children! Will you say grace? Please, Salmon?

[*All bow their heads while* SALMON *rises to say grace.*]

SALMON: We thank thee, O God, for thy bountiful mercy, which has brought us here together to enjoy thy gifts, garnered from this land of plenty, where we live in the protection of thy loving care. Grant, O Lord, the same mercy and protection to our absent ones. Watch over the father of this family and give him strength to do thy work. And grant the same care and bounty to our brothers John and Jason Brown, who are now with their wives and families in Kansas Territory. And keep us steadfast in the service thou has revealed unto us, in the name of Jesus Christ, our Lord.

ALL: Amen.

MRS BROWN: Thank you, Salmon. That was like your father.

ELLEN: Could I begin with cake as it's a party?

[*Talk and laughter now break out.*]

ANNIE: Help yourself to potatoes. Owen, pass the elderberry wine.

WATSON: I hope Martha has a good appetite. She'll need strength if Oliver's going to sing.

OWEN: She won't have any left when she's heard him.

[*In the midst of the merriment a distant shot is heard. There is a sudden silence.* SALMON *rises and takes his gun.*]

MRS BROWN: That was shooting.

SALMON: Keep still.

[*They all keep quiet. He listens at the door.*]

There's somebody running – this way.

[SALMON *draws back from the door, keeping his rifle ready. Suddenly the door bursts open and* JOHN BROWN *enters, dragging a negro after him.* JOHN BROWN *is a tall, square-shouldered man. He wears a military cloak and mud-spattered riding-boots. A fur cap, leather stock, and general bearing give him a soldierly appearance. He is fifty-nine years of age and wears a grey beard.* JOHN BROWN *shuts and bars the door, while the negro sinks exhausted to his knees.*]

JOHN: Draw the shutters.

[OWEN *draws shutters over the window.*]

MRS BROWN [*rising to greet her husband*]: John!

JOHN: No, dear. Sit down, please. All of you. You too, Salmon, and put that gun away. I want you all to behave as though nothing had happened. Annie, set a place at the table for me.

[*He takes a glass from the table and makes the negro drink. Then he sits by the fire and takes off his boots.*]

Here you, Green, put these on. This is the closest thing I've seen. They chased us through the Notch, but we gave them the slip in the pine-forest. They'll be on us any moment now. Stand up, Green.

[*The negro pulls on the boots. Then* JOHN BROWN *raises him and makes him stand to the side of the door, where a wooden coat-peg is driven in the wall.* BROWN *hangs his hat and cloak on the peg, covering the negro, with the exception of his feet, which look like an empty pair of riding-boots. Then* BROWN *listens at the door and unbars it. Horses are heard outside.* JOHN BROWN *takes his place at the table.*]

This looks like a wedding party. Which of you's married this time?

MRS BROWN: It's Oliver. I told you all about it, John, in the letter.

JOHN: To be sure you did. When were you married, Oliver?

OLIVER: Last Friday.

JOHN: Then you'll not take it ill if I propose your health?

OLIVER: I'll be glad . . .

JOHN: Listen, all of you. Not a word or a look that would give away yon poor fellow.

[*A knock.*]

JOHN: And now, my friends, I cannot pass over this occasion of a happy family reunion without some expression of our poor thanks to the Providence that has brought us together again. We live in a time of trouble, and though our hearts beat fast, they beat together.

[*As he speaks the door is flung open, and a* SOUTHERNER *strides in, followed by another man. Two men also stand guard outside the door. All are armed.*]

A wedding is indeed a happy occasion. We welcome a newcomer to the family, and you will agree with me when I say that Oliver has chosen well.

[JOHN BROWN *turns in surprise on the* SOUTHERNER.]

And where have you come from, sir?

SOUTHERNER: When you've finished, Captain Brown, I'd like a word with you.

JOHN: I'd have you know, sir, that you're interrupting an important ceremony.

SOUTHERNER: We can't help that. We hold a Federal warrant for the apprehension of Shields Green, a negro lately escaped from the slave territory of Missouri. And if it interests you, Captain Brown, we've a pretty shrewd notion it was you helped him to escape.

JOHN: If I was interested in what some men say of me, sir, I'd spend my days fighting slander actions in the courts. I'm sorry there's no room for you, but maybe you'll sit by the fire while I finish my speech.

SOUTHERNER: Where is he, you damned Abolitionist?

[*There is a movement among the sons, but* BROWN *waves them back.*]

JOHN: Abolitionist I may be, but God shall judge whether I'm damned or saved.

SOUTHERNER [*to his man*]: In there, you, and search. [*He covers the party at the table with his revolver.*] Don't move, any of you! [*He calls to the men outside*] Jones and Peterson, watch all the windows. He's in here somewhere. Oh, I know all about you, Mr Ossawatomie Brown. There's a rope waiting for you down in Kansas Territory. We haven't forgotten who killed Doyle and Wilkinson and Sherman. And we know a deal more about your Underground Railroad than you give us credit for. I guess you understand the penalty for helping an escaped nigger.

JOHN: I understand one thing, and one thing only. You people in the South are guilty of a great wrong against God and humanity. If I see fit to interfere with you, I think I do right. And so will others do right who seek to free those you wickedly hold in bondage. If you were to find a black man in my house tonight, I should defend him with my life.

SOUTHERNER: Ah, you're crazy, John Brown!

[*The searcher returns.*]

Well?

MAN: Nothing.

SOUTHERNER: Bah! Come on, we'll go.

> [*At this moment shouting is heard outside.*]

PETERSON [*outside*]: We've got him!

SOUTHERNER: Keep John Brown covered! [*Calling outside*] Bring the dirty skunk in here.

> [*The two men enter struggling with* UNCLE JEREMIAH, *who is clad in his nightdress. He protests loudly.*]

JEREMIAH: This is an outrage! How dare you attack an American citizen . . .?

MRS BROWN: Jeremiah! Your legs!

> [*The* CURTAIN *falls quickly.*]

SCENE 2

The same. Some hours later.

> *The table has been cleared and now stands in the middle of the room, bearing an oil-lamp.* JOHN BROWN *sits at the table, writing.* GREEN, *the negro, is huddled beside the fire.* OWEN *stands in the background, listening.*

JOHN: Now, Shields Green, I want you to pay attention. You will have to swear before God that all these things are true. Then you will have to make your mark at the foot of the statement, and my son and I will sign as witnesses. [*Reading*] 'Five hundred lashes on your bare back. Salt and water in the wounds. Feet in irons. Fainted after blows from your master's cane. High fever. Sent to work in the cotton-fields. Red-hot nails placed on your naked flesh.' You are sure of all this?

> [GREEN *nods.*]

And you know nothing of your wife?

GREEN: They took her away.

JOHN [*writing*]: '– wife – taken – away.' Owen, give him the Bible.

[OWEN *puts a Bible in* GREEN'S *hand.*]

Now stand up. You know what a serious thing it is to take an oath on the Bible?

GREEN: Yes, Mas'r Brown.

JOHN: Then say this after me. I swear – before Almighty God – that the things I have said – are true.

[GREEN *repeats the words.*]

Now, make a mark here.

[GREEN *takes the pen and makes his mark.* JOHN BROWN *signs after him, and* OWEN *witnesses the signature.*]

Well, Green, you're safe enough in this house for tonight and tomorrow. Sit down again. When you're well rested, Owen will lead you on through the mountains. The way is by easy stages, and you'll cross the lake into Canada. Nobody can touch you there.

GREEN: Mas'r Brown, are you going back to Missouri?

JOHN: Maybe I will.

GREEN: I'll go with you.

JOHN: Why?

GREEN: To kill.

JOHN: No, you're wrong, Shields Green. But I'll not blame you for wanting revenge. I claim no man has a right to revenge. It's a feeling that doesn't enter into my heart. But to strike a blow for human liberty – that's necessary.

GREEN: You *will* strike a blow, mas'r – a big blow?

JOHN: What would the other slaves do?

GREEN: They would rise up. They would make a big army.

JOHN: Would they kill their masters and burn their houses?

GREEN [*eagerly*]: Yes, mas'r.

JOHN: No, Shields Green, that's wrong. I shall never incite slaves to revenge. There shall be no murder or destruction of property. I have freed slaves without the snapping of a gun, and I shall do the same thing again on a larger scale.

All my life I've planned it. When I was a boy I played with Indian boys. That was in Ohio. They taught me smart things, things that have saved my life. They weren't the same colour, but I knew them for God's creatures. Then I went to stay with a Southern gentleman. I saw boys of my own age, niggers, cuffed and beaten and ill-used. They were black. They weren't God's creatures. A boy of twelve has no use for subtle reasoning. I asked if God was the Father of these niggers, and when they told me no, I said to myself, 'They're wrong', which may be a cantankerous argument, but it's stuck to me ever since. That's why I think it's an eternal disgrace to sit still in the presence of slavery. But revenge, and bloodshed for the hope of revenge, aren't in my way of thinking. There are other ways. Ways that need craft and cunning like the Indians use. Give me twenty men in the Alleghanies and I'll break slavery to pieces in two years. Owen, where are the boys?

OWEN: Out there, dancing in the barn with the others.

JOHN: Tell them I want them.

[OWEN *goes out.* ANNIE *comes in with a tray of food.*]

ANNIE: Mother says you're to eat this.

JOHN: Thank you, Annie. Set it down.

[ANNIE *takes a plate and cup over to the negro by the fire.*]

ANNIE: Father.

JOHN: Well?

ANNIE: You'll be staying at home now?

JOHN: It's the thing I hope and pray for, Annie. Sometimes when I'm in far places, and under strange roofs, the thought of home is like a pain, so that I cry out to be with you.

ANNIE: Mother's hoping you'll stay this time.

JOHN [*shaking his head*]: A man with harness on his conscience must go forward till God draws on the rein, and bids him halt. Young woman, there's a parcel of vanity hanging in my cloak. There, it's for you.

ANNIE [*opening a packet*]: For me?

JOHN: And some sweets for Ellen. I fancied you'd be too big for sweets.

ANNIE: Bracelets! Oh, thank you! They're beautiful!

JOHN: It's aiding and abetting Satan in his wickedness.

ANNIE: Well, why not, once in a way? We don't give Satan much chance at North Elba.

JOHN [*kissing her*]: When men say of John Brown that he's a square-toed old Puritan, I'll ask them if they've met his daughter. Ah, woman, woman . . .

ANNIE [*sitting on the arm of his chair*]: That's just it, father. I'm a woman now – and there isn't a man for miles around worth putting these bracelets on for.

JOHN: You'd best pray for one.

ANNIE: I do, but nothing ever happens. I wish you'd take me with you on your raids.

JOHN: What could a girl do?

ANNIE: I could cook and mend and wash. And by the look of your clothes you're needing a bit of mending this minute.

JOHN: And what of the danger?

ANNIE: Do you think *your* daughter's afraid of that?

JOHN: You're safer here with your mother.

ANNIE: Father, tell me – when you're on your travels do you never meet a young, dark, handsome man, with a serious face?

JOHN: I can't say that I've met him. Who is he?

ANNIE: I don't know.

JOHN [*laying down his knife and fork*]: You don't know!

ANNIE: I just dream about him.

JOHN: Annie, my child, this is a queer way to talk.

ANNIE: You've got a queer daughter, father.

[*There is a knock on the door.* GREEN *springs to his feet.*]

ANNIE: Who's that? Do be careful.

JOHN: Stand away.

[*He opens the door to admit* JOHN KAGI, *a handsome young American of Swiss extraction.*]

KAGI: Good evening, Captain Brown.

JOHN: Hello, Kagi! I thought you were in Maryland.

KAGI: I was. But I settled our business and rode through to find you.

JOHN: You've bought the farm?

KAGI: Here are the title-deeds.

JOHN: Sit down and rest. We'll get some food for you. This is my daughter Annie.

KAGI [*after a pause*]: Oh, glad to meet you, Miss Brown.
[ANNIE *is staring at him.*]

JOHN: Shake hands with Mr Kagi, Annie. Why, what's the matter?

KAGI: I suppose it's the resemblance to you, sir. I should have known her at once.

JOHN: Where's Owen and the boys? Annie, give Mr Kagi a bite while I find them.
[*He goes out.*]

ANNIE: Please sit down.
[*She goes to the cupboard and sets more food on the table.*]

KAGI: May I help?

ANNIE: Please sit down and eat it.

KAGI: Thank you, I will.
[*She watches him.*]

ANNIE: Father never told me about you.

KAGI: Didn't he? That's a pity. Maybe he didn't think I was worth mentioning.

ANNIE: Are you against slavery?

KAGI [*his mouth full*]: M-mm. Like hell!

ANNIE: Does father know you swear?

KAGI: Lord, no! Don't tell him.

ANNIE: You also speak with your mouth full.

KAGI: I'm sorry. [*Laughs.*]

ANNIE: Are you a serious young man?
[GREEN *turns round.*]

KAGI: Yes, about serious things. Why?

ANNIE: I just wondered. We're all serious here.

[*She slyly displays her new bracelets.*]

KAGI: Those are very charming bracelets, Miss Brown.

ANNIE: They're from father. Fancy you noticing them.

KAGI: Perhaps I shouldn't. . . . Was it rude of me?

ANNIE: We'll overlook it. You know, I expected you.

KAGI: You mean your father told you?

ANNIE: I dropped a knife.

KAGI: Dropped a knife?

ANNIE: Yes, when I was laying the table for the party, and I said to myself, 'That means there's a gentleman coming here,' and you see here you are.

KAGI: And do I come up to expectations?

ANNIE: No, not quite. You're uglier than I thought.

[GREEN *laughs.*]

KAGI: Oh, I'm sorry.

ANNIE: Perhaps you'll do.

KAGI: Thanks. Of course, I knew Captain Brown had daughters, but I never thought . . .

ANNIE: What?

KAGI: Well, I mean – I thought they were just daughters.

[*Enter* JOHN BROWN, *followed by his sons.*]

JOHN: Mr Kagi, meet my sons. Oliver you've met. This is Owen. This, Salmon. And this is Watson.

KAGI: Glad to meet you, gentlemen.

JOHN: Annie, I've an idea your mother wants you. Tell her we shan't be long. Owen, clear the table.

[ANNIE *goes out.*]

Oliver, give me the map of America.

[*The map is unrolled on the table.*]

Owen, do you remember what I said a while back – about breaking slavery?

OWEN: Yes, sir, you said that twenty men in the Alleghanies could break slavery to pieces in two years.

JOHN: And I mean exactly so, gentlemen. Give me twenty

men of good principles. Men who respect themselves. Men like Oliver Cromwell had. The sort of man who fears God too much to fear anything human, and I'll oppose the whole South. You see where my finger is pointing?

OLIVER: That's Maryland.

JOHN: Five miles from the Virginia border. I've bought a farm there. It's called Kennedy's Farm. Here are the title-deeds. Kagi has brought them. I'm going to raise a strange crop on it.

WATSON: If it's another slave raid, we're with you, father.

JOHN: This is the biggest thing we've ever done. I mean to strike such a blow in Virginia that will shake slavery to its foundations. I know every inch of the ground. I tell you that the mountains and swamps of the South were intended by the Almighty as a refuge for the slave.

OLIVER: Where will you strike?

JOHN: There, on the Potomac.

OLIVER: That's Harper's Ferry – the Government arsenal.

JOHN: Exactly. We seize the arsenal and arm the slaves. Give a slave a weapon and you make him a man. We'll march 'em into the mountains. Down through Carolina, Tennessee, Georgia, Alabama, Mississippi. A tiny spark will light a very big fire.

OWEN: This will take a lot of money.

JOHN: I can raise it.

OLIVER: Are the Abolitionists behind you?

JOHN: There's few of them know of my plan. And those who do are sworn to secrecy. There's little use talking of anti-slavery action to men who won't fight. The politicians will never be told of it. Slavery is no more to them than a party parrot-cry.

SALMON: I hear Mr Abraham Lincoln is standing for the presidency again. He's an anti-slavery man.

JOHN: Abraham Lincoln is a lawyer. Maybe he's a good law-yer, but what are laws against an evil that has its roots as deep as hell itself? Suppose the Senate passes an anti-slavery law tomorrow. Would slavery pass away? Not it. The South would fight, and I can't see the United States surviving civil war. I've seen enough of military life to know that it eats at the very heart of a country. Militarism is a disease you can't easily throw off. I flatter myself that the thing can be done my way – the right way – with the shedding of very little blood.

SALMON: This is to be a raid into the slave States, and an armed insurrection of the slaves?

JOHN: Yes.

SALMON: Don't think I'm lukewarm. I'll follow you anywhere. So will we all. But how is that insurrection to be controlled?

JOHN: I mean to give them leaders, and a constitution laid down by a provisional government. We shall respect the rights of white men in exactly the same degree as the coloured.

SALMON: I'm satisfied.

WATSON: When do we start?

JOHN: Give me three months to raise more money in the big towns and Canada, and we'll get settled at Kennedy Farm. Salmon, you'll have to stay here.

SALMON: I hoped to be with you.

JOHN: I know. But there's your mother and the girls. And the Underground Railroad. We need that more than ever now. Perhaps we can take Annie to cook for us, and maybe Oliver's new wife will join us.

OLIVER: Yes, father.

JOHN: We'll send them home before the trouble starts. Will you be ready?

[*They assent eagerly.*]

Good. I wish I had twenty sons. Now I must write letters. Good night.

[*The sons go out, bidding him good night.* KAGI *goes with them.* JOHN BROWN *busies himself with his papers.* MRS BROWN *comes in.*]

MRS BROWN: John.

JOHN: Well, Mary?

MRS BROWN: I came to wish you good night.

JOHN [*kissing her*]: Good night, Mary, and God bless you always.

MRS BROWN: John.

JOHN: Yes?

MRS BROWN: There's a thing I want to ask.

JOHN: What is it?

MRS BROWN: You can answer it or not, as you please. Did you kill those men down in Kansas?

JOHN: They were killed by my order, and in doing so I believe I was doing God's service.

MRS BROWN: Is it true God uses you as an instrument in his hands to kill men?

JOHN: I think he has used me to kill men, and if I live I am afraid he will use me to kill a good many more.

MRS BROWN: That is all I want to know, John. Just that you feel right. Because then I know that it *is* right. Good night. [*She presses his arm and turns to go slowly from the room.* JOHN BROWN *is left standing alone.* GREEN, *the negro, who has been sitting gazing into the fire, rises and comes over to* JOHN BROWN. *He drops on his knees and kisses* JOHN BROWN'S *hand.*]

CURTAIN

ACT TWO

SCENE I

Autumn 1859. The main entrance-hall of the Kennedy Farmhouse in Maryland, five miles from the Virginia border. It is a spacious room in the Southern style. The door in the centre and the square-paned Georgian windows look out upon a veranda, beyond which is an orchard, and, in the far distance, the mountains of Virginia. The furniture is simple and suggests a temporary occupation. Packing-cases lie about the room. A couple of men come into the house and go up the stairs on the left. GREEN, the negro, sits outside the door, on an upturned box, playing a banjo. KAGI sits at a table, poring over papers. He speaks to the men mounting the stairs.

KAGI: Are all the men in now, Stevens?

STEVENS: Yes, Mr Kagi. But I reckon they're getting kind of irritable, spending their days up there.

KAGI: I know it's hard. Keep 'em busy if you can.

STEVENS: It's a great help when Captain Brown comes up and gives 'em a word or two.

KAGI: I'll ask him, Stevens. You should have fifteen up there. Better call the roll.

STEVENS: Yes, Mr Kagi. And I say, if you've finished with that nigger, send him up. The men like a sing-song.

KAGI: I'll see if Miss Annie wants him. Then I'll send him.

STEVENS: Thank you, sir.

[STEVENS *and the other man go upstairs.* ANNIE *comes in through the door on the left. She carries a slate and pencil.*]

KAGI: Good morning, Miss Annie.

ANNIE: Good morning, Mr Kagi.

KAGI: Some more orders for me?

ANNIE: Yes. I want a lot of things for the kitchen.

KAGI: You've got a big family.

ANNIE: The men are easily pleased. That's a great blessing. Here are the things I want from the store.

KAGI: I'll make a list.

ANNIE: Another sack of flour. Molasses. A hundredweight of sugar. Do you think we ought to have another flitch of bacon?

KAGI: It all depends.

ANNIE: You mean on how long we'll be here?

KAGI: Yes. And we've got to be careful with the money.

ANNIE: Father told us to pack up a week ago. He said Martha and I must be ready to leave at a moment's notice.

KAGI: We shall miss you, Miss Annie.

ANNIE: You'll have to do your own cooking then.

KAGI: That means bully beef and biscuits.

ANNIE: Do you think he'd let me stay?

KAGI: I'm afraid that's impossible, Miss Annie. You – I don't think I can possibly put into words how I – how we shall all miss you.

ANNIE: That's very nice of you, Mr Kagi.

KAGI: If you knew what this friendship means to me, Miss Annie. If only I could be sure that we could go on being friends – somewhere else, afterwards. You must forgive me if I'm too blunt and outspoken. But our friendship is a real friendship, isn't it? I mean – you do understand me, don't you?

ANNIE: Oh, I think so. Do you think we ought to order that bacon or not?

KAGI: Bacon? Oh, yes, we must have a great deal of bacon. Especially if you say so. See, I've written it down already.

[GREEN *comes in from the veranda.*]

GREEN: Any orders, Miss Annie?

ANNIE: Yes, Shields Green, thank you. There's an order for the stores.

KAGI: Stevens was asking if they might have Green upstairs to play for them. It keeps the men happy.

ANNIE: Why, of course. I'll take this order myself. Martha and I are just going out.

KAGI: Good. We must keep Green inside as much as we can. There's a price on his head.

GREEN: Thank you, Miss Annie.

KAGI: You're wanted upstairs, Green.

[MARTHA *comes in from the left with a basket.*]

MARTHA: You ready yet, Annie? Gossiping as usual. Keeping Mr Kagi from his work.

KAGI: No, I assure you, Mrs Oliver – we've been talking business practically all the time.

MARTHA: Then it's about time you two talked about something else.

ANNIE: Hush! Be quiet, Martha!

MARTHA: Come along, Annie. We've a lot to do.

[MARTHA *and* ANNIE *go out into the garden.* GREEN *plays a sudden chord on the banjo.*]

KAGI: What are *you* grinning at? Get out!

[GREEN *disappears, laughing.* OLIVER *comes in from the room on the right.*]

OLIVER: Morning, Kagi.

KAGI: Good morning, Oliver.

OLIVER: Where's father?

KAGI: Usual place. Under the apple-tree, reading his Bible.

OLIVER: He's spending a lot of time out there these days.

KAGI: He says the Bible gives him strength.

OLIVER: All the men upstairs?

KAGI: Yes, Stevens has just gone up.

OLIVER: How d'you think they're standing it?

KAGI: Not too badly.

OLIVER: How long do you think we'll have to wait?

KAGI: Our plans are all made. You know that. But I can't say when John Brown means to strike. Of course, if people are suspicious of anything queer going on here, we'll have to move at once. By the way, that's a case of gunpowder you're sitting on.

[OLIVER *moves to another box.*]

OLIVER: What's in this one?

KAGI: Bully beef. It's slower in action than the other.

OLIVER: So long as Annie and my wife are here, there's no chance of moving. Father means to send them home about a week before the raid. I don't want them to go, all the same.

KAGI: I can't think what we shall do without Annie.

OLIVER: Annie's a useful girl.

KAGI: I say she's splendid. It must have been fine to be her brother – to know her so long, I mean.

OLIVER: Well, I hadn't looked at it that way. But she's a very useful girl to have about the house.

KAGI: She's an angel. . . .

OLIVER: Hello? I didn't know it was so bad.

KAGI: It isn't. At least, I mean, she knows nothing whatever about it.

OLIVER: About being an angel?

KAGI: No, about . . . Oh, I'm a fool to say these things. But I can trust *you*, Oliver?

OLIVER: Sure, you can. Hello, here's Watson.

[*Enter* WATSON.]

WATSON: Any mail arrived yet?

KAGI: Not yet, Watson. We're expecting a letter from Frederick Douglass. Ought to be in now.

OLIVER: Is that the negro preacher?

KAGI: Yes, he may be coming here, along with Higginson, the Abolitionist.

OLIVER: Douglass is a big influence with the niggers.

KAGI: Yes, but I'm afraid he's against the raid.

OLIVER: Then father will talk him round. There never was a plainer case.

KAGI: Why this anxious look, Watson? I thought you had news from home only yesterday.

WATSON: That's just it.

OLIVER: Why, Kagi, don't you know Watson's dread secret?

KAGI: No.

OLIVER [*to* WATSON]: Shall I tell him?

WATSON: I suppose you'd better.

OLIVER: Watson is about to become a father, and he's feeling it very acutely. In fact, he may be one already.

WATSON: It may be serious.

KAGI: Ah, I see. Now I understand the homesick look.

WATSON: God! I wish I could see Bell again.

[ANNIE *and* MARTHA *appear on the veranda.* ANNIE *has a bunch of flowers, and* MARTHA *has apples in her basket.*]

Hello, Martha! Hello, Annie.

ANNIE [*holding up letters*]: The mail! There's one for you, Watson.

WATSON: Quick! Let me see it.

ANNIE: The others are all for you, Mr Kagi.

KAGI [*taking them*]: Thank you, Miss Annie. You're very kind to bring them.

ANNIE: Aren't these nice roses? And we've got some apples for the men.

WATSON [*hoarsely*]: I say, it's a boy!

ANNIE: Oh, Watson, you're wonderful!

WATSON: And everything's all right.

OLIVER: Of course, I told you it would be, all the time.

KAGI: Congratulations, Watson.

MARTHA: Bell *will* be pleased.

WATSON: Excuse me, will you? I want to tell father. Where is he?

ANNIE: You'll find him down in the orchard.

WATSON: I must go at once. We must decide what to call it – I mean *him*.

[WATSON *goes. The others laugh.*]

OLIVER: Well, that's a load off his mind, anyway. And if you ask me, it was just as well he was down here, out of the way.

MARTHA: I want to give these apples to the men, Oliver.

OLIVER: Run upstairs, then. They'll be glad to see you.

MARTHA: I can't go alone. [*She indicates the other two.*] You come with me.

OLIVER: Right. But you'll have to give me an apple if I do.

MARTHA: There – just one. Don't let that girl interrupt you, Mr Kagi.

[OLIVER *and* MARTHA *go upstairs.* ANNIE *has filled some jam-jars with fresh water, and begins to arrange the flowers.* KAGI *follows her, but nervousness overcomes him whenever he is about to speak. The banjo and the singing are heard in the room above.*]

ANNIE: There. Aren't they beautiful?

KAGI [*gazing at her*]: They're divine.

ANNIE: But you aren't looking at them!

KAGI: Of course. No. They're wonderful. They smell, too. Splendid. I say, why are you so good to me?

ANNIE: Am I?

KAGI: Roses on my table. It's like heaven.

ANNIE: I expect they have much better roses in heaven.

KAGI: Yes. But don't let's talk about heaven.

ANNIE: No. There's time for that when you're old. [*Goes to the door.*] What a lovely place this is. I shall be sorry to go.

KAGI: You will?

ANNIE: I think the South is very beautiful. It's strange that a terrible thing like slavery can exist here. Look at the orchards and the mountains.

KAGI: They call them the Blue Ridge Mountains. They're over the border – in Virginia.

ANNIE: Virginia? That's where you're all going?

KAGI: Yes, for a time. Then we sweep further south. Carolina and Georgia.

ANNIE: It's a great and a brave thing. But it's strange that men should fight in all this beauty.

KAGI: There is wickedness here, and unless we fight against it, we do wrong ourselves.

ANNIE: And yet, if you and I had been born in the South, we should not have thought slavery a great wrong. Martha and I have met with Southerners on our walks round here – and they're dear, kind people.

KAGI: There was another murder not a mile away yesterday. That's five murders and one suicide since we've been in this place. All of them slaves.

ANNIE: Some owners must be very cruel. God forgive them. They can't know what they do.

KAGI: Miss Annie, you're a dear forgiving girl. I think America will need more children like you before we reach the end of this business.

ANNIE: Tell me, is there great danger?

KAGI: It's no child's play. But there's a good chance for all.

ANNIE: You'll come back . . . Jack?

KAGI: Of course I will.

ANNIE: But I know there's danger – terrible danger. Father has never been so serious before. I'm afraid . . .

KAGI [*taking her in his arms*]: Please don't cry, Annie. I may call you Annie now, mayn't I?

ANNIE: Yes, please.

KAGI: Your father will be safe enough. I swear that I shall defend him with my life.

ANNIE: Oh, Jack, Jack – it's you, you I want most! Oh, what am I saying?

KAGI: Annie, darling! Please don't. . . . I shall take care of myself. I never knew you cared that way.

[*He kisses her.*]

ANNIE: Jack, I love you.

KAGI: Annie . . . angel . . . I've waited weeks to say I loved you, and my stupid tongue said other things. Or was my tongue wiser than I?

ANNIE: Wiser?

KAGI: Your father engaged me as a secretary.

ANNIE: He likes you. He said so.

KAGI: He didn't know I loved his daughter.

ANNIE: But he'll understand. I'm sure he will.

KAGI: He might think it likely to interfere.

ANNIE: Will it?

KAGI: No. I shall fight better for your sake. Annie?

ANNIE: Yes?

KAGI: Will you be my wife?

ANNIE: Yes.

KAGI: What a child you are! And I've been so terribly afraid of you.

ANNIE: I don't mind. Martha says men are better managed that way. You'll tell father?

KAGI: Yes, I must.

[MARTHA *comes downstairs with the empty basket.*]

MARTHA: Now, you two. You've had long enough.

ANNIE [*running to her*]: Oh, Martha! Dear Martha!

KAGI [*clearing his throat*]: The fact is, Mrs Oliver . . .

MARTHA: What?

KAGI: Well, we were just saying that the orchards and the mountains . . .

MARTHA: Are exactly like they've been every morning since we came. And I've never heard you mention it before. Come along, Annie. We must see to the cooking.

ANNIE: I must go, Jack. You'll see father?

KAGI: Yes – first thing.

[ANNIE *follows* MARTHA. KAGI *goes to his desk and picks up the letters. But he deserts them for the roses.* JOHN BROWN *comes in.*]

JOHN: Any letters, Kagi?

KAGI: Yes, sir. One from Mr Douglass, I think.

JOHN: Did the pikes get through from Collinsville?

KAGI: Yes, sir. They're in the cellar of the school-house at the ferry.

[JOHN BROWN *reads the letter*.]

JOHN: Ah, good. Douglass is bringing Higginson. We may have them here any time now.

KAGI: There's a case of rifles come in from Chambersburg this morning, Captain.

JOHN: Have we paid for them?

KAGI: Yes, we've paid. But we haven't much money left.

JOHN: Money. That's the thing I fear most. Higginson might help. We must sacrifice personal feeling when lives are at stake.

KAGI: Stevens was asking if you'd go up and see the men, sir. He says you put spirit into them to tide over the long hours of waiting.

JOHN: Perhaps it won't be so long as we think.

KAGI: You mean, a change in plans?

JOHN: We must be ready for it, that's all.

KAGI [*indicating a parcel*]: These came through from the printer this morning. One thousand copies.

JOHN: Let me see one. The provisional constitution. That's important. Every man must carry one of these when we go into action. It's good proof we're not just outlaw ruffians.

KAGI: There's another thing I want to ask you about, Captain Brown. It's a personal matter.

JOHN [*taking a seat*]: Oh? Sit down, Kagi.

KAGI: Thank you, sir. Do you mind if I stand, sir?

JOHN: That's all the same to me. You look worried. Nothing wrong, I hope?

KAGI: No, sir. Not exactly wrong. But, on the other hand, I'm not sure it's exactly right.

JOHN: Now, Kagi. I like plain speaking and plain dealing. I've admired the same qualities in you. I'll thank you not to give me any riddles.

KAGI: The fact is, sir, I'm in love.

JOHN: That's a pity.

KAGI: With Annie.

JOHN [*after a pause*]: That's a downright pity.

KAGI: I was afraid you'd take it badly, sir.

[*There is another pause.*]

JOHN: Don't misunderstand me, Kagi. At any other time I should have been glad. I love you as one of my own sons. Does she care for you in the same way?

KAGI: Annie has promised to be my wife, sir, subject to your approval.

JOHN: I should do wrong to forbid it, maybe. But I should fail in my duty if I didn't show you the need for discretion.

KAGI: I don't follow, Captain.

JOHN: You know the chances of this raid. You know every detail of my plans. There are some would call it a gambler's throw. I believe it will be a blow struck for God and humanity, but I don't flatter myself Providence will take more especial care of our lives on that account. In fact, Providence may have good reason for taking our lives.

KAGI: You mean . . .?

JOHN: I mean that I think we shall all be killed.

KAGI: Captain Brown!

JOHN: I thought you knew.

KAGI: I did. At least I knew there was danger, but . . . not so bad.

JOHN: I am opposed to bloodshed, but if we, believing in God's purpose on this earth, are prepared to give our lives, I don't think the sacrifice will be in vain.

KAGI: I'm not afraid. I'll die gladly for the cause. But I don't understand . . .

JOHN: I know your courage and your devotion. I had those qualities in mind when I asked you to join me. But there was another thing. So far as I have been able I have engaged men who could fight and die with neither wives nor families on their consciences. Now do you understand me?

KAGI: Yes, but will Annie understand?

JOHN: If there is bloodshed at the end of this business I ask you to consider that my family will suffer heavily enough. Would you make the sacrifice heavier?

KAGI: But what can I do? We love each other. Is that something that can be undone now?

JOHN: Very easily. You can obey my orders.

KAGI: And what are your orders, sir?

JOHN: Tell her that I forbid the marriage. Avoid her. Don't speak to her.

KAGI: But I can't do that!

JOHN: You can if you're a good soldier. Is this your devotion to the cause?

KAGI: No, Captain Brown! You've no right to interfere between us!

JOHN: I only speak for God.

KAGI: Yes, that's all you ever say! Isn't it a nice easy road through life – to say that it's God's will whenever it suits your purpose? Isn't it God's will that Annie and I were brought together? Tell me that!

JOHN: God's way is often the harder way.

KAGI: But you can't – even if I am to die – we love each other. I think, sir, you're mad. This raid has driven every human thought out of your brain. God doesn't want madmen to fight his battles.

JOHN: It is generally the madmen who do, and the madmen who win.

KAGI: But you must have loved once yourself.

JOHN: Young man, I've loved many things in life. I rejoice in the love of a good woman and a fine family. I love my home. I love the hills and forests of the Adirondacks. I love comfort, and the prosperity of honest work. I'm of an age now when a man might turn to a chair in his chimney corner, and read books, and leave the mending of the world to others. But God has stirred my spirit, and made me travel an uneasy road. There's a hangman's rope waiting for me in six counties. I have chosen to be an outlaw because there is a great wrong in America. If the road is too hard for you, Kagi, we must part company.

KAGI: No, sir, I don't want that. . . . I didn't think . . .

JOHN: Lovers were never meant to think. Before many days are passed, Annie and Martha must be escorted north. You will go with them.

KAGI: But the raid . . . ? I can't leave you now, sir.

JOHN: Those are my terms. They're hard, but this is a hard business. Which is it to be?

KAGI: I'll stay, sir.

JOHN: I'm glad. Annie's young, and she'll soon forget.

KAGI: But if we get through alive . . . ?

JOHN: If we get through alive, it means we shall have lost.

[KAGI *bows his head.*]

You're still going with me?

KAGI: Yes, sir.

JOHN: I've trusted no one else with the truth. Not even my own sons. Do you understand me better now?

KAGI: I understand, sir.

[*The sentry appears on the veranda.*]

SENTRY: Two men to see you, sir. One a coloured gentleman of the name of Douglass.

JOHN: That's all right. Ask them to step inside.

SENTRY: Yes, sir.

[*He salutes and goes.*]

JOHN: Kagi, ask Shields Green to come downstairs. I'd like to have him meet Mr Douglass.

KAGI: Yes, sir. I'm sorry, sir.

JOHN: That's all right.

[KAGI *runs upstairs. A sentry ushers in the two men and goes. The coloured gentleman is* FREDERICK DOUGLASS, *the*

black preacher, a white-haired old negro. He is accompanied by
T. W. HIGGINSON, *a worker for Abolition, and later a friend
in need to the* BROWN *family.*]

Welcome to Kennedy Farm, Mr Douglass. And you, Mr
Higginson. Pray be seated.

HIGGINSON: You're in a state of war here, I see.

JOHN: We have to be careful. I presume no one knows of
your visit.

DOUGLASS: We, too, have been careful, Captain Brown. I
am on a preaching mission in Maryland.

JOHN: Good.

[KAGI *returns with* SHIELDS GREEN.]

This is Mr Kagi, my secretary. And this is Shields Green.
We live on terms of equality here, Mr Douglass.

DOUGLASS: How do you do, Mr Green?

GREEN: Very well, thank you, Mr Douglass.

DOUGLASS: This is one of my people that you have saved, I
think.

JOHN: God used me for that purpose, Mr Douglass. But I
shouldn't be surprised if Green is the means of saving me
some day. Sit down, all of you. There's a great deal to say.

HIGGINSON: I'll cut a long matter short by saying that
Douglass here has told me of your plans. If we can help we
will. If we can't, we shall go away and keep our mouths
shut.

DOUGLASS: Is it still your intention to capture Harper's
Ferry, Captain Brown?

JOHN: It is.

HIGGINSON: What is the size of your troop?

JOHN: Twenty-two men.

HIGGINSON: And you plan to seize the United States arsenal
with an army of twenty-two men?

JOHN: That is my settled intention.

DOUGLASS: But the plan of running off slaves – your original
plan – what of that?

JOHN: This will be the greater blow.

DOUGLASS: But the risk!

KAGI: We have considered that. All of us.

HIGGINSON: Captain Brown. You plan to seize an American town. A town not a hundred miles from Washington, and, what is more, an important military depot. Do you know what that means? It's an attack on the Federal Government. The whole country will be arrayed against us.

JOHN: Then I am more certain than ever that Harper's Ferry is the place to attack.

HIGGINSON: You want to rouse the nation?

JOHN: Exactly. The blow must be startling, or it will be in vain.

KAGI: We think the attack will be like a trumpet-call to the slaves. Do you agree, Mr Douglass?

DOUGLASS: But my people are powerless.

JOHN: We have arms for them.

DOUGLASS: But years of slavery. Generations of humiliation and chains. That treatment does not breed a fighting race.

JOHN: Look at Green. He's as brave as a lion.

DOUGLASS: Those are exceptions. You white people, who glory in liberty, do not know how blessed a thing it really is. Slavery breeds slaves.

JOHN: The Lord will put a sword into their hands.

DOUGLASS: But your old plan. You remember. Twenty men in the Alleghanies, who would gradually and secretly draw off the slaves from the plantations, until slavery was broken.

JOHN: I am an old man, and that kind of work is slow. We shall strike such a blow at Harper's Ferry as shall rouse the whole country.

HIGGINSON: Captain Brown, you are walking into a steel trap. There will be no way out alive. You will be surrounded, and escape will be impossible.

JOHN: Mr Higginson, I respect your views. But my knowledge of military matters is not small. Even if surrounded, we can cut a way out.

HIGGINSON: And if you fail?

JOHN: Whatever happens, we cannot fail.

KAGI: We have another source of strength. The best citizens of the neighbourhood will be captured at the start, and we shall hold them as hostage, and so dictate terms.

HIGGINSON: Virginia will blow you and your hostages sky-high rather than let you hold Harper's Ferry for an hour.

DOUGLASS: There will be terrible bloodshed.

HIGGINSON: Aren't you forgetting, sir, that these people are American citizens? Virginia is a proud old State, and Virginians are mighty plucky when they're roused.

JOHN: I am not forgetting, sir, that the Virginians believe in slavery.

DOUGLASS: Captain Brown, forgive me if I talk strongly on a thing so near your heart. Have you considered the lives that will be lost?

JOHN: Slavery will never go from this country without the letting of blood. If you are prepared to wait, and strike no blow, you will never kill slavery. But a day will come when the business must be fought to the bitter end. Maybe it will mean a civil war. The Union of American States will crumble, and there will be such bloodshed as the world has never seen in modern times. That is where your non-resistance, and your legislation, and your presidential elections will lead you. I want to make no idle talk of sacrifice, but a blow struck now, and the loss of a few lives, will bring the eyes of the world upon us, so that the South will abolish slavery out of very shame. I believe in the Golden Rule, sir, and the Declaration of Independence. I think they both mean the same thing, and it is better that a whole generation should pass off the face of the earth – men, women, and children – by a violent death than that one jot of either should fail in this country. I mean exactly *so*, gentlemen.

DOUGLASS: Remember, Captain Brown, it is written that they that take the sword shall perish by the sword.

JOHN: Matthew was right. The slave-owners have taken the sword and they must perish by it. The slaves are prisoners of war. They are held by the sword. It makes me very angry when men say that we are attacking inoffensive people. They're ruffians, sir.

HIGGINSON: You understand that I can get no support for you, either political or financial?

JOHN: I would have welcomed financial support. But political support – never.

HIGGINSON: You do not like politicians? Why?

JOHN: They act according to their instincts, that's all.

DOUGLASS: Mr Abraham Lincoln is a good man.

JOHN: But if they make him President his hands are tied. He couldn't force Abolition with twenty men as I hope to do. No, I want no support from politicians. They suppose every man wants to lead, and they're jealous of every scheme that isn't their own.

HIGGINSON: But what about democracy and the ballot-box – have you lost faith in all that?

JOHN: I have lived in Kansas, sir. I went there with my sons as free soil settlers. Do you know what happened to the settlers who voted against slavery? Have you ever heard of stuffed ballot-boxes, Mr Higginson? There is no democracy where an election is fought at the point of the bowie-knife.

HIGGINSON [*rising*]: I see your mind is made up, Captain Brown.

JOHN: Fifty years ago, Mr Higginson, when I first saw slavery.

HIGGINSON: Then I'm afraid I must go.

JOHN: You'll stay and eat with us?

HIGGINSON: Thank you, but you must excuse me. There's a train for the North at noon. I can catch it at Harper's Ferry if I leave now. Captain Brown, I respect you and admire you, but I think you are wrong.

JOHN: But I can trust you?

HIGGINSON: My word for that, sir. I must thank you for the talk.

JOHN: Talk, Mr Higginson, is a national institution in America. But it doesn't free the slaves. Mr Douglass, you'll stay?

DOUGLASS: It will be better for me to go.

JOHN: Come with me, Douglass. I'll defend you with my life. We want you for a special purpose. When I strike, the bees will begin to swarm, and I want you to help me hive them.

DOUGLASS: I cannot do that. What does Mr Green mean to do?

GREEN: I go with the ole man.

[*A horse heard galloping. Then* OWEN *runs excitedly over the veranda into the room.*]

OWEN: Father!

JOHN: Well, Owen? What is it?

OWEN: I want a word with you. It's urgent.

JOHN: You can speak before these gentlemen. They have our full confidence.

OWEN: I've been into Harper's Ferry. They've got wind of something going on here at the farm. They say the Federal Government will issue a search-warrant.

KAGI: A search-warrant?

OWEN: I overheard it at the depot.

KAGI: What's to be done, sir?

JOHN: There's only one thing to be done. We attack at once.

KAGI: But the women? Annie and Martha?

JOHN: Mr Higginson. Will you do me an especial favour which may be of some trouble to you?

HIGGINSON: Anything I can do as a man of peace.

JOHN: My daughter and my son's wife have been house-keeping for us. Will you escort them back to the North?

HIGGINSON: Gladly.

JOHN: How long before your train?

HIGGINSON: I must leave here inside ten minutes.

JOHN: Owen, warn the girls. Say they must pack and be ready inside ten minutes. Green, tell Oliver and Watson to step this way.

[OWEN *goes out on the left.* GREEN *up the stairs.*]

HIGGINSON: Your womenfolk must be well trained in the alarms of war, Captain Brown.

JOHN: My daughter has seen much prompt action in her short life. Besides, I asked them to be in readiness a week ago. I've been expecting this.

[OLIVER *comes down the stairs and* WATSON *enters from outside.*]

Oliver, we're moving as soon as we can. Martha and Annie are going with Mr Higginson.

OLIVER: A change in plans, sir?

JOHN: The rumour of a search-warrant, that's all. Oliver, you'll escort Mr Higginson to the Maryland border. Give the girls a hand with their baggage.

[WATSON *and* OLIVER *go out on the left.* KAGI *goes to his desk and gathers up the papers.*]

DOUGLASS: Captain Brown, let me make one last effort to turn you from this raid. I believe that you and your sons, and all the other brave men, are going to certain death. If you do not fall by Virginian bullets, they will hang you as outlaws. You count on a rising of the slaves. I beg you, I implore you – do not overestimate the fighting quality of crushed and beaten slaves. And suppose you do raise such a rebellion, do not think you would easily control it. My people have been treated like beasts. They will avenge themselves like beasts. Captain Brown, it will be horrible, horrible!

JOHN: I thank you, Mr Douglass. My answer to that is simple, and it is one you should understand. It was not John Brown who ordered this raid, it was God, and I am only his humble servant.

DOUGLASS: But if they kill you?

JOHN: Then it will greatly advance the cause of Christ. Besides, an old man should have more care to end life well than to live long.

DOUGLASS: You make me very humble, Captain Brown. I think your strength can only come from God.

KAGI: There'll be no help from Ohio now, sir.

JOHN: No? Perhaps Ohio will be more sorry than we are. Are you a judge of apples, Mr Higginson?

HIGGINSON: Apples? I think I know a good one.

JOHN: Then you must visit the orchard, and fill your pockets for the journey. Come, Mr Douglass. There's a tree in the garden of which I've never seen the like. Ask the girls to hurry, Kagi. See the apples? There's a great crop to be gathered by those who come after us. I hope they won't leave it rotting on the ground.

[JOHN BROWN *goes out talking to* HIGGINSON *and* DOUGLASS. WATSON *comes from the room on the left carrying a tin trunk on his shoulder.*]

KAGI: Are they ready, Watson?

WATSON: They're coming now.

[*He goes out.* KAGI *sits at his desk and pretends to write.* OLIVER *comes in, carrying* MARTHA'S *bag.* MARTHA *and* ANNIE *are dressed for the journey.*]

OLIVER: Where's Mr Higginson?

KAGI: You'll find them in the orchard. You'll have to hurry to catch that train.

MARTHA: Good-bye, Mr Kagi.

KAGI: Good-bye, Mrs Oliver.

MARTHA [*going towards the door*]: And don't you trust the climate, Oliver, even if it is the South. Promise me, no going out at nights without your greatcoat, and if it does turn cold, don't forget that flannel thing I made for wearing next to your chest. [*Over her shoulder*] Don't be long, Annie. [*She goes out.*] And dear Oliver, do be careful, whatever you do . . .

[*She and* OLIVER *have gone, leaving* ANNIE *standing in the doorway.* KAGI *glances up.*]

KAGI [*carelessly*]: You really will have to be quick to catch that train, Miss Annie.

ANNIE: Jack!

[KAGI *tries to write, but he is unable to keep it up, and runs to her.*]

KAGI: Annie!

[*The banjo upstairs is playing 'Polly Wolly Doodle', and the men are singing in chorus.*]

CURTAIN

SCENE 2

The same, a day later. Night of Sunday, 16 October 1859. A shaded oil-lamp hangs in the centre of the room and throws a bright light on the table under it. JOHN BROWN *stands speaking to* OLIVER, WATSON, OWEN, KAGI, GREEN, *and* STEVENS, *who are seated round the table. In the shadows of the room the rest of the party can be dimly seen. All carry rifles and wear hats ready for departure.*

JOHN: That, I think, disposes of every difficulty. Owen will remain in charge here, because I need a good man in command of supplies. We shall proceed to the school-house and form a second depot, which will also serve as a rendezvous in the event of any calamity at the bridge. Stevens, you will take two men and cut the telegraph wires.

STEVENS: Yes, sir.

JOHN: The watchman on the Potomac bridge must be captured silently. Oliver, I leave that to you.

OLIVER: Yes, sir.

JOHN: Kagi, you provided crowbars for breaking in the armoury door?

KAGI: They're all ready, sir.

JOHN: Few people will be abroad in the town, but I want all stray citizens rounded up; they will be our hostages, and out of harm's way. You understand that, Watson?

WATSON: Yes, sir.

JOHN: Then you will proceed to the house of Colonel Washington, and, with all possible courtesy, place him under arrest.

WATSON: I understand, sir.

KAGI: There's the question of the midnight express for the North. Shall we take up the rails?

JOHN: That would wreck the train. I want no innocent people to suffer. Let it go through.

KAGI: It's a risk.

JOHN: We must take it.

KAGI: Very good, sir.

JOHN: And now, gentlemen, let me press one thing on your minds. You all know how dear life is to you, and how dear your lives are to your friends. Remember that, and consider that the lives of others are as dear to them as yours are to you. Do not take the life of any man if you can possibly avoid it. But if it is necessary to take life to save your own, then make sure work of it. When they attack us, as they most certainly will, don't yell and make a great noise, but keep perfectly silent and still. Wait till they get within twenty-five yards of you. Get a good object, be sure you see the hind sight of your gun, then fire. A great deal of powder and lead is wasted by firing too high. If all the bullets ever aimed at me had hit me, I would be as full of holes as a riddle. And now as to the purpose of this raid, and the questions that men may ask, or the doubts that may lie in your own conscience. We go into Virginia to put a sword into the hand of the African negro. Let that be firmly planted in your minds. The slaves who join us we shall organize for defensive operations. We shall maintain them in freedom until such a time as the United States reforms the slavery laws. Until that time you will be their leaders. I could have found a hundred, nay a thousand, men to follow me in this raid. I choose to go with twenty, because I want men of principle to carry out this work. We have no place for ruffians and bullies in our ranks. I have chosen godly men to do God's work. A few men in the right, and knowing they are right, can overturn a king. And, lastly, remember this: that whatever the end of this night's work may be, we shall have lighted such a torch in America that men now groping in darkness will see the road of righteousness.

[*A murmur of applause.* JOHN BROWN *takes up his Bible and reads. The men stand bareheaded.*]

'And the Lord said unto Gideon, "By the three hundred men that lapped will I save you and deliver the Midianites into thine hand." . . . And the three companies blew the trumpets, and brake the pitchers, and held the lamps in their left hands, and the trumpets in their right hands to blow withal; and they cried, "The Sword of the Lord, and of Gideon." . . . And they stood every man in his place round about the camp. . . .'

[BROWN *closes his Bible and takes off his spectacles. Then he kneels, and all the men kneel with him, a little noisily because of their rifles. They begin to recite the Lord's Prayer as the* CURTAIN *falls slowly.*]

ACT THREE

SCENE I

Before dawn on 18th October. We look into the corner of the fire-engine house of the Government Arsenal at Harper's Ferry. In the wall, left, are the big doors, slightly ajar, with moonlight streaming through. Some packing-cases form a barricade. The main source of light is from a lamp, high up and out of sight. Against the longer right-hand wall is a bench, on which lies OLIVER BROWN, *mortally wounded and groaning. Downstage is a door to an out-house.*

There should be not more than ten of the raiders present; only six unwounded. The rest are killed or captured. Some of them, including WATSON, *are guarding the door.* JOHN BROWN *sits by* OLIVER. STEVENS *is calling the roll.*

STEVENS: John Cook.
COOK: Here.
STEVENS: Shields Green.
GREEN: Here.
STEVENS: Stewart Taylor.
TAYLOR: Here.
STEVENS: Watson Brown.
WATSON: Here.
STEVENS: Oliver Brown.
JOHN: Yes, he's here.
STEVENS: Coppoc.
COPPOC: Here.
STEVENS: Anderson.
ANDERSON: Here.
STEVENS: Thompson.
THOMPSON: Here.
C

STEVENS: That's ten of us, sir. Only eight of us fit for action. Seven killed or taken prisoner. No news yet of Owen and the others, but I understand they're holding the school-house across the river, sir.

JOHN: Thank you, Stevens. Go in to the prisoners and ask Colonel Washington to be good enough to step this way.

STEVENS: Yes, sir.

[*He goes through the door on the right.*]

[*There is some firing outside. The men at the barricade duck their heads.*]

WATSON: Keep your heads down.

JOHN: Watson!

WATSON: Sir?

JOHN: Hold your fire. We can make better use of our powder in the morning.

WATSON: Yes, sir.

[STEVENS *enters with* COLONEL WASHINGTON.]

WASHINGTON: Well, who's the leader here?

STEVENS: This is Captain John Brown.

[WATSON *comes from the barricade.*]

JOHN: Ossawatomie Brown of Kansas. Perhaps you know me better by that name, Colonel Washington?

WASHINGTON: Well, Captain Brown, or whatever you call yourself, on behalf of myself and the other prisoners in there I want to lodge a protest against this business.

JOHN: I expected that.

WASHINGTON: You're a cool fellow, Brown. Do you know it's an outrage to drag an American citizen out of his bed at midnight?

[*A shot.*]

JOHN: If you'll be so kind, Colonel Washington, I should like you out of the line of that doorway. There's a lot of bullets flying about.

WASHINGTON: You seem very anxious for my safety.

JOHN: You're a hostage, sir, and a dead hostage will be no use to any cause. Besides that, I want you for the name you bear. I honour all of the name of Washington.

WASHINGTON: Then I must say you've a queer way of show-ing it.

[OLIVER *groans*.]

Who's this poor fellow?

JOHN: That is my son, Oliver Brown.

[WASHINGTON *examines him*.]

WASHINGTON: Good God! You know he's dying?

JOHN: Yes, Colonel, I know.

WASHINGTON: What devilment are you planning, John Brown?

JOHN: It's not devilment. It is a plan to free slaves.

WASHINGTON: A slave raid? Well, it isn't a great success.

JOHN: Only time will tell us that.

WASHINGTON: Don't you think, Brown, that a man with your grey hairs would do better to think less of this world and more of eternity?

JOHN: I am prepared for eternity. I have travelled further along that road than you, Colonel Washington. I am ready.

[*One of the men motions to* WATSON.]

WATSON: Sir!

JOHN: What is it!

[*There is some excitement among the men at the door*.]

WATSON: They're showing a white flag, sir.

JOHN: Be careful! It may be a trick.

WATSON: There's an officer coming forward, sir.

[STEVENS *runs over to the door*.]

JOHN: Keep him covered, Watson. But don't shoot.

WATSON: No, sir.

STEVENS: He's carrying a letter in his hand. That'll be terms of surrender.

JOHN: Stevens. That's a word I don't like to hear.

STEVENS: I'm sorry, sir. But this is a pretty bad hole we're in.

WATSON [*shouting outside*]: All right. Hand it over.

[*A letter is thrown through the doors.* STEVENS *picks it up and hands it to* BROWN.]

JOHN: Tell the man to go back – we'll signal our reply.

WATSON: You can go back. We will signal our reply.

JOHN [*reading*]: This is from Colonel Lee. He demands the surrender of the persons in the armoury building. 'If they will peaceably surrender themselves, they shall be kept in safety to await the orders of the President. Colonel Lee represents to them, in all frankness, that it is impossible for them to escape; that the armoury is surrounded on all sides by troops; and that if he is compelled to take them by force he cannot answer for their safety.'

WATSON: What are you going to do, father?

JOHN: I know what I am going to do. What do you men say?

STEVENS: Colonel Lee's right. We can't escape.

WATSON: You can't surrender now!

STEVENS: I don't want to die like a rat in a trap.

[*Some of the men seem to agree with* STEVENS, *and talk among themselves.*]

WASHINGTON: John Brown, and all you men here, let me advise you to surrender without delay. The longer you hold out the worse your punishment will be.

JOHN: The longer we hold out, the more notice men will take of our action.

WATSON: That's right, father.

WASHINGTON: You know what that action is. It's high treason against the State.

JOHN: I don't acknowledge the laws of the State. We are fighting for a higher power.

WASHINGTON: You know the penalty for treason.

JOHN: I think we all know that. Now, gentlemen, I want you to consider our position. If we surrender now, the lives of good men on both sides will have been wasted in vain. The purpose of this raid, the purpose of freeing slaves, has failed. I admit that. But that other purpose, our intention to make a great noise in America – that cannot fail if you will stand by me now.

WATSON: Of course we'll stand by you!

JOHN: Do not misunderstand me, Watson. Death is the price of victory.

WATSON: Yes, father.

JOHN: What do you say, Stevens?

STEVENS: Is it high treason, or isn't it?

[*The men murmur.*]

JOHN: Yes. This is what men call high treason. I am more concerned with the judgement of God.

GREEN: I'm with you, Mas'r Brown. I fight on.

JOHN: Thank you, Shields Green. And you, Stevens?

STEVENS: I do what you do, Captain.

[*General agreement.*]

WASHINGTON: John Brown, I urge you, I implore you, to surrender!

JOHN: I thank you, sir, because I think your advice is meant for kindness. But here's my answer to Colonel Lee and Virginia, the slave State!

[*He fires his revolver up into the air through the open door. Immediately comes a reply from distant rifles.* WATSON BROWN *leaps up at the barricade.*]

WATSON: Get back, father.

[*He is shot and falls dead.* WASHINGTON *kneels beside him.*]

JOHN: What?

WASHINGTON [*rising*]: Dead!

JOHN [*after a pause*]: Wait until they are within twenty-five yards and then fire.

[*The men move quietly into position.*]

CURTAIN

SCENE 2

The Telegraph Office at Harper's Ferry, Virginia.

About dawn on the morning of Tuesday, 16 October 1859. We see only two walls of the hut, which is lighted by an oil-lamp on the wall. Down on the right a doorway leads outside. A notice gives the time-table of the Baltimore and Ohio Railroad.

A TELEGRAPH OPERATOR *stands in the doorway. A* VIRGINIAN MILITIAMAN *sits at a table, left-centre, cleaning his gun.*

As the curtain rises we hear the shouting of an angry crowd and a bugle-call.

OPERATOR: The marines are charging. They're smashing in the door.

SOLDIER: Then I reckon the war's about over.

[*The telegraph ticks.*]

OPERATOR: Hey! They've joined the wires! The telegraph's working. [*Runs over to telegraph.*]

SOLDIER: Don't jump about like that – when a soldier's in a state of war his nerves is on edge.

[*Enter* GALLAGHER, *a newspaperman.*]

Halt! Who goes there?

GALLAGHER: John P. Gallagher, of the *New York Herald*.

SOLDIER: Well, I don't know you. I guess I'll have to shoot you.

GALLAGHER: There's my pass. Signed Robert E. Lee. They tell me you've a telegraph working here.

OPERATOR: What do you want?

GALLAGHER: I've come to put this funny little town on the map. Great story. Battle of Harper's Ferry. The whole world's waiting for it.

SOLDIER: The last Yankee newspaperman who came nosing round here was hung on a tree.

GALLAGHER [*sits at the table and produces a notebook*]: I want you to tell me all you know about this raid. Story of eye-witness.

SOLDIER: But I didn't see any of it myself.

GALLAGHER: Splendid. That's all the better. You'll be able to use your imagination.

SOLDIER: Well, it started early yesterday morning.

OPERATOR: John Brown's men surrounded the town.

GALLAGHER [writing]: Surrounded – the – town. How many men had he?

OPERATOR: About a hundred – I guess.

SOLDIER: No, two hundred.

GALLAGHER: Call it two thousand. Looks better in a headline. Go on.

SOLDIER: He cut the telegraph wires, and he captured about fifty citizens for hostages.

OPERATOR: Then our boys began shooting. We got ten of their men and they killed six of ours.

GALLAGHER: That's sixteen killed. Didn't anything exciting happen?

SOLDIER: Well, John Brown and his men shut themselves up in the fire-engine shed over at the arsenal.

OPERATOR: But we'll soon have 'em out of there. What with the militia and Colonel Lee's marines, there's two thousand men under arms in the town.

SOLDIER: We've got 'em like rats in a trap.

GALLAGHER: Rats in a trap. That's good.

[It is growing lighter outside.]

Just a minute. If John Brown cut all your telegraph wires, how did you get any message through?

SOLDIER: The railroad, of course. The old fool was so soft-hearted he wouldn't wreck the train, and he let it go.

GALLAGHER: Do you know the names of any of those sixteen killed?

OPERATOR: One of the men – his body fell in the river. I

helped fish him out; full of bullets he was – his name was
Kagi – John Kagi.

GALLAGHER: I've never heard of him.

SOLDIER: Say, if you're mentioning any names, mine's
Robinson.

GALLAGHER: Robinson. Killed or wounded?

SOLDIER: No, that's me. Eyewitness.

GALLAGHER: Thank you, general. I'll remember you.

[*Some shooting.*]

SOLDIER [*at the door*]: If you want to see a real battle, come in
and watch it.

GALLAGHER: Aw, never mind the battle. Fiction is stranger
than fact. Come along and get this story on the wire.

OPERATOR: But I'll miss the fun.

GALLAGHER: You'll read it all in tomorrow's *New York
Herald*. That's nothing to the story I'm writing. Come on,
now, get busy.

OPERATOR: All right.

[*They go to the telegraph instrument and the* OPERATOR
begins to tap.]

GALLAGHER: Special Press Message. *New York Herald*.
Harper's Ferry. Tuesday. Got that?

OPERATOR: Hold on, not so fast.

[*A roar from the crowd.*]

SOLDIER: They've got John Brown. They're dragging him
out.

GALLAGHER [*dictating*]: Bullets are flying around me as I
write.

SOLDIER: Why, he's quite an old man!

GALLAGHER [*to* SOLDIER]: Shut up! [*To* OPERATOR] This
little old-world Virginian town . . .

SOLDIER: Say, I think the crowd are going to lynch him.

GALLAGHER: Lynch? What do you say? Gee, what a
story!

SOLDIER: No, the marines have got him.

GALLAGHER: Ah, that's a pity. [*He goes back to the* OPERATOR.] Where was I?

OPERATOR: Old-world Virginian town . . .

GALLAGHER: . . . is the scene of the most sensational outrage in American history.

[*The shouting of an excited crowd is heard.*]

SOLDIER: There's only seven of 'em, with John Brown. Couldn't have had more than twenty men!

GALLAGHER: For a day and a night terror has reigned supreme.

SOLDIER: Look out, boys. Here's Colonel Lee. He's coming this way.

GALLAGHER: Hold the line, operator. I'll give you the story later.

[*The* SOLDIER *stands to attention by the door.*]

[*The angry voices come nearer. Words of command are heard.* COLONEL ROBERT E. LEE *enters, followed by* COLONEL WASHINGTON.]

WASHINGTON: That crowd's in an ugly temper, Colonel Lee.

LEE: Yes, they want the prisoners. [*He calls through the doorway*] Captain Smith.

VOICE: Yes, sir.

LEE: Clear those people away.

VOICE: Yes, sir.

[*The noise subsides.*]

LEE: I shall want this office.

OPERATOR: Do you want me to go, sir?

LEE: No. This is a most unusual affair, Colonel Washington.

WASHINGTON: It's unprecedented.

LEE: You've suffered no injury?

WASHINGTON: I must admit I received nothing but courtesy at John Brown's hands.

LEE: It's the queerest business I ever struck. It goes clean against all the rules for a handful of men to seize a town and attempt to hold it against trained soldiers. It simply isn't in the book. Is the fellow mad?

WASHINGTON: Well, sir, I've had a fair opportunity of studying John Brown over in the engine-house, and I'll say this for him, he's the coolest man in the face of death I ever saw. One son lay dead, and the other – Oliver, I think he called him – lay dying fast, and believe me, sir, he commanded his men like a general.

LEE: What kind of bee has he got in his bonnet, then?

WASHINGTON: It's slavery, of course. That question's getting pretty acute, Colonel Lee.

LEE: I know. Still, the South can't alter its laws to suit every psalm-singing Yankee who knows how to handle a gun. I believe the slavery question will settle itself – if we give it time.

WASHINGTON: What are we to do with these men?

LEE: I shall hand them over to the civil authorities. They'll bungle the business as usual. [*To the* SOLDIER] Are the prisoners outside?

SOLDIER: Yes, sir.

LEE: Bring in John Brown.

[*The* SOLDIER *goes out.*]

[LEE *and* WASHINGTON *sit at the table.*]

[GALLAGHER *and the* OPERATOR *are listening at the back. The* SOLDIER *reappears, supporting* JOHN BROWN. *His head is bandaged and he can scarcely walk.*]

Sit down.

SOLDIER: These papers found on the prisoner, sir.

[WASHINGTON *takes them.* WASHINGTON *gives his chair to* BROWN, *who sinks into it.*]

LEE: Your name is John Brown?

JOHN: That is so. Of North Elba, in the State of New York.

LEE: You are the responsible leader of these men?

JOHN: I am.

LEE: On what authority do you attack a United States town?

JOHN: On the authority of God Almighty.

LEE: John Brown, I've no reason to doubt your integrity of purpose in this matter. But I'll thank you to remember you'll be called to account before an earthly tribunal. What made you do it?

JOHN: I repeat. God was my authority.

LEE: I'm a soldier, sir, and I've never found it in my conscience to say I was doing God's work. I'm paid to do man's work, and some of it's damnably dirty. Do you shed blood on God's authority?

JOHN: I believe the Lord put a sword in my hand.

LEE: With your permission, John Brown, we'll put that little point of theology on one side. Colonel Washington and myself are plain men. We'll thank you for plain answers. Who provided the money for this raid?

JOHN: It was chiefly my own.

LEE: Are you a wealthy man?

JOHN: No, sir.

LEE: Yet you had arms and equipment enough for a regiment. That took a lot of money.

JOHN: I have laid money by for years.

LEE: For this purpose?

JOHN: Yes, sir.

LEE: You had no help from politicians?

JOHN: No, sir.

LEE: Nor from the Abolitionists?

JOHN: They would not support me.

WASHINGTON: These papers were found in your possession. 'The Provisional Constitution and Ordinances for the People of the United States.' Do you recognize them?

JOHN: I wrote them.

LEE: You intended a revolution?

JOHN: I intended a new Declaration of Independence.

LEE: Was that your object in coming?

JOHN: My object was to free slaves and only that.

LEE: Then yours is a religious rather than a political movement?

JOHN: That's so.

LEE: How do you justify your acts – apart from divine guidance?

JOHN: I believe in the Golden Rule, sir.

WASHINGTON: Oh! And what is the Golden Rule?

JOHN: 'Do unto others as you would have them do unto you.' . . . I pity the poor in bondage who have none to help them. That's why I am here. I have neither animosity nor revenge towards you. I have respected the rights of the wealthy just as I respect the rights of the poor and oppressed.

LEE: You have killed Virginian citizens.

JOHN: That is a pity. I would not allow my men to fire on innocent persons if I could help it.

WASHINGTON: That's true, sir. I know he took every care.

LEE: John Brown, do you know what I ought to do with you?

JOHN: That's for you to judge. I'm ready.

LEE: As a good soldier I ought to take you out quietly and shoot you. Then we'll not be troubled by you when you're in the grave. But I'll tell you what *will* happen. I shall have to hand you over to the civil authorities. They will go through the farce they call trial by jury. The jury will be packed with Southerners and pro-slavery men. The lawyers will wrangle and fight like turkey-cocks. Your name will become a household word through the length and breadth of the land. Then, when the farce is over, they'll hang you. And when your body's rotting in the grave you'll be the most dangerous man in America. There won't be nails in all Virginia strong enough to hold your coffin down.

JOHN: You're a generous conqueror, Colonel Lee.

WASHINGTON: How many men had you?

JOHN: Twenty-two.

LEE: Your sons are dead. You know that?

JOHN: Yes. They were fine sons. It was a fine cause.

LEE: On a point of tactics, didn't you show some want of foresight in bringing so small a party to capture Harper's Ferry?

JOHN: Probably our views on military matters would differ
materially, sir.

WASHINGTON: Don't forget, Brown, that Colonel Lee has
learned his soldiering at a military academy.

JOHN: While I have had to be content with the writings of
Oliver Cromwell and Napoleon Bonaparte. But I have
received no little enlightenment by visiting their battle-
fields.

LEE: You've been to Europe?

JOHN: I sold wool at the London Exhibition in 1851.

LEE: Did you raise money for your cause?

JOHN: No. The English boiled with indignation, but they
kept their money in their pockets.

LEE: But why the madness of so small a party?

JOHN: The sacrifice has been less.

LEE: You expected to be beaten?

JOHN: It is always a military possibility, sir.

WASHINGTON: Didn't you expect reinforcements?

JOHN: Yes, sir. I put too much faith in human nature.

LEE: Isn't that the trouble with all you reformers? You put
too much faith in human nature?

JOHN: I think, sir, that unless some of us set a high standard
by expecting more than we get, the world will be a poorer
place to live in.

LEE: Have you anything more to ask, Colonel Washington?

WASHINGTON: No, sir. This photograph was found among
his papers.

LEE [*taking it*]: A little girl. [*To* BROWN] Yours?

JOHN: Yes.

LEE [*hands it over*]: Thank you, Captain Brown. I am sorry
that our only meeting has been so unpleasant for both of us.
I must now commit you to the town jail.

[LEE *motions to the* SOLDIER *to help* BROWN *to his feet. The sun has risen and golden light floods the doorway.* JOHN BROWN *turns painfully.*]

JOHN: I have failed, gentlemen. You may dispose of me very easily. I am nearly disposed of now. But all you people of the South had better prepare yourselves for a settlement of this question. It may come up for settlement sooner than you expect. This negro question, I mean. The end of that is not yet.

[JOHN BROWN *goes out. There is a howl from the mob.*]

LEE: That's one of the finest men I ever met, Colonel Washington.

WASHINGTON: They'll hang him.

LEE: Of course they will. And leave us soldiers to reap the whirlwind. Hark at the mob! They're the same the world over – from Jerusalem to Virginia.

WASHINGTON: You think he *is* inspired by God?

LEE: I think he believes so. And I'm hanged if I know the difference.

WASHINGTON: Do you think there are many in the North would act as he has done?

LEE: I'm a soldier. They don't pay me to think.

WASHINGTON: If it comes to blows, where will honest men be fighting?

LEE: I know where you and I will fight, Colonel Washington. We'll be fighting for Virginia. She's got us body and soul.

WASHINGTON: Yes, Virginia comes first. She's worth fighting for. And now, Colonel Lee, you'll have breakfast with me?

LEE: I thank you, sir, gladly. Ah, the air smells good! It's a grand morning for October.

[*They have gone.* GALLAGHER *waves his notebook.*]

GALLAGHER: Say, operator. Did you get it? History in the making. John Brown's Challenge to the South. *The end of that is not yet!* Come on, operator, get busy! What a story for the world!

[*The telegraph clicks.*]

BLACK OUT

THE CURTAIN FALLS

COURT SCENE

May be played behind curtain immediately before Scene 3. Not to be mentioned on programme. (A loudspeaker was used in the London production.)

VOICE: Gentlemen of the jury, do you find the prisoner guilty or not guilty?

FOREMAN'S VOICE: Guilty!

JUDGE'S VOICE: John Brown, have you anything to say before I pronounce sentence upon you?

BROWN'S VOICE: I have, may it please the court, a few words to say. I deny everything but what I have all along admitted – that I came here to free slaves. I suppose this court acknowledges the validity of the word of God. I see a book kissed here which I suppose to be the Bible. That book teaches me that what I would have men do to me, even so should I do to them. It teaches me further to remember them that are in bonds as bound with me. I have always tried to act up to that instruction. I am yet too young to understand that God is any respecter of persons. I believe that to have interfered on behalf of the despised poor, as I have done, is no wrong, but right.

[*There is a peal of thunder, and* BROWN'S *words grow fainter from this point.*]

Now if I am to lose my life to satisfy the ends of justice, and mingle my blood with the blood of my children, and with the blood of millions in this cruel slave country – I say, let it be done. . . .

[*The speech is now taken up by* SALMON BROWN.]

SALMON: 'I ask all righteous men to carry on the fight against that sum of all villainies called Slavery. I am content to die on the scaffold for God's eternal truth. I have enjoyed life much. Why should I complain on leaving it?'

[*While* SALMON *is reading, the lights come up on Scene 3.*]

SCENE 3

North Elba. Late November 1859. JOHN BROWN'S *home.*
It is night.

MRS BROWN *sits knitting beside the table, on which lies a pile of newspapers.* SALMON BROWN, *in his shirt-sleeves, sits near her, reading a newspaper.*

SALMON: Shall I read any more?

MRS BROWN: Go on, Salmon.

SALMON [*reading*]: 'The judge then pronounced sentence on the prisoner, who remained calm, as he had done throughout the trial. The counsel for the defence gave notice of appeal to the Governor of Virginia.'

MRS BROWN: What paper is that?

SALMON: The *New York Herald*. It's a week old, but the latest we could get this morning in Keesville.

MRS BROWN: Yes, I can bear with the *Herald*. It's against us, but it's cleanly against us, and its mistakes are those of some poor misguided creature.

SALMON: You know Mr Higginson rode down again this evening for the latest news? He should be back again soon.

MRS BROWN: Mr Higginson is a great help to us. I am sorry for him. The poor man frets now because he would not join John Brown. I tell him he has no cause for worry. God has chosen his instruments and maybe Mr Higginson is saved for other work.

SALMON [*taking up another paper*]: There's a letter here from a Frenchman. Victor Hugo. He says: 'John Brown is to be hanged. His hangman is not Judge Parker, nor the little State of Virginia – his hangman is the whole American Republic.' And a Mr Longfellow, a poet, he says: 'December 2nd will be a great day in our history, the date of a new revolution, quite as much needed as the old one.' And Mr Emerson – they tell me he's well known – he's been speaking in Boston.

MRS BROWN: Who?

SALMON: Emerson. Ralph Waldo Emerson.

MRS BROWN: What does he say?

SALMON: He says: 'John Brown's execution will make the gallows glorious like the Cross.'

MRS BROWN: That's a terrible thing to say. No doubt the poor man feels strongly. We must keep all those papers.

SALMON: There's no word of the appeal.

MRS BROWN: That's a poor hope. Nor will they prove John to be mad. I couldn't say, as they asked me to, that my husband was insane – even to save his life; because he wasn't.

SALMON: You saw they had captured Cook.

MRS BROWN: Yes, poor man.

SALMON: And there's a big reward still offered for Owen.

MRS BROWN: That means they haven't caught him.

SALMON: I'll trust Owen to escape them.

MRS BROWN: It's terrible to think of. They'll be chasing him with bloodhounds, like the slaves.

SALMON: If only I'd been there! At Harper's Ferry, I mean.

MRS BROWN: Your father wanted you here. You know how

much we needed you. And your father is easy in his mind about us. That's a great thing.

[ANNIE *comes in from the door on the right with a bowl.*]

How is she, Annie?

ANNIE: She's taken it all, and now she's sleeping soundly.

MRS BROWN: God be thanked for that. It's sleep she needs. Is the child well?

ANNIE: Martha's nursing him. She says she'll sit and watch. Bell wakens easily and calls for Watson.

SALMON: She's taken the blow hardest of all. I don't think she knows he's dead.

ANNIE: Martha would be pleased to have one of the papers. She still hopes to find more news of the way Oliver died.

[SALMON *gives her some papers.* ANNIE *goes out.*]

SALMON: Poor Annie! She's a brave girl. It's hard for the other girls to lose a husband. But she's got a sorrow of her own.

MRS BROWN: You mean this Mr Kagi?

SALMON: I'm sure of it. I saw it the way she acted when I told her he was killed. She's lost father and brothers and the man she loved.

MRS BROWN: God's will is very stern.

[*A knock on the door.*]

Who's that?

SALMON: Maybe it's Higginson back from Keesville.

MRS BROWN: Take care, Salmon.

[SALMON *takes up his gun, and cautiously unbolts the door.* OWEN *staggers in, haggard and in rags.*]

Owen!

OWEN: Mother!

[*They support him to a chair.*]

MRS BROWN: Owen, you're home, safe. . . . God be praised for this.

OWEN: The door . . . is it bolted?

SALMON: That's all right, Owen.

OWEN: They're out there – hunting!

SALMON: Nonsense!

OWEN [*wildly*]: I heard drums beating.

SALMON: Drums?

OWEN: There was a man – riding up the road from the Notch.

SALMON: That'll be Higginson. He's all right.

OWEN: Is there . . . have you any news?

SALMON: You've heard nothing – of Harper's Ferry?

OWEN: I saw the battle. I saw them taken. They left me in charge of headquarters. Then I escaped. I've been hiding and travelling ever since.

SALMON: You've seen no papers?

OWEN: Nothing. I daren't ask questions in case they suspected.

SALMON: How did you travel?

OWEN: Trains sometimes. On foot mostly. Look at 'em.
[*He points to his feet.*]

SALMON: There's a reward offered for you.

OWEN [*starting*]: What!

SALMON: Steady. You're safe here.

OWEN [*after a pause*]: What happened – to father and the boys?
[*They are silent.*]
For God's sake, tell me! They're not all . . .

SALMON: Oliver and Watson were killed. They took father alive and tried him. They've sentenced him to execution. We're waiting the result of an appeal, so there's still hope.

OWEN: And the others?

SALMON: It's rather terrible, Owen. Five waiting trial. The rest killed. This paper gives it all.
[OWEN *reads a paper.*]

MRS BROWN: But the boy's starving. Quick, Salmon, blow up the fire. Move the soup-pan on the bar.

OWEN: We must save father.

SALMON: How can we?

OWEN: We'll find men in the North, and in Kansas. We'll rush the prison.

SALMON: We've gone over all that, and it can't be done. The whole South is against us.

OWEN: And isn't the whole North with us?

SALMON: Not yet.

OWEN: When will it be, then?

SALMON: When the South have murdered John Brown, not before.

OWEN: This is awful. Oh, why didn't I die with the others?
[*He groans.*]

MRS BROWN: Owen, my son. Please don't say that. Your father would never wish it.

SALMON: There's just a hope the appeal will succeed.

MRS BROWN: We pray God continually for that. I'm afraid in my heart, but I'm weak and foolish, and wanting in faith.

SALMON: Whatever happens, Owen, we know, all of us here, that father was right.

OWEN: It's a terrible price to pay.

MRS BROWN: We must give gladly, Owen, like your father.
[ANNIE *comes in.*]

ANNIE [*running to him*]: Owen!

OWEN [*embracing her*]: Well, here I am, Annie.

ANNIE: Thank heaven, Owen, you're safe now!

MRS BROWN: Hurry, Annie! He's dying of hunger. Get down those cakes.

[*Food is put before* OWEN, *who eats ravenously.*]

ANNIE: Is there any news of the appeal?

SALMON: Mr Higginson's not back yet. And Owen knows nothing. He's been hiding.

ANNIE: You've told him about . . . ?

SALMON: Yes, we've told him.

ANNIE: Did he see the fighting?

SALMON: He was in charge of headquarters. He saw them taken, and then escaped.

ANNIE: Did he see . . . ?

SALMON: We'll not ask him now, Annie. He's worn out.

OWEN: I've got something for Annie. Kagi gave it me. You know about him?

SALMON: Yes, Annie knows.

ANNIE: He was killed.

OWEN [*producing a letter*]: He gave it me the night before the raid. He said I was to give it to Annie if things went wrong.

[ANNIE *takes it.*]

ANNIE: From Jack?

[*She stares at it.*]

OWEN: I reckon it's a bad habit of mine, keeping letters in my pocket.

[ANNIE *goes slowly from the room.*]

I guess it's her first love-letter. They riddled him with bullets. Even when he was dead and his body in the river, they kept shooting him. The swine!

MRS BROWN: Owen, there's bitterness and malice in your heart.

OWEN: But, mother, I can't forget the things I saw.

MRS BROWN: Even now there's no bitterness in John Brown.

OWEN: God forgive me! But he sees things clearer, and thinks bigger than the rest of us.

MRS BROWN: John Brown tries harder to be good than any man I ever knew. We must learn to be like him.

[*A noise outside.* SALMON *goes to the window.*]

SALMON: Here's Mr Higginson.

MRS BROWN: Then we shall soon know.

[*She sits beside the table.* SALMON *opens the door and* HIGGINSON *enters, carrying papers and a letter.*]

HIGGINSON: Good evening. I'm real glad to get in, Mrs Brown. It looks as though we'll have a storm on us very soon now.

SALMON: Owen's come home, Mr Higginson.

HIGGINSON: That's wonderful. This will be a great comfort to you, Mrs Brown.

MRS BROWN: Yes, indeed.

HIGGINSON: You need sleep, Owen.

SALMON: He's travelled five hundred miles, mostly on foot.

HIGGINSON: He'll soon get new strength here.

MRS BROWN: Is there any news?

HIGGINSON [*gravely*]: I brought the usual papers. There's a letter for you, Mrs Brown. It bears a Charlestown postmark.

MRS BROWN: Is it from John?

HIGGINSON: I think it's from the Virginia State authorities.

SALMON: That will be the result of the appeal.

MRS BROWN: Let me have it.

HIGGINSON: Mrs Brown. I suggest that you let your son open this letter. It may be good news, but it's more likely to be bad.

MRS BROWN: Let me have it, please.

[*She takes it and opens it slowly. As she reads it she bows her head and the letter slips to the floor. There is a rumble of distant thunder.*]

SALMON [*going to her*]: Mother!

[HIGGINSON *picks up the letter.*]

What is it, Mr Higginson?

HIGGINSON: The appeal has failed. The Governor of Virginia grants permission to Mrs Brown to take away John Brown's body after execution.

OWEN [*shouting hysterically*]: No! It's murder. They shan't do it! They shan't! They're hanging a saint!

SALMON: Steady, Owen.

[OWEN *sobs.*]

You must forgive him, Mr Higginson. He has passed through great suffering to escape.

HIGGINSON: I can forgive him very easily. Those thoughts are not far from the surface in all of us. Mrs Brown, I find it hard to speak to you of sympathy. Words are feeble things, but I wish you could hear what the men are saying down in the village. Their sorrow and their anger are flames that won't easily be put out. But most of all you should hear their pride. Pride that they knew John Brown. Pride in the things he once said to them. Pride in his great victory, for all men are saying that slavery was killed at Harper's Ferry.

MRS BROWN: First it was Frederick; Oliver and Watson too. And now it's John. Three sons and a husband.

SALMON: We must go on, mother, with your strength to help us.

MRS BROWN: We shall none of us be so strong again. I do not think we shall be the same people, now that John has left us. It is a new life before us, and we are like broken pieces. Lord, give us strength to mend ourselves and be new people. If I'm to see the ruin of my house, then I hope Providence will bring out of it some benefit to the poor slaves.

HIGGINSON: You will let me arrange things for you – and see to this [*he indicates the letter*].

MRS BROWN: You're very kind, Mr Higginson, but I mean to go to Virginia myself.

SALMON: No, mother. Father doesn't wish it.

HIGGINSON: That's a terrible long journey for you, Mrs Brown.

MRS BROWN: I must go. John would wish to be buried in the Adirondacks. He loves the mountains, and North Elba is his home.

HIGGINSON: I think, Mrs Brown, that heaven will look as kindly on the grave of John Brown wherever he may lie. Men will forget the old names. John Brown of North Elba, or Ossawatomie, or Harper's Ferry. Those names will die. He is John Brown of America now.

MRS BROWN: I fear men will say he's a traitor to America.

HIGGINSON: Mrs Brown, there is a harder patriotism than to

die fighting for your country. It's to die fighting against your country when you know your country's wrong.

[ANNIE *comes in quickly.*]

ANNIE: Salmon!

SALMON: What is it, Annie?

ANNIE: The signal!

SALMON: Where?

ANNIE: They're showing the light at Jackson's Farm.

[SALMON *opens the door and goes out.*]

SALMON [*returning*]: She's right. The Underground Railroad, mother.

[*He picks up his gun. Some shots are heard and the galloping of horsemen.*]

HIGGINSON: I suppose that means escaping slaves. Your father's work goes on.

SALMON: They've not stopped that, thank God!

MRS BROWN: Annie.

ANNIE: Yes, mother?

MRS BROWN: Put the lamp in the window.

[ANNIE *takes the lamp from the table and carries it to the window. There is a crash of thunder.* OWEN *springs to his feet.*]

OWEN: The drums! The drums are beating . . .

SALMON: Steady, Owen.

OWEN [*throwing him off*]: Let me go! They're marching . . .

[OWEN *seems to hear the beat of a drum. He runs to the door and flings it open. There is a blinding flash of lightning.*]

Look at 'em marching! Over the mountain-tops – down through the clouds – the army of the Lord! And John Brown's leading 'em! Glory Alleluiah!

[OWEN *shouts and waves into the sky. The thunder peals out, and as the curtain falls we hear the echo of a drum-beat in the thunder, and men singing the famous tune as they march.*]

CURTAIN

S. I. HSIUNG

Lady Precious Stream

AN OLD CHINESE PLAY DONE INTO
ENGLISH ACCORDING TO ITS
TRADITIONAL STYLE

PROPERTIES OF A SPECIAL NATURE
NEEDED FOR THE PRODUCTION OF THIS PLAY

Prop. box: Black wooden box, no top, 18 in. wide, 30 in. long, 24 in. deep.

Chairs: Chinese chairs.

Cushions: Red, flat, tufted, denim, 15 in. square.

Wine jug: Small, china, with spout.

Snow effect: Square of black silk 30 in. rolled around stick with paper snow inside.

50 taels of silver: Block of carved wood painted silver – to look like silver coins melted together.

Embroidered ball: Just that, with tassel, 6 in. diameter.

Broom: Round, rustic, with red handle.

Newspaper: Modern Chinese daily paper.

Firewood: Small twigs bound with cord, 15 in. long, 6 in. diameter.

Bag of rice: White canvas, size of 5 lb. sugar bag.

Horsewhips: 1 red, 1 blue. Tassel at end, fringe every 6 in.

Horse effect: Coconut shells and marble slab.

Carriage effect: 3 in. cymbals (2), on springs at end of red stick.

Bundle of clothing: Black bag, stuffed, same size as rice bag.

Square of blue cloth: Silk, 40 in.

Red and green swords: Wood, in sheath, ornamentally decorated.

Bamboo pole: 5 ft 6 in. long, painted gold.

Executioner's axe: Wood, wide blade, silver, blue handle.

Handcuffs: Wood, one piece, two large ovals joined together by small strip, gold colour.

Pavilion: 2 bamboo uprights, one cross-piece from which hangs embroidery piece about 5 ft 6 in. high, 6 ft long bamboo painted gold.

Lanterns: Wood frames, square, silk between frames, carried at end of 18 in. gold stick, electrically wired.

Small stool: Red, 12 in. by 12 in.

Carriage: 2 squares of silk 30 in., ornate embroidered wheel in centre, attached to sticks, short handles at one end to carry with.

Inkstone: Flat, soapstone, small depression in it for mixing ink and water, 4 in. square. Dark colour.

Table: Black, wood, 24 in. wide, 36 in. long, 30 in. high.

The Pass: Cloth, blue and white bricks, small doors in centre. 5 ft 6 in. high, 5 ft wide. Sticks at sides of pass and doors to help keep rigid.

Cloth letter: White silk, 12 in. by 6 in., red characters on it.

Archer's bow: Ornate gold bow, no string.

Yellow flag: 24 in. square on stick.

Royal seal: 6 in. block, covered with red cloth, drawn together and knotted at top.

LADY PRECIOUS STREAM

First produced at the Little Theatre, Strand, London, on 27 November 1934, presented by the People's National Theatre with the following cast:

HIS EXCELLENCY WANG YUN, *the Prime Minister*	Esme Percy
MADAM WANG, *of the Chen family, his wife*	Louise Hampton
SU, THE DRAGON GENERAL, *their eldest son-in-law*	Andrew Leigh
WEI, THE TIGER GENERAL, *their second son-in-law*	Morris Harvey
GOLDEN STREAM, *their eldest daughter, Su's wife*	Mary Casson
SILVER STREAM, *their second daughter, Wei's wife*	Vera Lennox
PRECIOUS STREAM, *their third daughter*	Maisie Darrell
HER MAID	Amy Dalby
HSIEH PING-KUEI, *their gardener*	Roger Livesey
SUITORS	David Lewis, Douglas Allen, James Penstone, Robert Syers
DRIVER	William Bell
HER ROYAL HIGHNESS THE PRINCESS OF THE WESTERN REGIONS	Fabia Drake
MA TA, KIANG HAI } *Her A.D.C.s*	Maxwell Reynolds, Michael Osler
HER MAIDS	Jane Fey, Elinor Powell, Candida John, Betty Anderson
MU	Andrew Leigh
WARDEN	Jack Twyman
EXECUTIONER	Geoffrey Wilkinson
HIS EXCELLENCY THE MINISTER OF FOREIGN AFFAIRS	Jack Twyman
PROPERTY MEN	Raymond Farrell, Thomas Clarkson
Chinese Attendants, Western Attendants, Soldiers, etc.	
HONOURABLE READER	Harold Warrender

The play produced by Nancy Price and S. I. Hsiung

ACT ONE

SCENE 1: *The Garden of the Prime Minister.
On a New Year's Day.*

SCENE 2: *The same. The 2nd of February.*

ACT TWO

SCENE 1: *The Cave of Hsieh Ping-Kuei.
One month later.*

SCENE 2: *The same. Nine months later.*

INTERMISSION – FIFTEEN MINUTES

ACT THREE

SCENE 1: *The Western Regions. Eighteen years later.*

SCENE 2: *The Cave. A short time later.*

ACT FOUR

SCENE 1: *The Garden of the Prime Minister.
The next morning.*

SCENE 2: *The Temporary Court of the King of the Western
Regions. The next day.*

OPENING ROUTINE: *Stage lights set on dim marks. House lights out. Blue footlights on. When house lights out, gong No. 1. READER enters between curtains to in front of curtain. Spot on READER*

READER [*to audience*]: Good evening [afternoon], ladies and gentlemen. You are now introduced to the traditional Chinese stage, which, according to our humble convention, is not in the least realistic. Scenery is a thing we have never heard of, and the property men who are supposed to be unseen by the audience, are taking an active part in the performance. The success or failure of a production is sometimes in their hands. They provide chairs for the actors to sit on and cushions for them to kneel upon; and when the hero is to die an heroic death he can fall down majestically and without any hesitation, for the never-failing hands of the property men are always on the watch and will promptly catch him before any disaster can take place. Nevertheless they sometimes, in an excess of zeal, overdo their duty by even looking after the worldly comforts of the players. When the actor has just finished some long lines, they would present him with a cup of tea to ease the throat. These actions would certainly be condemned by a western audience but we accept or rather pretend not to see them. There is, at least, one advantage; if some accident happens to the actor or property they can come forward and put it right before the audience can decide whether it is part of the play or not.

[*Gong No. 2 – curtain up.*]

Now let us imagine that this unfurnished stage represents the scene of the picturesque garden of the Prime Minister, Wang Yun, who appears wearing a long black beard which indicates that he is not the villain of the piece. In spite of his very long beard, His Excellency is a middle-aged man who has always found life easy and happy. As he is a man of peppery temper he is sometimes cross when he has really nothing to find fault with. He is a strict master of his home; which he rules with an iron hand, though his wife says that he should have someone at his elbow. In Government he finds that to rule a nation is much easier than to rule a family. That is, no doubt, why we have so many prominent statesmen in history.

Madam, his wife, is a kind lady of uncertain age. To her children she seems to be more than a hundred, while to her husband she is but a mere child. She is one of the women who know the importance of the ancient female virtues. To obey your father when young, to obey your husband when married, and to obey your children when a mother. By obeying people all her life she has acquired a benign look and a soft voice.

Their eldest son-in-law, Su, the Dragon General, is a famous warrior, because he always wins the battle when the enemy's General knows less about making war than he does. He knows nothing, but enough to be aware of his own ignorance.

Their second son-in-law, Wei, the Tiger General, is also a famous warrior because he always has the best of luck though it would be impossible to find a worse soldier. He knows nothing and does less, but he talks endlessly and has consequently become famous.

As for the daughters of the family, they are such charming young ladies that the author finds his English inadequate to describe their charms. However, charming ladies need no introduction – but we must warn you against Lady Precious Stream, our heroine, because she could make you put the halter willingly around your neck – if she chose to lead you along with her.

The hero of the piece, Hsieh Ping-Kuei, gardener to His

Excellency, is a man of deeds rather than words. So it would not do him justice if we vainly try to describe his merits, which, we hope, will prevent him from putting that halter willingly around his own neck.

[READER *bows and exits* D.L.]

ACT ONE

Gong No. 3 – Stage lights up. PROPERTY MEN *enter* L. *and* R. *and bow to audience – sit at their places. Gong No. 4 – music. Enter* 1ST *and* 2ND ATTENDANTS *from* R. *They go downstage* R. 1ST ATTENDANT *crosses front of stage to* D.L. 2ND ATTENDANT *stays* D.R. WANG *follows* ATTENDANTS *on, going* D.C. *Bows to audience.* PROPERTY MAN L. *brings on table and places it* D.L. *As* WANG *starts to speak music stops.*

WANG: I am your humble servant, Wang Yun, the Prime Minister of the Emperor's Court. My consort's name is Chen. Although we have been happily married for twenty years, we are still childless. It is true that we have three daughters, but that doesn't count; as you know, daughters leave their parents and become other people's property. My eldest daughter is called Golden Stream, who married Su, the Dragon General; the second is called Silver Stream, who married Wei, the Tiger General. The one dearest to my heart is the youngest, called Precious Stream – [PROPERTY MAN R. *places arm-chair* C.] – who will be sixteen next February. I have a mind to choose for her amongst the rich and young nobles for a son-in-law, but the little minx is as wilful as she is pretty, and refuses to obey my wishes.

[ATTENDANTS *come to* C. *Pantomime opening large double door. They return to* D.L. *and* D.R.]

[WANG *enters garden, stepping over threshold, and sits* C.] However, today's New Year's day; I will spread a feast here in my garden and have all my family present, and let my wife, my two sons-in-law and my two elder daughters try to persuade her to come to reason. Attendants!

ATTENDANTS [*kneeling*]: Yes, Excellency!

WANG: Request Madam to come here.

ATTENDANTS [*rising*]: Yes, Excellency.

[*They go* U.R. *and* U.L., *face off* R. *and call.*]

His Excellency requests the presence of Madam.

MADAM [*off* R.]: Yes, I will come.

[*Music starts.* 1st *and* 2nd MAIDS *enter from* R. *Go* D.S. *to* D.R., 1st MAID *crosses front to* D.L., 2nd MAID *stays* D.R. MADAM *follows them in to* D.C. *Curtsies to audience.* ATTENDANTS *return to* D.L. *and* D.R. *Music stops.*]

I am Chen, the wife of the Prime Minister, Wang.

[*She turns* U.S., *steps over threshold, curtsies to* WANG.]

My respects to Your Excellency.

[PROPERTY MAN L. *places arm-chair* L. *of* WANG.]

WANG: And mine to you. Be seated.

[*She sits* L. *of* WANG. MAIDS *cross to* D.C. *Step over threshold,* 1st MAID *goes* L. 2nd MAID *goes* R. *to stand over* MADAM'S *chair.*]

MADAM: May I know what is your wish in asking me to come to see you in the garden?

WANG: Today is New Year's Day. I want to celebrate it in some way. It looks as if it is going to snow. I propose that we have a feast here in the garden to enjoy the snow. And during the feast I hope you will try your best to persuade our youngest daughter to consent to marry one of the young nobles whose suit I have approved.

MADAM: Your orders will be obeyed. But I am afraid it will not be of any use, for the young minx is very obstinate. She insists on being allowed to choose for herself.

WANG: Nonsense! It is scandalous for a young girl to choose a husband herself. Our young generation is becoming hopeless. What are the teachings of Confucius and Mencius coming to? They study them and then act in defiance of them.

[*He shows a trifle of anger.*]

MADAM: She says that 'Not to impose your will upon others' is one of the most important teachings of Confucius and she hopes you will not forget it.

WANG [*blowing his long beard in a rage*]: Ph-ew! You have utterly spoiled her. For heaven's sake do not encourage her to rebel against me.

[*He turns aside and calls.*]

Attendants!

ATTENDANTS [*kneeling*]: Yes, Excellency!

WANG: Tell General Su, General Wei, and the ladies to come here at once.

ATTENDANTS: Yes, Excellency!

[*They rise – cross upstage* R. *and* L. *and call aloud.*]

His Excellency asks General Su and General Wei and his three daughters to come to see him.

VOICES: Yes, we are coming.

[*Music starts.* MADAM *receives cup of tea from* PROPERTY MAN L., *gives it to* WANG, *who drinks and returns cup to* MADAM. *She returns it to* PROPERTY MAN, *who retires to his place. During the above business* SU *has entered followed by* WEI. SU *to* D.L.C. WEI *to* D.R.C. *Both face audience. Music stops.*]

SU [*bows*]: Your humble servant Su, the Dragon General.

WEI [*bows*]: Wei, the Tiger General, at your service.

[PROPERTY MAN R. *places two chairs* R. *of* WANG.]

SU [*they face each other*]: Just a moment ago our father-in-law, the Prime Minister, asked us to come to the garden to see him. I wonder what is the reason.

WEI: So do I. Let us go up and find out. [*Bows.*]

SU [*stretching out his* R. *arm. Bows*]: You first.

[*They enter together and bow to* WANG.]

SU and WEI [*bowing*]: Your sons-in-law beg to pay their respects to you.

WANG and MADAM: Don't stand on ceremony, but please be seated.

SU and WEI: Thank you!

[*Music starts. They move* R., *bow to each other, sit,* SU *next to* WANG; WEI R. *of* SU. GOLDEN STREAM *and* SILVER

STREAM *enter* R. *They pause at entrance and bus. of arranging hair. They come down* C., *curtsy to audience. Music stops.*]

GOLDEN S. [L.C. *to audience*]: Your humble maid, Golden Stream, the eldest daughter of the Wang family. My husband is Su, the Dragon General.

[PROPERTY MAN L. *places two chairs* L. *of* MADAM.]

SILVER S. [R.C. *to audience*]: The second daughter, Silver Stream, at your service. My husband is Wei, the Tiger General, and the most handsome man in the kingdom. When we were talking in the reception room our father called us to come here.

[*She peeps over her shoulder, looking right and left.*]

It seems there is going to be a family council, and I believe I know the reason why.

[*The* TWO SISTERS *now face each other.*]

My eldest sister. [*Curtsy.*]

GOLDEN S.: Yes, my youngest sister. [*Curtsy.*]

SILVER S.: Do you know why father has called us to come here?

GOLDEN S.: No, I don't know.

SILVER S. [*speaking very rapidly*]: Because of our minx of a sister. I'm sure it's about her. . . . She is not very young now and she is choosing a husband for herself. No wonder, I would do the same if I were in her place. But father is also choosing one for her, and no wonder, I would do the same if I were in his place. And mother – –

GOLDEN S. [*interrupting her*]: All right, don't talk so much. Let us go in.

[*They enter up to* WANG *and* MADAM, *curtsy.*]

GOLDEN S. and SILVER S. [*together*]: Your daughters have come to pay their respects to you, dear father and mother.

WANG and MADAM: Don't stand on ceremony. Be seated.

GOLDEN S. and SILVER S.: Thank you.

[*They both sit,* GOLDEN STREAM *next to* MADAM, SILVER STREAM L. *of* GOLDEN STREAM.]

SILVER S. [*quick and sharp*]: Are you calling us here to discuss the case of my youngest sister, Precious Stream ?

WANG: Eh – yes; no, not exactly. Today is New Year's Day. I want to celebrate it in some way. It looks as if it is going to snow. I propose that we have a feast here in the garden to enjoy the snow. And during the feast, well – –

SILVER S.: Oh, I know! And during the feast we will try our best to persuade our youngest sister to consent to marry one of the young nobles whose suit you have approved. Isn't that so?

WANG: Yes, that is exactly what I wish you to do.

GOLDEN S.: But if she has a suitor in her own mind – –

WANG: Nonsense, I won't allow it.

GOLDEN S.: Is that fair, dear father?

MADAM: Yes, is that fair, dear?

WANG: Well – a daughter's duty is to obey.

SILVER S.: Father knows everything of consequence, and if our youngest sister's secret suitor is a desirable person, then he must be on father's list. Otherwise, it must be some unsuitable creature whom it would be well and proper to avoid. When I was young I left my choice entirely in dear father's hands, and, you see, I became the wife of the most handsome man in the kingdom.

[*Rises, curtsies, and sits.*]

WEI: Oh, I thank you.

[*Hides face with sleeve.*]

GOLDEN S. [*sarcastically*]: But father can't find another man as handsome as your husband for her now.

WEI: Yes, that's true.

SILVER S.: Not another word, please, she is coming.

[*Music starts.* PROPERTY MAN L. *places chair* L. *for* PRECIOUS STREAM. PRECIOUS STREAM *enters preceded by* MAID. MAID *to* L.C., PRECIOUS STREAM *does bus. of arranging hair, then down to* C. *Music stops.*]

PRECIOUS S.: I am your humble maid, Precious Stream, the

third and youngest daughter of the Wang family. When I
was doing my embroidery work in my boudoir, I heard
my father calling to me to come to the garden to see him.
My maid, lead the way to the garden.

MAID: Yes, my lady.

[MAID *enters the garden and goes* L. *followed by* PRECIOUS
STREAM. PRECIOUS STREAM *up to* C. *to* WANG, *curtsies.*]

PRECIOUS S.: Your daughter's respects to you, dear father
and mother.

WANG *and* MADAM: Don't stand on ceremony, be seated.

PRECIOUS S.: Thank you. And my compliments to my
brothers-in-law and my dear sisters.

[*Sits* L., 3rd MAID *crosses behind* PRECIOUS STREAM'S *chair.*
ATTENDANTS *close door and cross* U.R. *to behind chairs.*]

ALL: Thank you. The same to you.

PRECIOUS S.: May I know why I am called to come here,
dear father?

WANG: Yes. Ahem! Well – the fact is, eh – today – eh – today
is – eh – –

At this point the stage picture is:

C

2nd		2nd and 1st		3rd		1st
ATTENDANT		MAIDS		MAID		ATTENDANT
WEI – SU – WANG – MADAM – GOLD. S. – SIL. S. – PREC. S.

c

SILVER S.: Allow me, father. [*Rapidly as if reciting a poem.*] Today is New Year's Day. Father wants to celebrate it in some
way. It looks as if it is going to snow. Father proposes that
we have a feast here in the garden to enjoy the snow. And
during the feast he wishes – –

WANG [*uneasily*]: Ahem! – Ahem! That will do, thank you.

PRECIOUS S.: Splendid. Call the servants to arrange the table
at once. And when the snow is falling we shall have the
gentlemen to write poems for the occasion. I think my
brothers-in-law will be glad to do so.

su and wei [*looking at each other and shaking heads*]: No.

wang: Attendants!

    [ATTENDANTS *downstage* R. *and* L. *and kneel.*]

ATTENDANTS: Yes, Excellency.

wang: Remove that big rock to the centre, and let it serve
as our table.

    [*Points to table* D.L.]

ATTENDANTS: Yes, Excellency.

    [*They go to table* L. *one above and one below it. They try to
lift it, pause, take breath, try again, but are unable to move it.
Kneel.*]

Excellency, the rock refuses to be moved!

wang: Nonsense! What useless creatures you are!

    [ATTENDANTS *cross* U.L., *returning to places*, U.L. *and* U.R.]

MADAM: But, my dear, it is too heavy for them.

wei: Cowards! If it refuses to be moved why don't you
kick it.

SILVER S.: Yes, why don't you kick it?

PRECIOUS S.: Dear father, I do think it's too heavy for them.
Why don't you ask my brothers-in-law to remove it? They
are renowned all the world over for their strength. It would
be real sport.

wei: My dear relative, as our greatest sage Confucius said:
'To kill a little chicken, why use a big knife which is made
for killing horses!'

wang [*correcting him*]: '. . . for killing oxen' is the ancient
text.

wei: So, to lift this little rock is too small a feat for me, it is
also beneath my dignity. If there were a big rock, say ten
times as large as that, or even larger, then I would do it
with pleasure, and with great ease, I assure you.

SILVER S.: Yes, I can assure you too.

su [*a more truthful and practical man*]: As none of us can remove
that rock, may I make a suggestion?

wang: Certainly.

ALL: Yes.

SU: You know the gardener, Hsieh Ping-Kuei, before coming into our service was a street acrobat. I remember having seen him perform wonderful feats of strength by lifting up huge stones, now I . . .

WEI: Yes, I saw him lifting up a stone ten times as big as that one. Order him to remove it for us.

SILVER S.: Yes, order him to do it.

PRECIOUS S.: Then don't you think this rock is too small for him?

WANG: Attendants!

[ATTENDANTS *down* L. *and* R. *kneel.*]

ATTENDANTS: Yes, Excellency.

WANG: Order the gardener, Hsieh Ping-Kuei, to come here at once.

ATTENDANTS: Yes, Excellency.

[*Both go up* L. *and* R. *and call off* L.]

His Excellency orders the gardener, Hsieh Ping-Kuei, to come here at once.

HSIEH [*off stage*]: His Excellency's orders will be obeyed.

[ATTENDANTS *move to their places* L. *and* R. *behind chairs.* HSIEH *enters* L., *gets book from* PROPERTY MAN. *Down to* C., *addresses audience.*]

HSIEH: I am your humble servant, Hsieh Ping-Kuei, once a beggar, now the gardener to His Excellency the Prime Minister Wang. There is very little work to be done here, so I am always reading, hoping to make up the time I wasted in my youth. I hear that His Excellency is calling me. Let me go inside and see what are his orders.

[*He puts the book down his back. Enters garden and kneels before* WANG, R.C.]

Your humble gardener, Hsieh Ping-Kuei, begs to report himself for your Excellency's orders.

WANG: I want you to remove that rock to the centre.

MADAM: It will serve as a table, you see.

HSIEH: Very well, your Excellency.

[*He goes to table, picks it up, raises it up* L. *and behind row of chairs. He stumbles and almost falls.*]

ALL [*startled*]: Oooooooooooo – –

[HSIEH *brings table to in front of* WANG *at* C.]

HSIEH: Is that all right, your Excellency?

WANG: All right, you may go now.

[HSIEH *crosses* L.; *as he passes* PRECIOUS STREAM:]

PRECIOUS S.: All of us, and especially General Wei, thank you very much.

[HSIEH *bows.*]

That will do, you may go now.

[*He goes off* L.]

WEI: That's nothing. I can easily remove a rock ten times larger.

WANG: Attendants!

ATTENDANTS [*coming* D.L. *and* D.R., *kneeling*]: Yes, Excellency.

WANG: Serve the feast here.

[*Music starts.*]

ATTENDANTS [*rising*]: Yes, Excellency.

[PROPERTY MAN R. *gives tray with wine jug and seven cups on it to* ATTENDANT R. (2nd), *who carries it* C., *gives it to* ATTENDANT L., *who puts it on table, before* WANG.]

WANG [*rising. Music softer*]: Precious Stream, my dear daughter, serve the wine.

[*Music louder.* PRECIOUS STREAM *pours wine. Music softer.*]

Madam, my honourable sons-in-law, my dear daughters, please drink.

[*Music louder. As he names them, they come forward to table and pick up wine cups together.*]

ALL: Thank you.

[*They drink. Music softer.*]

WANG: The wine is excellent. Now once more.

[*Music louder.* PRECIOUS STREAM *repeats pouring business.*]

ALL: Thank you.

[*They drink. As they are drinking, the* PROPERTY MEN *bring chairs* D.L. *and* D.R., *face centre standing on chairs, unfurl flags and allow snow to fall, then return chairs and retire to their places. Music stops.*]

WANG: What a beautiful scene the snow makes.

[ALL *sit.*]

Having wine and snow, we must also have some poems to celebrate the occasion. Who is going to write them?

[*Looks to sons-in-law.* PROPERTY MAN R. *takes away wine jug and tray* — PROPERTY MAN L. *takes away table.*]

SU: I am a very poor scholar, my dear father-in-law, and I must ask you to excuse me.

GOLDEN S.: Father will, of course, excuse you.

WEI: Although I am known as the most brilliant scholar, my dear father-in-law, I regret to say that I am not in the right mood for poetry now. I remember some poet said: 'To write good poems, one needs inspiration!' It is very cold now, you see. We can't expect any perspiration until summer comes.

[ALL *except* WANG *and* SILVER STREAM *smile.* SILVER STREAM *is upset.*]

WANG: Perspiration? You mean inspiration.

PRECIOUS S.: If it's only perspiration you need, then you must be the greatest poet of the age!

WEI: Oh, thank you.

SILVER S.: For shame to chaff my dear one like this.

SU: As none of us can write any poetry, may I make another suggestion?

ALL: Yes.

WANG: Certainly.

SU: I remember having heard the gardener, Hsieh Ping-Kuei,

sing beautiful songs in the street, and I was told they were composed by himself.

GOLDEN S.: Yes, I remember, too.

WEI: No, I don't think he composed them.

WANG: Yes, he did, and that's why I took a fancy to him, and gave him the post of my gardener, as a just reward for his talent.

WEI: Truly, you are the most just Prime Minister in history. Now let him repay some of your kindness by entertaining us with his songs.

SILVER S.: Yes, if he really can.

WANG: Attendants!

ATTENDANTS: Yes, Excellency.

　　[*They come down* L. *and* R. *and kneel.*]

WANG: Order the gardener, Hsieh Ping-Kuei, to come here again.

ATTENDANTS: Yes, Excellency.

　　[*Go up* L. *and* R. *Call off* L.]

His Excellency orders the gardener, Hsieh Ping-Kuei, to come here again.

HSIEH [*off stage*]: Coming.

　　[ATTENDANTS *retire to their places.* HSIEH *enters* L., *returns book to* PROPERTY MAN *and comes to below* PRECIOUS STREAM'S *chair, and kneels.*]

WANG: As we are drinking wine and enjoying the snow here, we find we need a little poem to celebrate the occasion. As I have heard that you are somewhat of a poet in your own way, I order you to give us one of your poems.

HSIEH: If Your Excellency will excuse my being forward – –

WANG: Certainly.

HSIEH: I must beg to point out to Your Excellency that I am one of your labourers and my duty to Your Excellency is limited to labour.

WEI: Bravo! I said he couldn't!

SILVER S.: So did I.

SU: Wait a moment – what do you mean?

GOLDEN S.: Tell us candidly.

HSIEH: If it is not my labour but my talent you want, then I must beg you to treat me as a gentleman and I must be invited, not ordered.

WEI: Impossible! What impudence!

SILVER S.: The man ought to be thrashed.

PRECIOUS S.: Why, this is most reasonable. A true poet must not be treated as a workman. Why shouldn't we treat him with proper respect?

WANG: Well, to show that I am a just man I will give you a seat in that corner, and request you to write a short poem of four lines on the subject of 'Wine, Snow, and Poetry'. If your poem proves to be good, I will give you a reward; if your poem is bad, or you can't write at all – –

WEI: I'll have him punished for his impudence!

SILVER S.: That's exactly my view.

WANG: Do you hear, man?

HSIEH: Yes, your Excellency.

[*He rises, crosses to* D.L. *and calls*]

Attendants, bring me pen, inkstone, and paper!

WEI: What insolence!

WANG: Really, this is too much!

[PROPERTY MAN L. *gives pen, inkstone, and paper on tray to* PRECIOUS STREAM'S (3rd) MAID.]

PRECIOUS S.: Why, this is but the true attitude of a poet. If no one will bring you what you want, allow me.

[*Music starts.* PRECIOUS STREAM *rises and goes to* HSIEH, MAID *follows to* PRECIOUS STREAM'S R. PROPERTY MAN L. *brings* PRECIOUS STREAM'S *chair to* HSIEH. *He sits.* PRECIOUS STREAM *prepares ink on inkstone, points the pen, hands paper to* HSIEH, *gives him prepared pen. She gets behind chair.* MAID *to her* L. *Music stops.*]

HSIEH [*as he writes*]: 'Wine brings a double cheer if snow be here.'

WANG: 'Wine brings a double cheer if snow be here.'

HSIEH: 'Snow takes a brighter white from song's delight.'

WANG: 'Snow takes a brighter white from song's delight.'

HSIEH: 'Ah, but when cups abound, and song is sweet,
    And snow is falling 'round, the joy's complete.'

WANG: '. . . the joy's complete.'

[*While this is being written, all nod their heads in time to the
rhythm, with the exception of* WEI. PRECIOUS STREAM
takes back pen, gives it to MAID – *returns to her place.* MAID
follows. HSIEH *rises, crosses to* WANG. PROPERTY MAN L.
brings back PRECIOUS STREAM'S *chair and takes tray from*
MAID.]

HSIEH: Here you are, your Excellency.

[*Hands him the paper and backs to* D.L.)

WANG: Well, it is very good indeed.

[*Passes paper to* SU.]

SU: Yes, very good.

[*Tries to pass paper to* WEI.]

WEI: I don't think so. I could write a much better poem.

SILVER S.: Yes, I'm sure you could.

WANG [*to* HSIEH]: Thank you – you may go now. A reward
will be given to you – later on.

MADAM: I will order the steward to give it to you.

HSIEH [*bowing*]: Many thanks, your Excellency.

[*Starts to leave.*]

WANG [*to his wife*]: You see, my dear, our family needs a
poet.

[*At this point,* HSIEH *stops, bows to* PRECIOUS STREAM.
WANG *sees and is indignant.* HSIEH *exits* L.]

When we want to celebrate an occasion like this, we find
that none of our family can write anything. Now those
suitors whom I have approved all write first-class poems.
All the poems they have *shown* to me are excellent.

PRECIOUS S.: My brother-in-law Wei also used to show you
very good poems before he married my sister.

WEI: I can still show you good poems if I am allowed.

SILVER S.: Yes, I am sure he can.

PRECIOUS S.: I should like to see you write them in my presence.

WEI: Impossible!

SILVER S.: Imposs – –

[*All snicker.*]

WANG: How unreasonable. But these young suitors are also all rich and of high birth; indeed, one couldn't find anyone better than they are in every way.

PRECIOUS S.: May I ask you, dear father, is everyone of them rich and noble?

WANG: Yes, certainly.

PRECIOUS S.: Are there not one or two among them not so rich and noble?

WANG: No. None. They are all equally rich and equally noble.

PRECIOUS S. [*rises and curtsies*]: Then, dear father, how can I choose? By choosing one, it will be unfair to the others. To be fair, I think I must refuse them all.

[*She sits.*]

WANG: Oh!

[*He puts his hand to his forehead.*]

MADAM [*laughs*]: You have outwitted your father, dear child.

GOLDEN S.: Very clever, indeed.

SILVER S.: Very silly.

PRECIOUS S. [*coaxingly*]: Dear father, you are the Prime Minister and therefore the most clever man in the kingdom!

[WANG *is rather flattered and looks pleased.*]

When the most clever man in the kingdom is at a loss to say who is the most suitable, then how can I, a stupid young girl without any experience, make a decision?

MADAM: That's true.

GOLDEN S.: Yes, dear father, it's quite true.

SILVER S.: No! When I was young I was neither stupid nor without experience.

[ALL *react*.]

WEI: Why don't you refer the matter to the imperial counsellors, so that they may hold a conference?

SU: Nonsense! Our dear father-in-law will settle it sooner or later. In the meantime, let us drop it.

PRECIOUS S. [*she rises, curtsies.*]: Thank you, dear brother-in-law.

[*Sits.* SU *smiles at her, rises and bows.*]

WANG [*rises*]: I think I have a very good plan for settling it.

ALL: Marvellous! How clever! So soon!

WANG: Listen, my dear. On your birthday, the second of February, there will be a festival. Let us build a beautiful pavilion here in the garden, and let all the suitors come beneath it. You, in the pavilion, take an embroidered ball and throw it down from the pavilion. The one who catches it will be your bridegroom.

PRECIOUS S.: Is that a wise way to settle such a problem?

WANG: It is the only way. And I am quite determined.

[*Sits.*]

MADAM: It is romantic, too!

ALL: Yes, very romantic.

PRECIOUS S.: When even careful judgement is not sufficient to settle such a problem, is it wise to settle it by lottery?

WANG: It will not be a lottery. It will be the will of God.

WEI: The suitor who is hit by the embroidered ball can well call his case one of *force majeure*.

[*He laughs.* SILVER STREAM *laughs also.* MADAM *looks at* WEI, *who stops. Then at* SILVER STREAM, *who also stops laughing.*]

MADAM: I see! Whenever we find a situation which cannot be dealt with by mortals we ask the help of God. We always turn to God when we are in distress.

ALL [*raise* R. *hand, fingers close together, tip of first touching*

mouth. Thumb to face and little finger farthest away and say]:
'La, Mo, Cho, Me, To Fu.'

MADAM: Well, now that we have put our responsibility upon
God, shall we retire?

WANG: Yes, let us retire.

[*Music starts.* ATTENDANTS *open doors and stand aside.* ALL
rise. WANG *down* C. *followed by* MADAM. *He bows to
audience and goes off* L.; *she curtsies and follows him, then the*
TWO MAIDS *follow her.* ALL *step over threshold as on entering. As family moves downstage,* PROPERTY MEN R. *and* L.
place chairs R. *and* L. *in their original places. Music softer.*]

SU: We have some business at my house if you will excuse us.

[*He and* GOLDEN STREAM *bow and curtsy to audience and
exit* L. – *he first, she following him.* WEI *crosses to* PRECIOUS
STREAM.]

WEI: Now, dear sister-in-law, allow me to give you a little
advice.

PRECIOUS S. [*pointing out to audience*]: Look, there is a rock
ten times as large as the one used for our table. I think you
said a moment ago you could lift such a rock with ease.
Now, will you please – –

[SILVER STREAM *to* L. *of him, pulls his sleeve.*]

WEI: I think we have some important business waiting for us,
too. Good morning.

[*Music louder.* WEI *and* SILVER STREAM *down* C. *bow and
curtsy to audience and exit* L. ATTENDANTS *follow them
and close doors of garden, exit* L. PROPERTY MAN L. *places
chair* C. *Music stops.*]

PRECIOUS S. [*goes* R.]: What shall I do?

[*Goes* L.]

What shall I do?

[*Taps her forehead, then up centre, sits.*]

My maid – ask the gardener Hsieh Ping-Kuei to come to me.

MAID: Yes, my lady.

[*To upstage* L. *and calls.*]

Lady Precious Stream wishes the gardener, Hsieh Ping-Kuei, to come here immediately.

HSIEH [*off stage*]: Yes, I am coming.

[MAID *to* L. *of* PRECIOUS STREAM. HSIEH *enters and kneels* L. *before* PRECIOUS STREAM.]

May I know your orders, my lady?

PRECIOUS S.: Stand up, please.

[*He rises.*]

My maid. Provide a seat for Mr Hsieh.

[PROPERTY MAN L. *places chair behind* HSIEH.]

HSIEH: How can I sit down before you, my lady?

PRECIOUS S.: The best of manners is obedience.

HSIEH [*bows and sits*]: Then I must thank you.

PRECIOUS S.: My maid. Go to my boudoir and fetch some fifty taels of silver for me.

[MAID *curtsies and goes down* C.]

Go as quickly as possible.

[MAID *opens door, goes* C., *closes door and stoops as if listening.* PRECIOUS STREAM *comes down* C. *opens the door and says*]

And return as slowly as possible.

[MAID *jumps up, moves* L. *and says*]

MAID: Yes, my lady.

[*Exits* L.]

PRECIOUS S. [*returns and sits*]: Mr Hsieh, I now know that you are a man of both high literary and military abilities. I wish to help you, but first of all you must tell me about your family.

HSIEH: Thank you, my lady. Do you really want to know about my family? Well, I am of a very poor family.

PRECIOUS S.: That I know. I want to hear about the members of your family.

HSIEH: My father and mother are both dead.

PRECIOUS S.: I see. Is there anyone else in your family?

HSIEH: Being poor, I only had one father and one mother!

PRECIOUS S.: I mean those of your own generation.

HSIEH: I had a brother who died at five. I have no sister.

PRECIOUS S.: Did anyone of your family marry?

HSIEH: Yes.

PRECIOUS S. [*taken aback*]: Oh! Who?

HSIEH: Well, my father married my mother.

PRECIOUS S. [*relieved*]: Of course! And your brother?

HSIEH: As he died at five he did not marry.

PRECIOUS S.: I see. Well – and did – did your parents have a daughter-in-law at all?

HSIEH: No, they had none.

PRECIOUS S.: Then I have something to tell you, but I find it hard to do so. *Well*, do you understand riddles?

HSIEH: A little.

PRECIOUS S.: On the second of February it will be my sixteenth birthday, and I am going to marry the man who is hit by the embroidered ball which I shall throw down from a beautiful pavilion to be erected here. It will be a case of the will of God, but I have resolved to take it into my own hands. I have in mind a suitable person. Now, this person, if you look far – –

[*Pointing away in the distance.*]

HSIEH [*continuing her speech*]: . . . is a thousand miles away – –

PRECIOUS S.: Yes, and if you look near – –

[*Pointing near to her.*]

HSIEH: Then he is before you!

[*Rises.*]

PRECIOUS S.: Thank you! That is exactly what I mean.

[MAID *enters* R., *comes downstage, takes silver from* PROPERTY MAN R.]

HSIEH: If my lady bestows on me such an honour I will never fail her!

PRECIOUS S.: My maid is returning. Not another word. Be sure to be present on the second of February.

[MAID *opens door.*]

HSIEH: The second of February.

MAID [*up to* R. *of* PRECIOUS STREAM]: Here you are, my lady.

PRECIOUS S.: Give it to Mr Hsieh.

[MAID *crosses to* HSIEH *and gives him the piece of silver, then stands* U.L. *of* PRECIOUS STREAM.]

HSIEH: Thank you. I shall never forget your kindness.

[*Down* C.]

The second of February.

[*Goes up* L., *gives* PROPERTY MAN *the piece of silver and exits.*]

PRECIOUS S. [*rises*]: Let's retire to our boudoir and wait for the will of God.

[*Exits* L.]

MAID NO. 3: [*crosses* D.C. *To audience*]: The Will of God.

[*Music starts.* MAID *laughs, moves* U.L. *laughing as she exits. Music stops. Lights fade. Lights up immediately after they have come down. Music starts. Enter* ATTENDANTS, *followed by* WANG. ATTENDANTS *cross to* D.R. *and* D.L., WANG *to* D.C.]

WANG: Today *is* the second of February, the day on which I am going to take a new son-in-law into my family.

[*Crosses* U.C. *and sits.*]

[*During the exit of the* MAID *and the entrance of* WANG *the* PROPERTY MAN L. *places the two chairs* L.C. *and* R.C. *with backs to audience.* PROPERTY MAN R. *places arm-chair* C. *for* WANG. PROPERTY MAN L. *goes off* L. *and returns with table, which he places between the* L.C. *and* R.C. *chairs.* PROPERTY MAN R. *goes off* R. *and brings on embroidery attached to bamboo sticks. This he and* PROPERTY MAN L. *tie to outside of the two chairs.*]

WANG: I have been looking forward to it enormously, and I am very happy to find the weather is so fine. It is now quite near the hour of throwing the ball, and I must give the necessary instructions. Attendants!

ATTENDANTS [*kneeling*]: Yes, Excellency.

WANG: You must stay in the garden and guard the gate. Admit only those young gentlemen you know I like.

[*Enter* FOUR SUITORS *from* R. – 1st *and* 2nd *to* D.L.C., 3rd *and* 4th *to* D.R.C.]

As soon as the embroidered ball has been thrown I will come back at once.

ATTENDANTS [*rising*]: Yes, Excellency.

1st SUITOR [*to audience, bowing*]: Lady Precious Stream is as beautiful as the flowers of May.

2nd SUITOR [*same business*]: The second of February is her wedding day.

3rd SUITOR [*same business*]: The young suitors come here happy and gay!

4th SUITOR [*same business*]: Who will be the lucky one – –

WANG [*rises*]: Nobody can say.

[*He exits* L. PROPERTY MAN R. *removes arm-chair from* C.]

1st SUITOR: Here we have arrived. Let us knock at the gate.

[*They turn and knock at gate.*]

1st ATTENDANT: Yes, I am coming.

[*He opens the door, coming* C. *with* 2nd ATTENDANT.]

Good morning, my young lords. Have you young gentlemen come to await the lucky ball?

SUITORS: Exactly.

1st ATTENDANT: Come in, please.

[1st ATTENDANT *shows the way to the* L. *round stage, below pavilion to* R., *they imitating his movements.* 2nd ATTENDANT *closes door. Both return to places* D.R. *and* D.L.]

ALL (4): Lady Precious Stream is coming.

[*Music starts.* LADY PRECIOUS STREAM *enters* R. TWO MAIDS *before and* TWO MAIDS *after her. She goes to* C., TWO MAIDS R. *and* TWO MAIDS L. *of her – all standing facing her. She carries an embroidered ball, given her by* PROPERTY MAN R. *Music stops.*]

PRECIOUS S.: Time flies and today is the fatal day of the

second of February. Although I am anxious to be free from suspense, the idea of going up to the pavilion and throwing down the embroidered ball while the crowd looks on makes me feel very shy, and I don't know how I shall ever manage to carry on. My maids!

MAIDS: Yes, my lady.

[*Curtsy.*]

PRECIOUS S.: Lead the way to the pavilion, please.

MAIDS: Yes, my lady.

[*Curtsy. Music starts. The* TWO MAIDS L., *come* C. *and go round stage, below the pavilion, followed by the* TWO MAIDS R. LADY PRECIOUS STREAM *follows them. They go round stage once, then up behind pavilion.* LADY PRECIOUS STREAM *goes in the pavilion. Music stops.*]

PRECIOUS S. [*surveying the crowd represented by the* SUITORS]: Now I must look carefully. There are princes dressed in red and there are young nobles dressed in blue. [*As the colour of each* SUITOR'S *costume is mentioned he steps out of line and then back.*] Those clad in yellow are the sons of rich merchants, and those in white are heirs to the great landowners! I must find where Hsieh Ping-Kuei is standing. I have looked from east to west, and now I must look from north to south. Again and again I have looked for him, and nowhere is he to be seen. I remember clearly when I gave him the silver, I told him to come on this day and he promised he would. But he has proved unfaithful.

[*Then to* SUITORS, *directly.*]

Oh, woe is me! I must retire without throwing the ball.

[HSIEH *enters* L., *crosses* D.L.]

1st SUITOR: No! You mustn't go back!

2nd SUITOR: Throw the ball before you go, please!

3rd SUITOR: How can you desert us?

4th SUITOR: I have been waiting all the morning!

PRECIOUS S.: Ah! I see him emerging from that corner.

[*Speaks to the* SUITORS.]

Now, gentlemen, please come near to the pavilion and listen to my words.

[SUITORS, *one step forward.*]

I want all of you to pledge your word of honour to me that you will uphold the man who, by the will of God, is going to be my husband, whoever he may be. And, moreover, that you will swear that you, one and all, will draw your swords against him who will not uphold the destined match!

ALL: We swear!

[*Step back.*]

PRECIOUS S.: This marriage is to be arranged by the will of God, and we mortals have to abide by this arrangement. Now, catch the ball.

[*She holds ball above her head, swings it, counts.*]

One, two, three!

[SUITORS *sway and reach upward each time she counts. She throws ball and* HSIEH PING-KUEI *catches it.*]

HSIEH: Here it is!

SUITORS: Oh!

[*They make a move forward.*]

PRECIOUS S.: Gentlemen, remember that all of you have pledged your word of honour to me and you must abide by it. Now, like decent folk, congratulate him and me.

ALL: Congratulations!

HSIEH: Thanks.

[PRECIOUS STREAM *has now got down from the pavilion. Curtsies to* HSIEH *then up to* SUITORS R. *When* PRECIOUS STREAM *gets down from pavilion,* PROPERTY MAN L. *takes table off* L., *returns, unties the pavilion. Takes chairs to* L. PROPERTY MAN R. *takes pavilion to* R. *then returns to his position* R.]

SUITORS: Our hearty congratulations.

PRECIOUS S.: Many thanks!

[WANG *enters* R., *downstage to* C.]

WANG: Where is my new son-in-law? Where is my new
son-in-law?

[*Bus. of* SUITORS *in rotation, upstage to downstage, turn-ing back on* WANG.]

HSIEH: At your service, my dear father-in-law.

[WANG *sees* HSIEH — *blows through beard.* PROPERTY
MAN R. *brings cushion forward and catches* WANG *as he faints.*
WANG *faints into the arms of* PROPERTY MEN *who lower
him on to the stage.* PRECIOUS STREAM *fans him with her
sleeve.*]

PRECIOUS S.: Oh, father, father!

SUITORS [*fanning* WANG *with sleeves*]: Oh, Your Excellency!
Your Excellency!

WANG [PROPERTY MEN *pick him up*]: Oh, my God!

PRECIOUS S.: Yes, dear father, this is indeed the will of
God.

SUITORS [*sarcastically*]: The will of God.

WANG [*to audience*]: But I won't have it. I will take the
matter away from God into my own hands.

PRECIOUS S.: But, father, aren't you glad? You said our
family needed a poet, and now we have one.

[*Crosses* L. *to* HSIEH.]

God has granted your wish.

WANG: We will see whether God will grant me a different
wish.

PRECIOUS S.: Now, my gallant suitors, did you not swear
that you would draw your swords against him who dared
not to uphold the destined match?

SUITORS: Yes, we did.

[*One step forward, bravely.*]

WANG [*to* SUITORS]: What!

[SUITORS *fall back* — WANG *turns to* PRECIOUS STREAM.]

You have conspired against your own father.

PRECIOUS S.: I never dreamt it would be you we should
have to deal with.

WANG [*to* SUITORS]: You fools, to think that I once liked
  you. I am a blind fool. Now get out, all of you.

> [ATTENDANTS *open doors.* HSIEH *and* PRECIOUS STREAM
> *go up to entrance* L. *and take tea from the* PROPERTY MAN.
> WANG *takes* SUITORS *one by one by the ear and ushers them
> out.*]

1st SUITOR: Lady Precious Stream is as beautiful as the flowers
  in May.

2nd SUITOR: The second of February is her wedding day.

3rd SUITOR: The young suitors come here happy and gay.

4th SUITOR: But when they are leaving they say – –

WANG [*kicking* SUITOR NO. 4, *against whom* PROPERTY MAN
  L. *holds a cushion*]: Woe is the day.

> [*They exeunt. Music starts.* PROPERTY MAN R. *places
> arm-chair* C. PROPERTY MAN L. *places two chairs* L. *of*
> WANG *then* PRECIOUS STREAM'S *chair.* PROPERTY MAN
> R. *places two chairs* R. *of* WANG. WANG *sits* C. *Enter*
> MADAM, GOLDEN STREAM, SILVER STREAM, SU *and*
> WEI. *They come up to* WANG, *curtsy, bow, and sit.* PRECIOUS
> STREAM *comes down* L. *to her chair, does not sit.* HSIEH *goes
> round back, down* R. *and stands opposite* PRECIOUS STREAM.
> *Music stops.*]

MADAM [*to* PRECIOUS STREAM]: Why don't you sit down,
  my dear?

PRECIOUS S.: So long as my future husband is not given a
  seat, I can't sit down, dear mother.

MADAM: Then be seated, both of you.

WANG: No! This is the house of a Prime Minister, not
  a beggar's hut. How can he be allowed to sit down
  here?

MADAM: Dear, you are only making the situation worse.
  Come, don't be headstrong. Let all of us sit down and talk
  over the matter, and see what is to be done.

WANG [*sulkily*]: All right. Have your own way.

> [PROPERTY MAN R. *places chair behind* HSIEH.]

MADAM: Now be seated, please.

[*Both sit.*]

HSIEH: Thank you, Madam.

PRECIOUS S.: Thank you, dear mother.

WANG [*gruffly*]: Say, man, on what conditions [MADAM *nudges him – then softly*] will you let her be free?

WEI: Allow me to arrange for you, dear father-in-law. I know how to deal with this sort of customer. Look here, my man; say, my friend! Hullo, Hsieh Ping-Kuei!

[*Rises.*]

Mr Hsieh Ping-Kuei.

HSIEH [*fiercely*]: What is your wish, my great General?

WEI: Don't be cross, my – er – Mr Hsieh. You know it would never do for Lady Precious Stream to marry you, a beg – –

[SU *nudges* WEI.]

Say – a poor man. I quite understand that this is, for you, a great chance, and that you must have a handsome price before you let go your hold.

HSIEH [*fiercely, rises*]: I don't quite understand your meaning.

SILVER S. [*rises, goes* R.]: You can't bully my husband. Bully him back, my dear.

[HSIEH *turns back to* WEI.]

WEI [*curtly*]: Be quiet, [*softly*] dear.

[SILVER STREAM *to* L., *curtsies and sits.*]

I mean, that if you will let us off quietly, without any scandal, I am sure my father-in-law is willing to give you, say – –

SILVER S.: One hundred taels of silver.

WEI [*watching* HSIEH]: No, say two hundred.

SILVER S.: Not a penny more.

WANG: I am a just and generous man. I will offer you five hundred taels.

WEI: Now, be sensible, my man.

[*Sits.*]

WANG: Well, how much do you want?

[MADAM *presses* WANG'S *arm.*]

How much do you want, Mr Hsieh?

HSIEH: I want nothing from you, sir. Even millions and billions could not buy me off. The decision lies with Lady Precious Stream. If she thinks that I am not her equal, and that this is but a lamentable mistake, just let her say the word, and I will go away without taking a penny from you.

PRECIOUS S. [*rises*]: Beautiful!

[HSIEH *and* PRECIOUS STREAM *sit.*]

SU: It's quite right!

MADAM: Dear, dear!

GOLDEN S.: He is playing the game!

WANG: My dear daughter, you know that to me you are dearer than all. Now, say the word and let us get out of this disgrace.

WEI: And, if – eh – Mr Hsieh actually refuses to take any money, then the five hundred taels you promised, dear father-in-law, ought to be given to me as a reward for my acting as a go-between.

SILVER S.: Of course father will reward you, dear.

PRECIOUS S. [*rises* – HSIEH *rises*]: I am sorry to deprive you of your reward. I will stick to my match.

[HSIEH *bows. All react.*]

To my sister [*curtsy*] I am not worth one hundred taels, and to my brother-in-law [*curtsies*] only two hundred, and even to my father [*curtsies*], who professes to love me dearer than all, I am worth only five hundred.

WANG: No. [*Beckons* PRECIOUS STREAM *to him. She goes.*] In my heart I was prepared to offer one thousand.

PRECIOUS S. [*crosses back of chair.*]: Thank you, father.

[*To audience.*]

I see I am getting on.

[*To family.*]

You seem to think that one would prefer to have, let us say, a thousand taels rather than to have me. And here is a man who refuses to take millions and billions and prefers me instead. Shall I be so ungrateful as to give him the go-by and to remain with those who value me so little? No, father, I decline!

[*Curtsies and sits –* HSIEH *sits.*]

GOLDEN S.: So would I!

MADAM: Dear, dear!

SU: Very noble.

SILVER S.: Very silly!

WEI: It's too bad. My five hundred taels are gone.

WANG: If you insist on marrying him, all I can say is that a beggar girl is going to marry a beggar and remain one. You need not expect any dowry from me. No – not even a penny.

PRECIOUS S. [*rises*]: No, father, Not a beggar girl to a beggar. But a working girl to a worker. We both can work.

WANG [*laughs*]: You? Work? Impossible!

SILVER S.: Don't you think it will soil your beautiful clothes?

PRECIOUS S.: No, because I will not wear them.

[*She goes* C. *The* FAMILY *crowd round her,* MADAM *and the* TWO DAUGHTERS L. *of her, the* MEN R. *of her with backs to the audience.* WANG *remains by his chair, turns his back upon them.* MADAM *helps* PRECIOUS STREAM *off with her clothes, hands them to* R. PROPERTY MAN. PRECIOUS STREAM *gives her jewels to* L. PROPERTY MAN. PRO-PERTY MAN R. *moves forward, takes* PRECIOUS STREAM'S *dress and puts it off* R. PROPERTY MAN L. *moves forward when he receives her jewels.*]

The ancient proverb says: 'A good son will not depend upon his father's wealth; and a good daughter will not depend upon her family for clothes.' Here I am giving back to you these fine clothes. And here are your jewels, too.

MADAM: Oh, dear, don't!

GOLDEN S.: My poor sister.

SU: A brave girl!

SILVER S.: I wonder how they will manage to live.

WEI: They will soon die of starvation.

WANG [*still in a rage*]: Do you mean that you will leave us? Probably you will come back to us when you find you are starving.

[*All sit except* PRECIOUS STREAM *and* HSIEH *whose chairs have been removed.*]

PRECIOUS S.: That's far from the case. If I come back to see you, dear mother, it will be when we can raise our heads higher than any of you can.

WANG: Poverty and failure will be your lot. But don't come to me for any help.

MADAM: Don't mind what your father says, dear. We shall always be ready to help you. But you're not really going to leave us for good, are you?

GOLDEN S.: Please don't, dear sister.

PRECIOUS S. [*crosses to* R. *below* HSIEH]: I am afraid I'll have to. My place is to be by my husband's side for better or for worse.

[PROPERTY MAN L. *comes forward with two cushions and puts one in front of* WANG *as* PRECIOUS STREAM *crosses to kneel.*]

My dear father, your humble daughter, Precious Stream, pays her respects . . .

WANG [*rising and snatching away cushion*]: No! You needn't consider me as your father.

[PROPERTY MAN L. *places second cushion.*]

PRECIOUS S. [*kneeling*]: Then I must at least thank you for your share in my birth.

WANG: It was a mere accident.

[*Sees* MADAM – *sits quickly*, PRECIOUS STREAM *rises and crosses to below* HSIEH *at* R.]

SILVER S.: And a sad one, too.

WANG: But I'll bet you'll be glad to leave him very soon.

PRECIOUS S.: Do you dare to lay a wager definitely by clapping hands three times with me, father?

WANG: Certainly, and do you dare?

PRECIOUS S.: Certainly.

ALL: Oh, please don't!

PRECIOUS S. [*to audience at* C.]: I call upon all of you here to witness. Today I hereby make a wager by clapping hands with my father three times, that my husband and I will never come back to the Prime Minister's house unless we are rich and successful.

[PRECIOUS STREAM *goes upstage to below and* R. *of* WANG. WANG *rises and they clap hands three times.* WANG *sits –* PRECIOUS STREAM *returns to below* HSIEH.]

ALL: It can't be helped now.

PRECIOUS S. [*to* HSIEH]: Now let us leave here for good and prepare for the wedding.

[*They go down* C.]

HSIEH [*to audience*]: I will always honour you.

PRECIOUS S. [*to audience*]: And I will obey you.

HSIEH [*turns* R., *to* PRECIOUS STREAM]: I will protect you.

PRECIOUS S. [*turns* L., *to* HSIEH]: I will love you.

[HSIEH *turns left and exits –* PRECIOUS STREAM *following.*]

WANG [*rising and going downstage –* MADAM *follows*]: Disgraceful!

WEI: Disgusting!

SILVER S.: Scandalous!

WANG: Let us retire!

[*Music starts. They all move downstage.* WANG *bows to audience and exits* L., MADAM *follows him after curtsying.* SU *and* GOLDEN STREAM *repeat the business. Then* WEI *and* SILVER STREAM *follow.* ATTENDANTS *and* MAIDS *come last but they do not bow or curtsy.* PROPERTY MEN *replace chairs to left and right and retire to off* L. *and off* R. *Music stops. Lights dim.*]

END OF ACT ONE

NO CURTAIN

(NOTE: *There is no pause between Act One and Act Two. As soon as the lights have faded on Act One the* READER *enters immediately.*)

ACT TWO

Gong No. 1. Enter READER *from* D.L. *Spot on* READER.

HONOURABLE READER: By some accident we missed the simple but romantic marriage ceremony. Perhaps we purposely avoided it because we thought it might not turn out successfully, so it would be better to have nothing to do with the matter. Nevertheless we are always desirous to hear what happened to Precious Stream and Hsieh Ping-Kuei, and so we have kept in touch with them somehow or other. We decided that we may condescend to pay them a visit. Now that their honeymoon is over we will certainly not be considered as intruders. (Even if they object to our calling, we will go and watch them afar.) We arrive at the outside of the city at an open space before a kind of cave where the newly married couple live. The open space in front of the cave and the interior of the cave are supposed to be represented here. And further, when circumstances render it necessary, the winding road on the little hill which leads to the cave is included in the scene. There is no decoration whatever on the stage and the audience must have recourse to their imagination.

[*Exit* READER L. *Gong No. 2 – Lights up.* PROPERTY MEN *enter from* R. *and* L., *bow, etc. Gong No. 3 – Music starts. Enter* 1st *and* 2nd SOLDIERS. TWO SOLDIERS *enter* R. *downstage to* R.C. *and* L.C., *face each other, picking up bag of rice and firewood from* PROPERTY MAN R. *as they enter. Music stops.*]

1st SOLDIER: Here we are.
2nd SOLDIER: Yes, I believe this is the place.
1st SOLDIER: Let us knock at the door.

[*He pretends to knock.* PROPERTY MAN L. *knocks on his box.*]

Is there anyone there?

[*Backs to audience.*]

PRECIOUS S. [*offstage* R.]: Yes, I am coming.

[*Enters* R. *down to* C., *addresses audience.*]

If you are rich, even the most distant relations come to visit you; if you are poor not even the closest will come near you. Since I married Hsieh Ping-Kuei we rarely have visitors. But just now I heard a strange knocking at the door.

[*Calls out.*]

Who is knocking at the door?

1st SOLDIER: We have brought some firewood and rice for our eldest brother Hsieh.

[PRECIOUS STREAM *goes round* R. *making a circle, as though descending steps, and comes to* C. *between them.*]

PRECIOUS S.: Much obliged.

[*Runs to door of cave.*]

Please bring in what you have brought.

[*They enter, and stand before her.*]

1st SOLDIER: Here are ten hundredweight of firewood.

PRECIOUS S.: Put it here, please.

[PROPERTY MAN L. *removes firewood.* PROPERTY MAN R. *removes rice.*]

2nd SOLDIER: Here are five hundredweight of rice.

PRECIOUS S.: Put it here, please. As your eldest brother, Hsieh, is not at home, you will excuse me for not asking you to stay and drink a cup of tea?

1st SOLDIER: Don't stand on ceremony.

2nd SOLDIER: Thank you all the same.

PRECIOUS S.: Thank you for your trouble. I won't detain you.

1st SOLDIER: Don't mention it. Good-bye.

2nd SOLDIER: Only too delighted. Good-bye.

E

PRECIOUS S. [*curtsies*]: Good-bye.

[PROPERTY MAN L. *places chair* C. PROPERTY MAN R. *does horses' hoofs for* HSIEH'S *entrance.* SOLDIERS *exit up* L. PRECIOUS STREAM *to* C., *sits and sews.*]

HSIEH [*offstage* R.]: Look out! A horse is coming!

[*Enters* R., *picks up whip from* PROPERTY MAN'S *box* R. *Gallops down* R. *to* C.]

To a newly married man an hour away from his home seems to be three years. So I feel I have been absent from my home for ages. As I have some important news for my dear wife, I must hurry on by whipping my horse.

[*He goes up* L. *round stage again, coming to* C.]

Here is my humble cave which I consider better than a splendid palace.

[*He ties horse* R., *giving whip to* PROPERTY MAN R. *He calls out and knocks as though to someone in a cave.*]

My dear third sister, will you kindly open the door?

PRECIOUS S. [*rises, goes up* R. *and round, comes out of cave*]: Is that you, my lord and master, Hsieh, who has come back?

HSIEH: Yes, I have come back with some important news.

[PRECIOUS STREAM *opens door – they enter cave.*]

PRECIOUS S.: Never mind about the news.

[HSIEH *enters, they both ascend stairs.*]

The most important thing is, do you want something to eat and drink?

[HSIEH *sits centre, she* L. *of him on stool placed by* PROPERTY MAN L.]

HSIEH: Thank you, I had a good dinner at the camp.

PRECIOUS S.: So that's why the two soldiers brought us ten hundredweight of firewood and five hundredweight of rice.

HSIEH: Yes, that is part of the good news, too. It is payment in advance of my salary, and we needn't worry about our food any more.

PRECIOUS S.: Good news, indeed!

HSIEH: I have just been appointed an officer of considerable rank.

PRECIOUS S.: That's fairly good.

HSIEH: You don't seem to be very enthusiastic about the good news.

PRECIOUS S.: Oh, yes, I am rather glad that you are now beginning to ascend the ladder of promotion. But this is only a beginning. To me, my husband ought not to be satisfied until he has at least conquered the world!

[*He taps his forehead.*]

And what else do you want to tell me? I perceive you've something on your mind that makes you uneasy.

HSIEH: Well, as I am now in government service, I can hardly consider myself as my own master. I am ordered abroad with the troops.

PRECIOUS S.: A man's ambition cannot be limited by space, as the old proverb says. You needn't be uneasy about telling me you must leave for a time, though we have been married for a month only.

HSIEH [*still uneasy*]: Oh, quite – quite! But the fact is – is – well, it is a very long journey. We are going on a campaign to the Western Regions.

PRECIOUS S. [*astounded*]: Oh! It is a long and dangerous journey even in peaceful times; and now we are at war with them.

HSIEH: That's why I am going.

PRECIOUS S.: Even those who go to the Western Regions as friends seldom return . . . I mean, seldom return satisfied.

HSIEH: No! They never return at all!

PRECIOUS S.: And are you going there as their enemy!

HSIEH: Yes, our aim is to conquer them.

PRECIOUS S.: When do you start?

HSIEH: Very soon.

PRECIOUS S. [*rising and crossing* L.]: Then I must prepare some winter clothes for you, because you may have to stay there over the new year.

HSIEH: You needn't make any preparations for me. I have something more to tell you.

PRECIOUS S.: Then tell me at once!
[*Sits.*]

HSIEH: It is very difficult to tell you at once.

PRECIOUS S. [*forcing a smile*]: Then tell me little by little. I won't mind.

HSIEH [*sits*]: The date of our general mobilization is fixed.

PRECIOUS S. [*anxiously*]: When?

HSIEH: Well, do you understand riddles?

PRECIOUS S.: A little.

HSIEH [*hand business*]: If I say the date is far, far away – –

PRECIOUS S. [*forcing another smile*]: A hundred years away!

HSIEH: And I say the date is quite, quite near at hand – –

PRECIOUS S. [*appalled*]: Today! My heaven!
[*She hides her face in her long sleeves.*]

HSIEH [*rises, to* R., *turns and faces her*]: There! There! Cheer up! Wouldn't you be glad to see me return triumphantly on horseback as a general! There is something to which you may look forward!

PRECIOUS S.: But to think we have only been married for a month, and you are leaving me today! So unexpectedly too! Why did you apply for such a post?

HSIEH: I didn't apply for it – it was conferred upon me.

PRECIOUS S.: How?

HSIEH [*resuming his seat* C.]: You know people have been talking about a monster with a red mane which has been devouring travellers in a wood nearby. Well, I thought I ought to do something, and I went to the wood this morning and shot the monster, which proved to be merely a tiger of enormous size.

PRECIOUS S. [*looks at him*]: A tiger of enormous size! And you say 'merely'.

HSIEH: Yes. I was quite disappointed.

PRECIOUS S.: Now, my dear hero, tell me how you did it!

HSIEH: Eh – oh – there is very little to tell. It was such a trifle. I went there, I saw a tiger, I shot it, that's all!

PRECIOUS S.: How fine! How grand!

HSIEH: Nonsense! Shooting an ordinary tiger when anticipating a monster is as disappointing as shooting a bird when hunting a tiger! One naturally feels a come-down. And the worst of it is that people go crazy and make a tremendous fuss about it.

PRECIOUS S.: And make trouble, too!

HSIEH: Yes, terrible trouble! They actually carried me to the Governor's yamen, where I was appointed a captain and ordered to join the Western Punitive Expedition. I found that Generals Wei and Su, our brothers-in-law, are the joint commanders-in-chief of this expedition, and I was ordered to mobilize with the first company immediately!

  [*Rises.*]

PRECIOUS S.: Immediately!

  [*Rises.*]

HSIEH [*gets cloth from* PROPERTY MAN R.]: Yes, I was with difficulty allowed to come back to bid you a hurried good-bye, and I am afraid I have already overstayed my time.

  [*Rolls cloth on floor and pantomimes packing.*]

PRECIOUS S.: Oh, no! You mustn't leave me like this!

HSIEH: I am afraid I must.

  [PROPERTY MAN L. *removes chair and stool.* HSIEH *looks up at her.*]

Don't worry about me, the commanders-in-chief are our brothers-in-law, you see.

PRECIOUS S.: I am more worried than ever on hearing that the wretch Wei is your chief. I don't trust him at all, and I hope you will take greatest care of yourself.

HSIEH: You needn't worry at all, for he is not going,

[*He gives cloth to* PRECIOUS STREAM, *who ties it on his back.*]

but staying behind to control the supply of ammunition and the paying of the soldiers. I have arranged that my pay is to be paid to you regularly in the form of rice and firewood, and he promised he would see to that. General Su will follow me with the main body of troops in a short time.

[*He goes out of cave, remains* R.]

PRECIOUS S. [*follows him, to* L. *of him*]: That is excellent. I know how to deal with the wretch Wei, and I am relieved to hear that our brother-in-law Su is going to follow you soon.

A VOICE [*offstage* L.]: Dear eldest brother, Hsieh, the troops are waiting for you!

HSIEH [*calling out*]: Thank you! I will come at once.

[*To* PRECIOUS STREAM.]

I must go now. My dear third sister allow me to salute you and bid you good-bye.

[*He bows to her – she curtsies. He gets whip from* PROPERTY MAN R.]

PRECIOUS S.: I must see my hero mount his steed.

HSIEH [*he mounts his horse*]: My dear third sister, good-bye.

[*He starts going round stage, she following. Two complete circles are made.*]

PRECIOUS S.: Farewell! I must see you riding along the winding road to the highway.

HSIEH: You will take care of yourself for my sake, won't you?

PRECIOUS S. [*following him carefully*]: Of course! And you will take care of yourself for my sake, won't you?

HSIEH: Of course! Now please go back, my dear third sister.

PRECIOUS S.: No, not until we reach the highway.

HSIEH [*stopping* D.L.C., *at end of second circle*]: Here is the highway. Go back and have a good rest.

PRECIOUS S.: Do let me follow you for another short distance.

HSIEH: No, no! Although I can't bear to leave you, we must part sooner or later. The road is rough, and you are already tired. Please go back and rest.

PRECIOUS S.: No, no! I must see you off from the camp.

HSIEH: Impossible! That's too far for you.

PRECIOUS S.: I must. I must.

VOICE [*offstage L.*]: We are starting, dear eldest brother, Hsieh.

HSIEH [*calling out*]: I come, I come!
      [*Pointing off R.*]
   Look! There is your sister, Golden Stream, coming.
      [PRECIOUS STREAM *looks off R.* HSIEH *draws his sword and cuts the reins, the cord on the whip, then gallops off.*]

PRECIOUS S.: Oh! He has gone!
      [*Exits L. Music starts as* PRECIOUS STREAM *exits. Music stops. Lights fade. Immediately following, music starts. Lights up.* MADAM *enters walking between the shafts of the carriage with* TWO ATTENDANTS *preceding her, followed by* DRIVER *and* TWO MAIDS. *They come downstage –* ATTENDANTS *to L.,* MADAM, C. *Music stops.*]

MADAM: Since the news of the death of my son-in-law, Hsieh Ping-Kuei, reached me, I have been greatly worried about my dear daughter Precious Stream. She is very obstinate, and her pride won't allow her to accept any help from her father. It is now eight months since she left our house. As the New Year is drawing near and she is very poor, I have brought something with me, and have come to pay her a visit which I ought to have done a long time ago. We must be near the place now. It's not far from here, is it, driver?

DRIVER: No, Madam.

MADAM: Faster, please.

DRIVER: Yes, Madam.

[*They go round the stage once and arrive*, MADAM *standing* R.C., DRIVER *and* MAIDS *behind her to* R., ATTENDANTS L.C.]

1ST ATTENDANT: This is the cave, Madam.

MADAM: Knock at the door, please.

1ST ATTENDANT [*knocking*]: Lady Precious Stream, please open the door.

PRECIOUS S. [*enters* L., *crosses to* C.]: I'm coming.

1ST ATTENDANT: Madam, your mother has come to visit you. [ATTENDANTS *go* L.]

PRECIOUS S. [C.]: Ah, this will kill me! Oh, how can I face my mother! [*Comes out of cave.* MADAM *gets out of carriage.*] Oh, my dear, dear mother.

MADAM [*puts arms round her*]: My Precious Stream!

PRECIOUS S.: How I have longed to see you, mother.

MADAM: And I to see you, but what a change. You, such a sweet-looking, innocent little lamb now become a hollow-faced, starved-looking ordinary person. Oh! I cannot bear this!

PRECIOUS S.: Dear mother! Allow me to kneel down and pay my respects to you.

MADAM [*stopping her*]: No, you mustn't stand on ceremony. Attendants, draw near and pay your respects to Lady Precious Stream.

ALL: Our respects to you, Lady Precious Stream. [SERVANTS *kneel and make curtsies.*]

PRECIOUS S. [*curtsies*]: Many thanks. Please don't stand on ceremony.

MADAM: Now you may all go and have a rest, but return again in a short time.

ALL: Thank you, Madam. [*They exeunt* L.]

PRECIOUS S.: Oh, dear mother, why do you condescend to come to our humble cave?

MADAM: I have heard that you are hungry and cold, and you are not well. So I wanted to see you and the place where you are living.

PRECIOUS S. [*barring the way*]: Oh, no! My humble cave would profane your dignity.

MADAM: Nonsense! I must go in and see what kind of a life you are leading.

PRECIOUS S.: It is a poor, wretched hole, and would only make you feel uncomfortable.

MADAM [*firmly*]: The place where my dear daughter can live for nearly a year is at least good enough for me to visit!

PRECIOUS S. [*giving in*]: Then let me go in first and have the place tidied for you.

MADAM: No, I want to see it just as it is. Lead the way, my darling.

[*They enter cave,* PRECIOUS STREAM *leading the way, taking* MADAM'S *hand. They go round stage, finish with* PRECIOUS STREAM L.C., MADAM C.]

PRECIOUS S.: Mind the steps, mother dear.

MADAM: So this is your place!

[PROPERTY MAN R. *places chair* C. PROPERTY MAN L. *brings stool, places it* L. *of* MADAM.]

Oh, you silly darling, fancy forsaking your beautifully decorated boudoir and coming to this horrible cave! How could you!

PRECIOUS S. [*offering her a chair*]: Make yourself comfortable in this poor chair, dear mother.

[PROPERTY MAN L. *brings bowl and chopsticks above* PRECIOUS STREAM. *She takes them from him, and gives them to* MADAM, *who gives them to* PROPERTY MAN R.]

I am afraid I have no tea or refreshments to offer you, except some poor rice.

MADAM: Fancy sacrificing the delicacies you enjoyed for this poor stuff! How could you! Now, sit down yourself.

PRECIOUS S. [*sitting on the left side*]: Thank you, dear mother! After those delicacies this plain fare seemed to be very palatable to me.

MADAM: You are under-nourished. That's why you are ill.

PRECIOUS S.: Indeed, it is not a question of food. The wretched Wei told me that my husband had been killed! It was this news that sent me to bed.

MADAM: This news may be false, my darling.

PRECIOUS S.: Oh, yes! I don't believe it at all. But, still, it makes me feel wretched. And father sends agents to try to persuade me to marry again, which makes me feel worse.

MADAM [*furious*]: The old rascal! He'll wish he'd never been born when I've done talking to him tonight.

PRECIOUS S.: Oh, no! Please don't quarrel with father on *my* account. It will only increase my sin against filial piety.

MADAM: Very well, then. He has you to thank if I let him off. How are you feeling now?

PRECIOUS S.: You see I have already recovered at the sight of you!

MADAM: But this is not the place for convalescence. Now be reasonable, and come back with your mother, where you need not worry about anything, and will have plenty to eat and plenty to wear.

PRECIOUS S.: No, dear mother. . . . I'd rather starve here than go back.

MADAM: Nonsense! Now tell me, when did you last hear from your husband?

PRECIOUS S.: I have never heard from him since his departure. The official news declared that there was a general defeat. Not long ago when the troops of the Western Region retired, our search party returned with the report that my husband was amongst those who were killed.

MADAM: Oh, my dear, let us hope that he has escaped somehow and will return safe and sound!

PRECIOUS S.: Thank you, dear mother! But I had hoped he would return victorious. To return as a deserter or an escaped prisoner would be worse than not to return at all.

MADAM: Oh, brave girl. I think the best way for you is to come back with me, and if your father tries to say anything against you he will have *me* to deal with.

PRECIOUS S. [*determined*]: No! I am afraid you'll have to go back alone, dear mother. And if father refers to me, tell him to regard me as dead or, still better, regard me as never having been born.

MADAM: Don't be stupid. Don't mind your father. Don't worry about your husband! Come to your mother! The place where your mother is, is the place for you; and the place where your mother goes is the place where you should go. Your mother will protect you. And when your mother dies you will be her chief mourner, won't you?

PRECIOUS S.: Of course, of course!

MADAM: And when your father dies don't mourn for him, and don't weep for him at all.

PRECIOUS S. [*coaxing her*]: No, no, I won't weep for him at all. It is you, and only you, whom I love and whom I will mourn and weep for. Do you feel satisfied now?

MADAM: Yes. But since you refuse to go with me, I will stay with you here instead.

PRECIOUS S. [*rises*]: Oh, no! You can't stay here.

MADAM: I am determined.

PRECIOUS S. [*crosses D.L.*]: This will never do!

[*The* SERVANTS, MAIDS, *and* DRIVER *return from* R. *and stop* D.R.]

MADAM: You can't force me to go.

PRECIOUS S.: I hear the servants coming. I think you ought to go now, dear mother.

[PROPERTY MAN L. *moves stool.*]

MADAM [*rises*]: No. My maids, bring in the silver and the rice and the clothes that you have brought with you.

MAIDS: Yes, Madam.

[*They enter and ascend stairs.*]

MADAM: Give them to Lady Precious Stream.

MAIDS: Yes, Madam.

[*They cross to* L. *of* PRECIOUS STREAM.]

MAIDS: These are for you, Lady Precious Stream.

MADAM: Put them down.

PRECIOUS S.: No, mother. I won't take anything from the Wang family.

[MAIDS *put down parcels. They are removed by* PROPERTY MAN L. MAIDS *return to positions* D.R.]

MADAM: Nonsense! These are presents from me to you. They have nothing to do with the Wang family. Besides, when I am staying with you, we shall need a little money to buy some extra food. You can't expect me to live on rice pudding all the time.

PRECIOUS S.: Dear mother, you can't stay here with me.

MADAM: Can't I? You'll see. Attendants!

ATTENDANTS [*kneeling*]: Yes, Madam?

MADAM: All of you may go home now, for I'm going to stay a few days here with Lady Precious Stream.

[*She sits.*]

ATTENDANTS [*rising*]: Yes, Madam.

PRECIOUS S.: Wait, please. What shall I do? What shall I do? [*Tapping her forehead.*] Ah! I have it. Well, mother, I have changed my mind. I agree to return with you rather than let you stay here with me.

MADAM [*rising*]: That's a good girl. Attendants! Prepare the carriage for us. Lead the way, my darling.

[*They commence to go out of cave.* ATTENDANTS *cross to* D.L. DRIVER *arranges carriage.* PROPERTY MAN R. *removes chair.*]

PRECIOUS S.: Mind the steps, mother. Oh, mother, I forgot something.

MADAM: What is it, my darling?

PRECIOUS S.: I forgot to put the silver, the clothes, and the rice in a safe place.

MADAM: They won't be lost if the cave door is locked.

PRECIOUS S.: But the rats – they will eat the rice and destroy the clothes.

[*Both enter carriage.*]

MADAM: They are worth very little. I can afford to get some more.

PRECIOUS S.: I can't allow anything from my dear mother to be destroyed. I won't be a moment.

MADAM: Then be quick.

[PROPERTY MAN L. *places cushion after* PRECIOUS STREAM *has gone into cave;* PRECIOUS STREAM *runs into the cave, bolts door and falls on her knees* C.]

PRECIOUS S.: Mother, I am not going back with you. And for my unfilial conduct I am kneeling inside the cave.

MADAM: Oh, my obstinate darling, how could you?

PRECIOUS S.: Dear mother, though I remain in the cave, my heart goes with you.

MADAM [*to the* MAIDS]: My maids, try to get Lady Precious Stream to open the door and come with me.

[MAIDS *cross* L. *to* R. *of* PRECIOUS STREAM. PROPERTY MAN L. *knocks on his box as* MAIDS *pretend to knock on cave door.*]

1ST MAID [*knocks at cave*]: Lady Precious Stream, will you please open the door and come back with us?

PRECIOUS S.: No, dear maids. I sincerely entreat you, instead of trying to persuade me to come out, to try your best to make Madam, my mother, depart as quickly as possible. The weather is cold and the north wind is bitter. If you will do this favour for me, you will have the eternal gratitude of an unfilial daughter.

MAIDS: We will, we will!

[*They move* R. *to above* MADAM.]

1ST MAID: Madam, Lady Precious Stream refuses to come

out. She entreats you to return as soon as possible for it is bitterly cold here.

2nd MAID: If you will allow me to say a word, Madam, I think she is quite determined, and we had better go home ourselves and come back some other time.

MADAM [*weeping*]: Oh, my poor darling daughter.

PRECIOUS S. [*weeping*]: Oh, my poor dear mother.

1st MAID [*to the servants*]: I think we had better start at once.
    [MAIDS *return to places behind* DRIVER.]

MADAM: Start!
    [*They go round stage once and exit* L. PRECIOUS STREAM *listens to them leave and comes out of cave to* C. PROPERTY MAN L. *takes away the cushion from* PRECIOUS STREAM.]

PRECIOUS S.: Oh, she has gone!
    [*Music starts. As* PRECIOUS STREAM *exits, music stops. Stage lights fade. House lights on.*]

END OF ACT TWO

NO CURTAIN

(*During the intermission the* PROPERTY MEN *rearrange their prop. boxes, sweep stage, etc.*)

ACT THREE

House lights out. Gong No. 1 – Enter READER *from* R. *Spot on* READER.

HONOURABLE READER: We are now coming to a strange land known as the Western Regions. It is believed that the customs here are exactly opposite those of China. For instance, the women wear long gowns whilst the men wear short coats and have their trousers showing. Their appearance, too, is unusual. They have red hair, green eyes, prominent noses, and hairy hands.

The stage represents the magnificent court of the King of the Western Regions. Probably they have very queer furniture and very strange decorations. Indeed we would be quite at a loss to prepare the properties of this scene had we not the advantage of leaving the audience to furnish them according to their imagination.

Everything in this scene is strange. But the most strange thing of all is that HIS MAJESTY THE KING is no other than our old friend the gardener, HSIEH PING-KUEI! He whom we believed the enemy killed long ago is still alive, and after his conquest of the Western Regions has proclaimed himself King. To our regret no records of this conquest exist and we regret even more having arrived just a day too late to see his coronation.

However, another great occasion is coming very soon. It has been arranged that a royal wedding is to take place to-morrow. The Queen Elect is a foreign Princess with whom our hero shares the laurels of his victories. She is another clever woman who has succeeded in making our hero put a halter willingly around his own neck. There is a general rumour to the effect that there is a reluctance on his part to the marriage, and the people wonder why such a beautiful maiden should not be snapped up with alacrity. But we know that the cause is not due to this excellent lady whom we are going to meet soon, but to HIS MAJESTY, who has some dark secret that he dares not reveal. That is why we find that the first gentleman of the kingdom is rather depressed in this hour of what should be great happiness.

He seems to know that among the audience many are doubtful of his identity, so he introduces himself to them once more.

[READER *exits* R.]

[*Gong No. 2. Stage lights up.* PROPERTY MEN *enter* L. *and* R. *Gong No. 3 – Music starts. Enter* 1st *and* 2nd ATTENDANTS *followed by* HSIEH. ATTENDANTS *cross to* D.R. *and* D.L. HSIEH *to* D.C. *Music stops.*]

HSIEH [*saluting*]: By the help of the Royal Princess I have now the honour to be your humble servant Hsieh Ping-Kuei, the King of the Western Regions. I have been away from my home for eighteen years. There are two things I desire perpetually: to return to my wife, Precious Stream, and to avenge myself on Wei, the Tiger General, who attempted to have me murdered and nearly caused my death. When I returned victorious, General Wei pretended to celebrate my triumph by giving a banquet in his camp, and having made me quite intoxicated with strong wine, tied me on to a horse and set it galloping towards the enemy.

[PROPERTY MAN L. *places table* C. PROPERTY MAN R. *places chair* C. *above table.*]

Luckily I was rescued by the Princess, who released me and helped me conquer all the Western Regions, from which she revolted for love of me. She wishes to marry me, an unusual proposal which I could not possibly refuse. Postponing it again and again I have at last been obliged to promise to marry her after my coronation.

[*Crosses* U.C., *sits.*]

Whilst everyone else in the kingdom seems to be rejoicing at the prospect of the coming wedding, I alone am troubled by it.

[PROPERTY MAN R. *places chair* D.R. *for* WILD GOOSE. WILD GOOSE *enters from* R. *crosses* D.R. *on to chair.*]

I have been vainly trying to explain to her that I am already married, but I can't bear to break her heart. What shall I do? What *shall* I do?

WILD GOOSE: Hsieh Ping-Kuei's unfaithful!

[*The* WILD GOOSE *continues to repeat this phrase over and over, sotto voce, until shot.*]

ATTENDANTS: We beg to report to your Majesty that a wild goose is flying over the palace, uttering strange sounds.

HSIEH [*rises, crosses* D.L.C.]: Show me where it is.

ATTENDANTS [*pointing*]: There is the bird, Your Majesty.

HSIEH: This is strange. It seems to keep uttering that I'm unfaithful. This is, indeed, a bad omen. Attendants, bring me my bow and arrows.

ATTENDANTS: Yes, Your Majesty.

[1ST ATTENDANT *gets bow from* PROPERTY MAN L. *and gives it to* HSIEH.]

HSIEH: I have never before heard a wild goose uttering sounds which seem to be like the words of a human being. With my bow and arrow I shoot it. There!

[*He shoots.* WILD GOOSE *makes movements as though shot and exits* R. 2ND ATTENDANT *gets piece of cloth from* PROPERTY MAN R.]

2ND ATTENDANT: I beg to report to Your Majesty that I found this piece of cloth on the bird.

HSIEH [*crossing to* C.]: Give it to me.

2ND ATTENDANT [*handing it to him*]: Yes, Your Majesty.

HSIEH [*after looking at cloth*]: Ah! Attendants, retire for a moment, please.

[ATTENDANTS *exit* L. *and* R.]

F

The words on the cloth, torn from her skirt, are written with her blood. They say: 'Precious Stream presents her respects to her unfaithful husband Hsieh Ping-Kuei and begs to tell him that since his departure she has been suffering every hardship in the humble cave. If he returns immediately, they may meet each other once more, but if he delays for only a few days, they may never see each other again.' Oh, my dear wife, my dear Precious Stream. I cannot stop the tears flowing from my eyes. Far, far away there is my home, my sweet home. My dear wife. I must get back in time to see you. Let me ponder and think of some plan. Ah! I have it!

[ATTENDANTS *enter from* R. *and* L. *to* D.R. *and* D.L.]
I must do it. I must do it at any cost. Attendants!

ATTENDANTS: Yes, Your Majesty.

HSIEH: Request Her Highness the Royal Princess to come to court.

[*He sits* U.R.]

ATTENDANTS: Yes, Your Majesty.

[*Crosses* U.R. *and* U.L. *and call off* R.]
His Majesty requests the presence of Her Highness the Royal Princess.

PRINCESS [*off* R.]: To hear is to obey.

[*Music starts. Enter* FOUR MAIDS *from* R. 1st *and* 2nd *cross* D.R. *and then go to* D.L. 3rd *and* 4th *cross* D.R. PRINCESS *follows to* D.C. ATTENDANTS *return to places* D.L. *and* D.R. *Music stops.*]

PRINCESS [*to audience, saluting*]: Your humble maid, the Royal Princess of the Western Regions, at your service. I have just returned from the parade grounds after reviewing my troops and have been told that His Majesty has commanded me to go to court.

[*To* MAIDS.]
My maids, lead the way to the court.

MAIDS [*saluting*]: Yes, Your Highness.

[*The* MAIDS *cross to* C. *and then go* U.L., *and make a large circle around the stage, returning to their original positions. The* PRINCESS *follows them, but stops at* R. *of table.*]

PRINCESS [*to* HSIEH, *saluting*]: Your humble maid, the Royal Princess of the Western Regions, offers her respects to Your Majesty.

HSIEH: Don't stand on ceremony.

[PROPERTY MAN L. *places chair at* L. *of table.*]

PRINCESS [*crossing below table to chair* L.]: Thank you.

HSIEH: You are at liberty to sit down.

[MAIDS *cross directly to* U.L.C. *and* U.R.C., *standing above chairs.*]

PRINCESS [*sitting*]: Thank you. May I know what important affair of State Your Majesty wishes to discuss with me?

HSIEH: There is no affair of State I wish to trouble you with. As you have been having a very hard time recently in reviewing all these troops, I have prepared a banquet in your honour, and I would be glad if you would consent to have a hearty carousal with me.

PRINCESS [*highly pleased*]: This would indeed be a great honour! Allow me to serve Your Majesty with wine.

HSIEH [*signals* ATTENDANT R.]: Oh, no, I couldn't possibly trouble you. Attendants! Prepare wine for me.

ATTENDANTS: Yes, Your Majesty.

HSIEH [*to* PRINCESS]: Let me have the pleasure of serving you.

[1ST ATTENDANT *gets tray with wine jug and two glasses from* PROPERTY MAN R., *puts them on table, then back to his place.* HSIEH *immediately pours out wine, hands glass to* PRINCESS. *She drinks.*]

Although I am very happy in drinking with you, the thought of our being attacked by the neighbouring states constantly troubles me.

PRINCESS: I beg your Majesty not to worry about the

invasion of other states, for I myself am able to cope with any invasion of the enemy, regardless of the numbers.

HSIEH: Regardless of number.

PRINCESS: Yes! But of course we entirely depend upon your blessing, without which there is no chance of victory.

HSIEH: Oh, no, you are the invincible Princess.

PRINCESS: Thank you. To Your Majesty's health!

[*She finds that her cup is empty.*]

More wine to Your Majesty!

HSIEH: How full of life and charm you are!

[*Pours more wine.*]

Do not hesitate to refresh yourself thoroughly. You have had a hard time reviewing the troops, and a good bumper of wine will greatly benefit you.

PRINCESS [*pleased*]: Oh, thanks, Your Majesty! But I can't drink as much as I could formerly.

HSIEH: How much could you drink formerly?

PRINCESS: A hundred cups at least!

HSIEH: And now?

PRINCESS [*smiling*]: Only fifty cups [*strikes two cups together*], multiplied by two.

HSIEH [*laughing*]: Ha, ha! Just the same! One hundred cups!

[*To* ATTENDANTS.]

Attendants! Serve the wine in large cups!

ATTENDANTS: Yes, Your Majesty.

[*Music starts.* ATTENDANT L. *removes tray and glasses from table, giving them to* PROPERTY MAN L. ATTENDANT R. *gets tray and two goblets and jug from* PROPERTY MAN R., *places them on table, then back to their places.* HSIEH *pours out and gives* PRINCESS *goblet of wine. She drinks it, hands it to* MAID, *who passes it along to the* MAID R., *who places it on table.* HSIEH *repeats business goblet passed round, replaced on table.* HSIEH *then gives the* PRINCESS *the jug, who sways in her seat and gradually sinks with head on table. Music stops.*]

MAIDS [*look first at* PRINCESS, *then at each other, then speak to audience*]: Her Highness is intoxicated.

HSIEH [*raising her head*]: So she is. [*Rises.*] She has fallen into my trap.

> [PROPERTY MAN L. *puts flag in* PRINCESS'S *belt.* HSIEH *moves to* R. *of* PRINCESS, *takes flag from her belt, then down to* C. *to audience.*]

Now I have done it. With this little flag I can go where I like, and get away from the Western Regions, but I shall have to leave without bidding her good-bye.

> [PROPERTY MAN R. *puts pen and paper on table, removes goblets and jug.*]

HSIEH [*sits at table*]: I will write a letter to her, I can't bear to say good-bye to her.

> [*Reading as he writes.*]

'I am going to the frontier to review the troops there. If you still love me, follow me with all your troops to the third pass; if you don't love me, stay where you are and don't think of me.'

> [*He rises.*]

Men of the Western Region, saddle my horse!

ATTENDANTS: Yes, Your Majesty.

> [2nd ATTENDANT *gets whip from* PROPERTY MAN R., *holds it for* HSIEH, *who takes it.* HSIEH *leaps on his horse and gallops off* L. MAIDS *step forward, waving hands.*]

MAIDS: Your Highness! Your Highness!

> [MAIDS *return to place upstage.*]

PRINCESS [*waking up*]: The wine has affected me a little. Where is His Majesty?

> [*Looks under table.*]

1ST ATTENDANT: His Majesty has gone to the frontier to review the troops there, Your Highness.

PRINCESS: Did he leave any orders for me?

2ND ATTENDANT [*picks up letter from table, hands it to her*]: His Majesty left this letter for Your Highness.

[PRINCESS *takes letter.*]

PRINCESS [*rising*]: Let me read it. What does he mean? What *does* he mean?

[*Pacing stage, tapping forehead.*]

Ah, I see! His Majesty has gone back to China. He wants me to follow him with all the troops to China. Attendants!

[*Turns back to audience.*]

ATTENDANTS: Yes, Your Highness.

PRINCESS: Order my two aides-de-camp Ma Ta and Kiang Hai to await my further orders before the palace gates with all my troops.

ATTENDANTS: Yes, Your Highness.

[PROPERTY MAN L. *clears chair* PRINCESS *has used.* PROPERTY MAN R. *moves arm-chair.* PROPERTY MAN L. *clears table to upstage* L. ATTENDANTS *cross* U.L. *and* U.R., *turn* R. *and call:*]

Her Highness orders her two aides-de-camp Ma Ta and Kiang Hai to await her further orders before the palace gates with all her troops.

MA TA and KIANG HAI [*offstage*]: To hear is to obey.

[ATTENDANTS *return to places* D.L. *and* D.R.]

PRINCESS [*facing audience*]: How unreasonable His Majesty is. He ought not to have gone away without bidding me good-bye. I will overtake him with my troops and ask him what is the reason.

[PRINCESS, *facing her maids, gestures them to precede her.* MAIDS *salute, face* L., *march off* L., *followed by* ATTENDANTS *and* PRINCESS. *Enter* MA TA *and* KIANG HAI R., *getting spears from* PROPERTY MAN R., *downstage to* C., *to audience.*]

MA TA: Our home is far, far in the North-West.

KIANG HAI: We are somewhat tongue-tied.

MA TA: Beef and mutton are what we like best!

KIANG HAI: Big camels are what we ride.

MA TA [*saluting*]: I am Ma Ta, at your service.

KIANG HAI: I am Kiang Hai, your humble servant.

MA TA: Glad to see you.

KIANG HAI: How goes it?

MA TA and KIANG HAI: We are here waiting for orders from Her Highness, the Royal Princess.

[*They take one step back, turn, face each other, two steps back. Enter* MAIDS, *two down* R., *two* L., *followed by* PRINCESS, *who comes* C. MAIDS *get spears and* PRINCESS'S *whip from* PROPERTY MAN R.]

PRINCESS: Oh, unfaithful Hsieh Ping-Kuei, I will overtake you and sue you for breach of promise.

MA TA and KIANG HAI [*saluting*]: Our respects to you, Your Highness.

PRINCESS: Don't stand on ceremony. Are the troops ready?

MA TA and KIANG HAI: Yes, Your Highness. We are waiting for your orders.

PRINCESS: Order them to march to the first pass.

MA TA and KIANG HAI [*calling*]: To the first pass.

[*Music starts.* MAIDS L. *turn upstage, start marching, followed by* MAIDS R. *They exit* L. *followed by* MA TA, KIANG HAI, *and* PRINCESS. *Pass brought on* R. WARDEN *comes on* R., *stands on chair behind it. Pass brought on by* SOLDIERS 1 *and* 2. *Music stops.*]

WARDEN: By the order of Her Highness the Royal Princess of the Western Regions, I am the Warden of the first pass.

[HSIEH *enters* R., *downstage to* D.L.]

HSIEH: Hey! Open the pass for me!

WARDEN: Where do you come from, and what is your business?

HSIEH: By the orders of Her Highness the Royal Princess, I have business of State to transact beyond the pass.

WARDEN: Have you the yellow flag from Her Highness?

HSIEH: Yes – here it is.

WARDEN: Soldiers, open the pass for him!

[*Music starts.* HSIEH *upstage, through the pass and off* L.

MAIDS enter, march to L., *make line up and down stage,* MA TA *and* KIANG HAI *following them. A division is left between the* FOUR MAIDS. PRINCESS *enters* R. *across to* L., *comes to* L.C. *through the division between* MAIDS. *Music stops.*]

WARDEN: The Warden of the first pass pays his respects to you, Your Highness.

PRINCESS: Don't stand on ceremony. I want to ask you, has His Majesty the King passed here?

WARDEN [*trembling*]: There was a man who passed through, but I don't know if it was His Majesty the King.

PRINCESS: Don't you even know your King? You are under arrest! To the second pass.

[*Music starts.* MAID NO. 1 *starts, followed by other* MAIDS, MA TA *and* KIANG HAI. *They march in front of* PRINCESS. *She follows them. All go through pass and exit* L. *Pass is moved to* C. *stage. Warden changes beard. Music stops.*]

WARDEN: By order of her Royal Highness, the Princess of the Western Regions, I am the Warden of the second pass.

[HSIEH *enters* R., *down* L.]

HSIEH: Hey! Open the pass for me!

WARDEN: Where do you come from and what is your business?

HSIEH: By the order of Her Highness the Royal Princess, I have business of State to transact beyond the pass.

WARDEN: Have you the yellow flag from Her Highness?

HSIEH: Yes, here it is!

WARDEN: Soldiers, open the pass for him.

[*Music starts.* HSIEH *goes through the pass and off* L. MAIDS *march in as before below pass to* L., *leaving division between them for* PRINCESS. PRINCESS *enters* R. *through the division to* L.C. *Music stops.*]

The Warden of the second pass presents his respects to Your Highness.

PRINCESS: Don't stand on ceremony. I want to ask you, has His Majesty the King passed here?

WARDEN: A man did pass here, but – –

PRINCESS: Excellent service you're rendering me. Report yourself for a court martial tomorrow morning. To the third pass!

[*Music starts.* MAIDS, MA TA, KIANG HAI *and* PRINCESS *march through pass and exit* L. *as before.* WARDEN *joins in the march after* MAIDS *and before* MA TA *and exits with them. Pass is moved to* L. MU *enters and stands on chair behind pass. Music stops.*]

MU: I am well known for my white helmet, white armour, and white banners. I also have a white moustache, white beard, and white eyebrows. After I have drunk plenty of white wine I will show you the whites of my eyes! I am old Mu, the White General, at your service. By order of His Imperial Majesty, the Emperor, I am the Warden of the third pass.

[HSIEH *enters* R. *down to* C.]

HSIEH [*to audience*]: Wait! This is now the frontier of my motherland. The third pass is the boundary. The man in the tower seems to be old General Mu. Let me call him by name.

[*Crosses up to pass.*]

My respects to you, old General Mu.

MU: Thank you. Thank you. Who are you to call me by name?

HSIEH: I am Captain Hsieh Ping-Kuei coming back from the Western Regions to report myself at headquarters.

MU: The pass is haunted! The pass is haunted!

[MU *gets down behind the pass.* SOLDIERS *shake the pass.*]

You were killed in the Western Regions. So this is your spirit which comes back to haunt us.

HSIEH: No, I was not killed. My enemy planned my death and thinks I am dead, but I am still alive.

G

MU [*poking head through pass*]: Is that so? I can hardly believe it.

MAIDS [*off.*]: Houp-hey!

HSIEH: There are troops in pursuit of me. Open the pass and let me in.

MU: All right. Open the pass for him, soldiers.
[*Music starts.* HSIEH *goes through pass and exits* L. MAIDS *enter from* R. *followed by* MA TA *and* KIANG HAI. *They form a line as before. The* PRINCESS *goes between them to* C. *All are very tired. Music stops.*]

MA TA and KIANG HAI: We beg to report to Your Highness that we have now arrived at the third pass, which belongs to China.

PRINCESS [*crossing* R.]: So we have! Go and ask them to let us pass through.

MA TA and KIANG HAI [*crossing* L.]: Yes, Your Highness.

PRINCESS [*turning* L.]: One moment. Come back!

MA TA and KIANG HAI [*turning* R.]: Yes, Your Highness.

PRINCESS: As we have come to the territory of another country we must be more polite in our speech!

MA TA and KIANG HAI: Yes, Your Highness.
[*They face old* MU.]

MA TA: Hey! My old man!

MU: Old moon? Can't see the old moon until midnight.

KIANG HAI: My master!

MU: Mustard! Go to the grocery for it.

MA TA: My Lord!

MU: He is in Heaven.

KIANG HAI: My Emperor!

MU: You are empty? This is not an eating-house. What are you two doing here? You are too ugly to be called human beings, and certainly too ordinary to be called devils. Go back, and get someone more presentable to talk to me.
[*They turn to* PRINCESS.]

MA TA and KIANG HAI: He requests the presence of Your Highness.

PRINCESS: All right. I'll go.

[*She goes to upper corner of the pass.* MA TA *and* KIANG HAI *return to their places in line.*]

My respects to you, old grandfather in the tower.

MU: Thank you, and mine to the little grandmother beneath it. What is your business here?

PRINCESS: May I ask you, has His Majesty the King of our country, Captain Hsieh Ping-Kuei of your country, passed through this way?

MU: His Majesty the King of your country has not passed, but Captain Hsieh Ping-Kuei of our country has passed.

PRINCESS: But he is no other than the King of our country. If he has passed here and is with you there, I entreat you to ask him to appear on the wall of the pass, so that we may say a few words to each other. Then I will withdraw with my forces, and I promise you there will be no trouble and no damage. Do you think this can be done, my old General?

MU: You bewitching little minx! Captain Hsieh Ping-Kuei of our country used to be a robust young giant, and now, after eighteen years' adventure in your country, he comes back the wreck of a man! How can I allow him to see you again, you little minx!

PRINCESS [*furious*]: What impudence! [*Crosses* R.] Ma Ta and Kiang Hai!

MA TA and KIANG HAI: Yes, Your Highness.

PRINCESS: Attack the Pass!

ALL: Houp-hey!

[*All take one step forward as if to attack pass with spears.*]

MU: Wait a moment! Wait a moment! The pass is made of cloth; it will be damaged if you don't take care.

[PRINCESS *motions them to stand at ease again.*]

If you withdraw for a short distance, I will ask Captain Hsieh Ping-Kuei to come out and speak to you. After all,

I am not his guardian, and I don't care what company he keeps!

PRINCESS [*crosses to pass*]: You must play fair!

MU: Of course! Fair play for a fair lady.

PRINCESS: The troops are ordered to withdraw to a short distance.

[*They all do a left turn.*]

MA TA and KIANG HAI: Yes, Your Highness.

[*They march off R., MAIDS going off first.*]

MU: Captain Hsieh! Captain Hsieh!

HSIEH [*appearing from the L.*]: May I congratulate you on your victory?

MU: Congratulate the lady, my enemy! The victory belongs to her. You are requested to go up to the tower; she wants to speak to you.

[*Gets down from chair.*]

HSIEH: Thank you for your trouble.

[*MU exits L.*]

I see the Princess coming alone.

PRINCESS [*appearing again*]: I see the unfaithful one standing alone.

[*To HSIEH.*]

What have I done to deserve this? Why did you desert me?

HSIEH: I will tell you everything now. The other day a wild goose brought a letter from Lady Precious Stream.

PRINCESS: What! Who is this Lady Precious Stream?

HSIEH: She is my wife.

PRINCESS [*appalled*]: What – your wife! So you are already married! You are going back to her now?

HSIEH: Yes.

PRINCESS: Oh, you have been deceiving me all these years!

HSIEH [*protesting*]: No. You wrong me there! I was desperately in love with you all the time, and I am still.

PRINCESS: Then why do you forsake me?

HSIEH: Because I am in honour bound to the other.

PRINCESS: But you ought to have told me this before.

HSIEH: I loved you too much to hurt your feelings.

PRINCESS: To deceive me and then desert me is most heart-less.

[*Crosses* D.R.]

I will never speak to you again. I hate you! I hate you!

HSIEH [*hurt*]: Please don't! I *still* love you. Will you be a sister to me, and go to China with me?

PRINCESS: Never. Never! I don't want to be near you now.

HSIEH: But I want to be near you. That's why I asked you to follow me.

PRINCESS: Yes, but at a safe distance.

HSIEH: Don't say that. I would gladly marry you if I could. Now, will you not be my sister and come with me?

PRINCESS: Never!

HSIEH: Then I must bid you farewell for ever, because I may never see you again!

PRINCESS: I don't want to see you again!

HSIEH: I have many enemies in China, and without your military protection I shall probably be murdered by them very soon!

PRINCESS: Oh, I never thought of that! Yes, your General Wei will try to murder you. I must go with you to protect you, even if I hate you.

[*Crosses few steps* L.]

HSIEH: No! I can't accept your protection if you still hate me.

PRINCESS [*crosses a step* L]: Well, I won't hate you.

HSIEH: And will be my sister?

PRINCESS [*crosses a step* L.]: No! At most your cousin.

HSIEH: No! Sister.

PRINCESS [*crosses a step* L.]: Let us say first cousin?

HSIEH: No! Sister.

PRINCESS [*crosses to* C.]: All right. Come down at once.

HSIEH: No! In Lady Precious Stream's letter she said she is in great danger, so I must hurry on. Order your troops to be encamped near the pass, and await a message from me. Good-bye till then.

[HSIEH *exits* L., *followed by* SOLDIERS *carrying pass.*]

PRINCESS: Good-bye.

[*Calling off* R.]

Ma Ta and Kiang Hai!

MA TA and KIANG HAI [*off* R.]: Yes, Your Highness.

PRINCESS: Order the troops to be encamped here.

MA TA and KIANG HAI: Yes, Your Highness.

[*Music starts.* MAIDS *enter from* R. *followed by* MA TA *and* KIANG HAI. *They cross stage and exit* L., *followed by the* PRINCESS. *Lights dim. Music stops. Lights up.*]

HSIEH: Look out! A horse is coming!

[*Enters from* R. *Crosses to* D.C.]

When one is anxious to get home one travels both in daytime and by starlight. Bidding good-bye to the Princess not long ago, I have now arrived at the little hill not far from my own door.

[*He dismounts to* R., *gives whip to* PROPERTY MAN R.]

Let me tie my horse under the shadow of a willow tree.

[*To audience.* PRECIOUS STREAM *enters from* L., *gets basket from* PROPERTY MAN L. *During the following speech she crosses* D.L., *then crosses stage to* D.R.]

There is someone coming. She looks rather like my wife, but I must be careful to avoid being guilty of taking another man's wife as my own. Now that I have arrived at my home, I must be very polite.

[*Crosses to* D.L., *faces* R. *and bows.*]

My respects to you, madam. May I have a word with you?

PRECIOUS S. [*faces* L., *curtsies*]: And mine to you. Have you lost your way, sir?

HSIEH [*crossing to* D.L.C.]: No one could be lost in such a place as this. I want to find someone.

PRECIOUS S. [*crossing to* D.R.C.]: Only famous people are known to me.

HSIEH: She whom I seek is a very famous person. She is the daughter of the Prime Minister Wang, and the wife of Hsieh Ping-Kuei. Lady Precious Stream she is by name.

PRECIOUS S.: May I ask why you are inquiring for her?

HSIEH: I have been serving in the same company as her husband, who has entrusted me with a letter for her.

PRECIOUS S.: Let me have the letter.

HSIEH: Oh, no, madam. Hsieh Ping-Kuei said this letter should be delivered in person – by me.

PRECIOUS S.: Please excuse me a moment.

HSIEH: Certainly.

[*He crosses* U.L. *to* PROPERTY MAN *and gets tea.*]

PRECIOUS S. [*crosses to audience*]: I should like to confess and get that letter at once, but I am in such rags that I am ashamed to do so, and if I don't he will certainly not give me that letter. Oh, how cruel that for eighteen long years' separation we have never met and have not been able to correspond. What shall I do?

[*Business of tapping forehead.*]

Ah! I have it.

[*Turns to* HSIEH, *who has come back* D.L.C.]

Well, sir, do you understand riddles?

HSIEH: A little.

PRECIOUS S.: Do you want to see Precious Stream?

HSIEH: Yes.

PRECIOUS S. [*hand bus.*]: Now, if you look far – –

HSIEH: – – she is a thousand miles away.

PRECIOUS S.: Yes. And if you look near – –

HSIEH: – – she is before me. Am I speaking to Mrs Hsieh, the famous daughter of the Prime Minister Wang?

PRECIOUS S.: Oh, no, not the famous, but only the humble wife of Hsieh Ping-Kuei.

HSIEH [*bowing*]: My respects to you.

PRECIOUS S. [*curtsying*]: You have already paid your respects.

HSIEH: Over-politeness does no harm.

PRECIOUS S.: Well said. Now my husband's letter, please.

HSIEH: One moment. Will you excuse me a minute?

PRECIOUS S.: Certainly.

[*Crosses* U.R. *to get tea from* PROPERTY MAN.]

HSIEH [*crosses to audience*]: Wait a moment! I was married to her for only a month, and I have been absent from home for eighteen years. I don't know what kind of a woman she really is. Let me try to flirt with her. If she proves to be a good and virtuous woman, I'll tell her who I am and we'll be happily reunited. But if she proves to be a woman of easy virtue, I'll disown her and go back to the Royal Princess of the Western Regions.

[*Crosses to* L.C. PRECIOUS STREAM *crosses to* R.C.]

Ah! Where on earth is that letter?

PRECIOUS S.: Where is it?

HSIEH: It is lost, madam.

PRECIOUS S.: Don't you know that a letter from one who loves you is worth all the money in the world! You should remember our sage said: 'I examine myself three times every day to see whether I have done truly and loyally my best to my friend.' And you have lost the letter of your friend. I am heartbroken!

HSIEH: Don't take it so seriously, madam. If you're so anxious about that letter, I'll tell you something I remember that is in it.

PRECIOUS S.: Please tell me what you do remember.

HSIEH: Listen carefully. 'On the mid-autumn night, under the bright moonlight, Hsieh Ping-Kuei presents his compliments to his dear wife. . . .'

PRECIOUS S.: And mine to him. How has he been lately?

HSIEH: Very well.

PRECIOUS S.: Safe and sound?

HSIEH: Safe and sound.

PRECIOUS S.: How about his meals?

HSIEH: They were badly cooked by the soldiers.

PRECIOUS S.: How about his clothes?

HSIEH: He has had to wash and mend them himself. '. . . and begs to tell her that he has been very unfortunate lately. He has suffered severe torture. . . .'

PRECIOUS S.: Ah, torture. He was beaten?

HSIEH: Yes, madam, beaten.

PRECIOUS S.: How many strokes did he receive?

HSIEH: Forty strokes in all.

PRECIOUS S.: Oh, my poor husband.

HSIEH: Don't cry, madam. There are still worse things coming. 'The other day a horse under his care was lost.'

PRECIOUS S.: Was it a Government horse or a privately owned one?

HSIEH: How can there be any privately owned horses in a camp? Of course it was a Government one.

PRECIOUS S.: That being so, I suppose he will have to pay for it.

HSIEH: How can he avoid paying for it?

PRECIOUS S.: But where can he find the money to pay for it?

HSIEH: He is sure to be able to find the money in some way or other. 'And because of having to pay for the horse, he has had to borrow ten pieces of silver.' [*Pointing to himself.*] Borrowed from me!

   [*Moves nearer her.*]

PRECIOUS S.: Stop! Allow me to ask you, what is your rank? [*Forces him* L. *one step.*]

HSIEH: I am a captain.

PRECIOUS S. [*another step* L.]: And my husband, Hsieh Ping-Kuei?

HSIEH: Also a captain.

PRECIOUS S. [*two steps* L.]: If you're both captains, you should get the same amount of pay, then how could you be able to lend him money whilst he had none?

HSIEH: Oh, there is a reason, madam! My eldest brother, Hsieh Ping-Kuei, is a born spendthrift, who squanders all

H

his pay, whilst I, having been born in a humble family, have been accustomed to save all I get. In this way I was able to lend him the money to pay for the horse.

PRECIOUS S.: That is not true. My husband was also born in a humble family, and he wouldn't know how to spend his money even if he tried.

[*Crosses* D.R.C.]

HSIEH [*laughing*]: Ha, ha!

PRECIOUS S.: Oh, dear, he is laughing at me!

[*To audience.*]

HSIEH [*crosses to* PRECIOUS STREAM]: The other day I went to his camp to demand the money and he said that he has a wife at home called Lady Precious Stream of the Wang family.

PRECIOUS S. [*furious, forces* HSIEH *one step* L.]: Stop! Let me ask you, has Precious Stream ever owed you anything formerly?

HSIEH: No, nothing.

PRECIOUS S. [*another step* L.]: Has she borrowed anything from you recently?

HSIEH: No, nothing.

PRECIOUS S. [*one more step* L.]: Why should her name be mentioned?

HSIEH [*forces* PRECIOUS STREAM *one step* R.]: Well, let me ask you now. As our old proverb says: 'Father's debts – –'

PRECIOUS S.: '– – the son pays.'

HSIEH [*another step* R.]: And the husband's debts?

PRECIOUS S.: The wife – the wife doesn't care a fig for them.

[*Turns her back on him.*]

HSIEH: Well said. But the wife has to pay for them in some other way. Having no ready money, my eldest brother Hsieh agreed to sell his wife, and you know, madam, he did not need to be afraid of there being no bidders, so a bargain was immediately made with a certain officer.

PRECIOUS S.: And who is this certain officer?

SIEH: Eh – eh – –

[*With a smile.*]

Do you understand riddles, madam?

PRECIOUS S.: Have you the audacity to say that it is you?

HSIEH: Eh – I haven't the audacity, but I have the proof.

PRECIOUS S.: What is your proof?

HSIEH: In the form of a marriage contract.

PRECIOUS S. [*to audience*]: Oh, cruel! No, I can't believe it!

[*To* HSIEH.]

Who are the witnesses to the contract?

HSIEH [*tapping forehead and crossing* L.]: They are – they are – Su, the Dragon General; Wei, the Tiger General; and Wang Yun, the Prime Minister.

PRECIOUS S.: Nonsense! I won't believe it, because they are all my near relatives, and they would certainly not allow my husband to sell me.

[PRECIOUS STREAM *doesn't look at* HSIEH. HSIEH *crosses* U.L. *and hides.*]

Though I am poor, my father is rich. Let me make out how much the capital and interest amount to now and I will send the money to you. I won't detain you now. Good-bye, and wait for the money in the Western Regions.

[PRECIOUS STREAM *crosses* U.R. *to be stopped by* HSIEH, *who has crossed from* U.L.]

HSIEH [*forcing her* D.C.]: No, no! It took me forty-eight days to travel from the Western Regions to here, and I have come here specially, not for the money, but for the beauty!

PRECIOUS S.: If you go on uttering nonsense and insulting me, I'll call for help and have you arrested.

HSIEH: But you are as good as my wife.

PRECIOUS S.: Oh, what impudence!

HSIEH [*rises on toes with arms outspread and lunges at her*]: I am going to capture you and carry you off to the Western Regions.

PRECIOUS S. [*retreating to* D.L. – *to audience*]: Oh, I'm frightened. The man is a beast! What shall I do? There is no help within reach. Let me think!

[*Taps forehead.*]

Ah! I have it. I'll throw dust in his eyes.

[*To imaginary person off* R.]

Hello, sir!

[*To* HSIEH.]

Someone is coming over there.

HSIEH [*turning* R. PRECIOUS STREAM *stoops to pick up dust*]: Where?

[*Turns back to* PRECIOUS STREAM.]

PRECIOUS S. [*rising and pretending to throw dust*]: Good-bye!

[*She crosses* U.L. *and around the stage.*]

HSIEH [*wiping eyes and crossing* D.R.]: Ah, ha! A virtuous woman indeed! No use flirting with her.

[*Gets whip from* PROPERTY MAN.]

It's not very far, so I will not ride but walk to my cave to meet her.

[*Crosses to* L. *and follows* PRECIOUS STREAM.]

PRECIOUS S.: It's too bad. He's following me.

HSIEH: I am your husband, Hsieh Ping-Kuei.

[PRECIOUS STREAM *enters cave, bolts door.* PROPERTY MAN L. *places chair with back to audience at* D.C. *beside her.* HSIEH *stops at* L.C.]

PRECIOUS S.: Let me shut the door and bolt it.

HSIEH: Open the door! You are shutting out your own husband.

PRECIOUS S.: You said but a short time ago that you were an officer of the same regiment as my husband, and now you are my husband. You are out of your senses.

HSIEH [*kneels down to talk through door.* PRECIOUS STREAM *is kneeling inside door*]: Oh, no! Don't you remember, you told me to be present on the second of February when I received the embroidered ball? We were driven out by your father and lived in this cave. Then I shot and killed the man-devouring tiger and was made a captain, joining the Western Punitive Expedition? I came back to tell you the news, I couldn't bear to leave you. Time was pressing, and I had to cut the reins of my horse which you held tightly in your hands. Then we parted, and that was eighteen years ago.

PRECIOUS S.: Did you receive my letter?

HSIEH: Oh, yes. That is why I hurried home.

PRECIOUS S. [*rises and peeks out*]: Let me look at . . . [*Closes door again*]. No. How can you be my husband with such a strange beard? My husband is a very handsome young man.

HSIEH: Thank you, my third sister. But you ought to say, he used to be a handsome young man. Take yourself, for instance, my dear third sister, you're quite different from the young girl who threw the ball from the pavilion. Consult a looking-glass and tell me what you think.

PRECIOUS S.: Don't you know there is no looking-glass in the humble cave?

HSIEH: Oh, I forgot! Look into a basin of water, as you always did formerly.

PRECIOUS S. [*crossing* R.]: It is a long time now since I looked into a basin of water, not caring how I looked.

   [*Kneels.*]

   Oh, horrible! I couldn't call myself Precious Stream now!

HSIEH: Now, open the door and let me in.

PRECIOUS S. [*opens door and puts out hand*]: Show me the letter first.

HSIEH [*hands letter to her*]: Here is the letter.

PRECIOUS S. [*closes door, crosses* R.]: Yes, this is the letter. Oh, my heavens!

HSIEH: Then why do you close the door again?

PRECIOUS S. [*kneeling*]: I will open the door only on one condition.

HSIEH: What is your condition, please?

PRECIOUS S.: A very simple one. I only want you to go backwards one step.

HSIEH [*he takes one step towards footlights*]: All right, I have done so.

PRECIOUS S.: Another step, please.

HSIEH [*doing so*]: All right. Now open the door.

PRECIOUS S.: One step more, please.

HSIEH [*his foot dangling beyond the proscenium*]: No, I can't! I have come to the end of things!

PRECIOUS S.: If you had not come to the end of things, I'm sure you would never have come back to me. And after you had deserted me for eighteen years you insulted me the moment you met me. What is there to live for? I'd rather die than take back such a husband!

HSIEH: Please don't say that. I entreat you to forgive me.

PRECIOUS S.: No.

[PROPERTY MAN L. *provides a cushion.*]

HSIEH: I entreat you on my knees.

[*He drops on right knee.*]

Look. I am paying you my highest respects in the presence of hundreds.

PRECIOUS S. [*peeking through door*]: No, I won't look at you. How about your other knee? I thought you said you were on your knees.

HSIEH: Oh, I beg your pardon.

[*Slaps left knee and puts it down.*]

PRECIOUS S.: Ah, that's better.

[*Rises, opens door by pulling chair which is removed by* PROPERTY MAN L.]

Come in, my dear!

HSIEH [*rising, handing the cushion to* PROPERTY MAN L. *and entering*]: Thank you, my dear!

[*He circles stage* L., *climbing the stairs, followed by* PRECIOUS STREAM.]

PRECIOUS S.: To what rank have you been promoted after all these years?

[PROPERTY MAN L. *places chair* U.C. *and stool to its* L.]

HSIEH: Eh? When your husband has returned from thousands of miles away, the first question you put to him is not about his health, nor his requiring food and drink, but about his rank. What is rank compared to food and drink?

[*He sits in chair.*]

PRECIOUS S. [*sits on stool*]: I haven't been very frequently in touch with food and drink during these eighteen years, so I am liable to forget them.

HSIEH: What do you mean? Do you mean to tell me that you haven't had enough to eat and drink during my absence? I remember having made a handsome provision for you just before my departure.

PRECIOUS S.: What was it?

HSIEH: Ten hundredweight of firewood and five hundredweight of rice.

PRECIOUS S.: Ten hundredweight of firewood and five hundredweight of rice? Even presuming they had everlasting qualities, how could they possibly outlast the wear and tear of all these eighteen years?

HSIEH: Granted. But you ought to have gone to your father and brother-in-law Wei for additional supplies.

PRECIOUS S.: They said that your pay had ceased, and offered to make me a loan, which I refused.

HSIEH [*rising*]: Splendid! Good-bye!

PRECIOUS S. [*rising*]: Where are you going?

HSIEH: To His Excellency the Prime Minister's house.

PRECIOUS S. [*crossing to* R. *of* HSIEH]: Don't go. My father is not very well.

HSIEH: What is the matter with him?

[PROPERTY MAN *removes chair and stool.*]

PRECIOUS S.: The common sickness of great men who don't like to see their poor relatives.

HSIEH: It doesn't matter. I haven't that kind of sickness, and I will condescend to see him.

PRECIOUS S.: What are you talking about? *You* condescend to see His Excellency the Prime Minister?

HSIEH: Yes, we have to sometimes.

PRECIOUS S.: What do you mean? The King is the only man in the world he would serve.

HSIEH: But I have not said that I am not a king.

PRECIOUS S.: *You* a king?

HSIEH: Yes – only the King of the Western Regions.

PRECIOUS S.: Only the King of the Western Regions!

[*To audience.*]

This seems incredible.

[*To* HSIEH.]

What proof have you?

HSIEH: What proof do you want?

PRECIOUS S.: Show me your royal seal.

HSIEH: Nonsense! Whoever heard of anyone having asked a king to prove himself a king by showing his royal seal?

PRECIOUS S.: I have never seen a royal seal, and I want very much to see one. Show it to me.

HSIEH: All right. If I have the royal seal . . .

PRECIOUS S.: Show it to me and I will believe you are a king.

HSIEH: And if I haven't the royal seal . . .

PRECIOUS S.: Then seal your lips so that you will utter no more nonsense.

HSIEH: Do you really want to see the royal seal?

PRECIOUS S.: Very much.

HSIEH [*paces L. a few steps*]: Then let me adjust my hat and dust my jacket.

[PROPERTY MAN L. *hands him seal.*]

Here is the seal of the King of the Western Regions.

PRECIOUS S.: Oh, indeed! The royal seal of the King of the

Western Regions! I must kneel down and ask your Majesty's favour.

[PROPERTY MAN R. *provides a cushion.*]

HSIEH [*returns seal to* PROPERTY MAN]: Who is she that kneels before me?

PRECIOUS S.: She is Your Majesty's humble maid, Precious Stream.

HSIEH: And for what purpose have you come?

PRECIOUS S.: To seek Your Majesty's favour.

HSIEH: You used very harsh and impolite words to me when you addressed me on the spot not far from the cave. I will not bestow on you any favour.

PRECIOUS S.: Your humble maid did not know it was Your Majesty then.

HSIEH: If you had known then, you would not have used such harsh and impolite words, would you?

PRECIOUS S.: Had she known then, she would have used more harsh and more impolite words.

HSIEH: Indeed! That settles the matter. No favours at all.

PRECIOUS S. [*rising and throwing the cushion to* PROPERTY MAN R.]: Then now she must use the most harsh and the most impolite words. Wretch that thou art!

[*Shakes finger at him.*]

HSIEH [*covering ears with hands*]: Speak no more! I am about to bestow on you some favour. Hear me!

PRECIOUS S.: Yes, Your Majesty.

[*Kneels.* PROPERTY MAN L. *gives her a cushion and* HSIEH *a sword.*]

HSIEH: By the order of His Majesty the King of the Western Regions, Lady Precious Stream of the Wang family is to be crowned Her Majesty.

[*He taps her on back with sword.*]

Queen of the Western Regions.

PRECIOUS S. [*rising and giving* PROPERTY MAN L. *the cushion*]: Thanks, Your Majesty.

[*Crosses* D.C. *to audience – sighs.*]

At last!

HSIEH [*returns sword to* PROPERTY MAN, *crosses to* PRECIOUS STREAM]: I have been neglecting you all these eighteen years.

PRECIOUS S.: And I have been thinking of you all the time.

HSIEH: Aren't you glad we are at last united?

PRECIOUS S.: Yes, but I'm afraid it is only a dream. Please pinch me to make sure.

HSIEH: Nonsense! Can't you see the bright sun shining? You're not dreaming.

PRECIOUS S.: I'm not dreaming. I'm not dreaming!

HSIEH: No!

[*Tries to kiss her right hand. She takes it away. Curtsy and bow.*]

Let us retire! My Queen!

[*Music starts. They exit* L. *Music stops. Lights fade.*]

END OF ACT THREE

NO CURTAIN

(*Follows immediately – no pause.*)

ACT FOUR

Gong No. 1. – Enter READER L. *Spot on* READER.

HONOURABLE READER: Early the next morning we once more have the honour of waiting upon His Excellency, the Prime Minister Wang, at his house. It happens to be his sixtieth birthday, an occasion indeed worthy of celebration. His Excellency gives a magnificent banquet to which nearly everybody of importance is invited. He also gives a special family party in his garden with which we are very pleased to renew our acquaintance. Perhaps it is because we hate the sight of hundreds of intoxicated people drinking toasts and paying compliments to each other in loud tones that sound like quarrelling that we slip out of the big banquet hall unobserved and steal into the garden seeking for tranquillity in spite of our not being members of the family.

The Prime Minister is still the same old obstinate man, quite unchanged after these long years, except the colour of his beard, now assuming a silver grey. He is probably bored by the numerous congratulations he has received from his many guests, and following our example, steals to the garden in search of a little peace. But, unluckily, he is to have some unexpected shocks very soon.

[*Exit* READER L. *Gong No. 2 – Lights up. Enter* PROPERTY MEN L. *and* R. *Gong No. 3 – Music starts. Enter* ATTENDANTS *and* WANG. TWO ATTENDANTS *enter* R., *cross to* D.L. *and* D.R. WANG *enters* R. *down to* C. *Music stops.*]

WANG: To be the Prime Minister is to be second to none and above all other officers! To most people my post is a very enviable one, yet as one who has had more than enough of it, I regard it as scarcely worth all the trouble it gives.

[PROPERTY MAN R. *places arm-chair* C.]

If you are unpopular you receive all the bricks – –

[*Up* C. *and sits.*]

and if you are popular, you receive endless congratulations which is even worse.

[PROPERTY MAN L. *gets table from up* L. *and puts it before* WANG.]

A famous statesman is like a famous actor, everybody wants to pat him on the back, and you must have at least a dozen secretaries to pick out the letters of your real friends from the thousands of others from people you don't know. The worst of all is your birthday. Once a year you must let thousands of people congratulate you on a matter which was no doing of yours. If there is another congratulatory ceremony I shall go mad!

ATTENDANTS [*kneeling*]: We beg to report to Your Excellency – –

WANG: What?

ATTENDANTS: – – that the Right Honourable gentlemen of the Cabinet present their compliments to you and – –

ATTENDANTS and WANG [*together*]: Come to congratulate you [me] on your [my] sixtieth birthday.

WANG: To the pit of hell with them!

ATTENDANTS [*rising*]: Yes, Your Excellency.

WANG: No, no, to the seats of honour with them, and say that I regret I can't receive them in person for I am not well – not at all well. I will thank them for their kindness – I shall have to say their kindness – tomorrow when we meet in court.

ATTENDANTS: Yes, Excellency.

WANG: I will kill the next one who comes.

ATTENDANTS [*kneeling*]: We beg to report to Your Excellency – –

WANG [*rises*]: What?

ATTENDANTS: – – that Lady Precious Stream has come to pay her respects to Your Excellency.

WANG: Show her in.

　　[*Sits.*]

ATTENDANTS: Yes, Excellency.

　　[*Cross* U.L. *and* U.R., *turn* R.]

　　Show Lady Precious Stream in, please.

PRECIOUS S. [*offstage*]: I am coming.

　　[*Music starts. She enters to* C. *Music stops.*]

Eighteen years have passed since I was last at the Prime Minister's house, which is now newly painted and beautifully decorated, and quite different from what it used to be.

　　[*Moves slightly* L. *Turns.*]

Well, here is the garden at last.

　　[ATTENDANTS *return to places.* PROPERTY MAN L. *puts cushion for* PRECIOUS STREAM *to kneel on. Up* C., *kneels before* WANG.]

The unfilial daughter, Precious Stream, presents her respects to her father.

WANG [*rises. Peers over table*]: You – Precious Stream?

PRECIOUS S.: Yes, Your Excellency?

WANG: Oh, my dear daughter!

PRECIOUS S.: Oh, my dear father!

WANG: Not having seen her for eighteen years, I cannot restrain the tears from flowing from my eyes the moment that we meet.

　　[PROPERTY MAN L. *puts chair* L. *of table for* PRECIOUS STREAM. *When* PRECIOUS STREAM *rises she hands cushion to* PROPERTY MAN L.]

I wonder what has made her come to my house? Don't stand on ceremony, my child. Be seated.

　　[*She rises and sits* L. *of* WANG.]

PRECIOUS S.: Thank you. How have you been lately, my father?

WANG: I have been very well. Now, my child, what has made you come to my house?

PRECIOUS S.: To congratulate you on your birthday, dear father.

WANG: Oh! Why should you remember my birthday when you have no wish to remember me?

PRECIOUS S.: There are things which one cannot forget even if one tries.

WANG [*in a temper*]: Yes! Yes!
    [*Calms down.*]
No! no! Go to the inner chamber to see your mother.

PRECIOUS S. [*rises*]: Yes, your orders will be obeyed.
    [PROPERTY MAN L. *removes* PRECIOUS STREAM'S *chair. Crosses* D.L.C. *to audience.*]
My father is still annoyed with me, and does not wish to speak to me. I now go to the inner chamber to see my dear mother.
    [*Exits* L.]

ATTENDANTS [*kneeling*]: We beg to report to Your Excellency – –

WANG: What!

ATTENDANTS: – – that your two sons-in-law, the great Dragon General and the great Tiger General – –
    [WANG *rises and glares at them. Whispering as they rise.*]
have come to congratulate you on your sixtieth birthday.

WANG: Show them in!

ATTENDANTS: Yes, Excellency.
    [*Cross up and call.*]
Show the Generals in, please.
    [*Music starts. Enter* SU *and* WEI *down* R., *to* C., *bow to audience, then up* C. *to* WANG. *Bow before him. Music stops.*]

SU and WEI: How are you, my dear father-in-law?

WANG: Much as usual, thanks! Be seated!
    [*He waves them to seats* R. *of him. They sit.* SU *next to him;* WEI R. *of* SU. ATTENDANTS *return to places.*]
Now, my two excellent sons-in-law, don't tell me that you

have come to my house to congratulate me on my birth-day.

SU and WEI: That is exactly what we have come for.

WANG [*deep sigh*]: My heavens! Now let us talk about some-thing else. Do you know that we have a rare visitor here today?

SU and WEI: No, dear father-in-law.

WANG: And that is the great difference between this and past years, it is an occasion worthy of celebration.

SU and WEI: Why?

WANG: My third daughter has come back to me at last.

SU and WEI: Who?

WANG: Precious Stream, my third daughter. Don't you remember her?

SU and WEI: Oh, yes!

[*They both nod to* WANG.]

Of course!

[*They nod to each other.*]

WANG: She has come back to me at last.

WEI: Ah ha! Now, old Su, I feel sure that our third sister-in-law is tired of her lonely life in her cave, and has come back to find a second husband. We live and we learn.

SU: We live, it is true, but learn nothing.

WANG: Attendants!

ATTENDANTS [*kneeling*]: Yes, Excellency!

WANG: Request Madam and the three young ladies to come here.

ATTENDANTS: Yes, Excellency.

[*Cross upstage and call:*]

Show in Madam and the three ladies.

LADIES [*offstage*]: Yes, we are coming.

[*Music starts.* MADAM, SILVER STREAM, GOLDEN STREAM *and* PRECIOUS STREAM *enter* R., *come down-stage, speak to audience, preceded by* 1st *and* 2nd MAIDS. *Music stops.*]

MADAM: Lofty and majestic is our house.

> [*Up* C. *to* WANG. *Sits on his left.*]

GOLDEN S.: With gold and silver us heaven endows.

> [*Up* C. *Curtsies to* WANG. *Sits next to* MADAM.]

SILVER S.: Handsome and noble is my spouse.

PRECIOUS S.: But poor am I as a church mouse.

> [*Curtsies, sits in end chair* L. MAIDS *cross upstage and behind*
> MADAM.]

WANG: Attendants!

ATTENDANTS [*kneeling*]: Yes, Excellency.

WANG: Serve the wine at once.

ATTENDANTS [*rising*]: Yes, Excellency.

> [*Music starts.* ATTENDANTS *place wine on table.* WANG
> *pours out wine. Music softer.*]

WANG: Drink, my dear sons-in-law.

> [*All rise.*]

SU and WEI: Thank you, dear father-in-law.

ALL: Here's to you, father.

> [*Music loud.* WANG *shakes jug, pours out for himself only.*
> *Music softer.*]

WANG: Here's to the whole family.

> [*He drinks. Music loud.*]

ALL: Thank you.

> [*All sit.* ATTENDANT R. *removes tray and gives it to*
> PROPERTY MAN R. PROPERTY MAN L. *moves table to*
> *up* L. *Music stops.* ATTENDANTS *retire to* U.L. *and*
> U.R.]

WANG: Now, Precious Stream – –

PRECIOUS S.: Yes, Your Excellency.

> [*Stands, curtsies.*]

WANG: My dear daughter.

PRECIOUS S.: My dear father.

> [*Sits.*]

WANG: I have something to say to you, but I don't know
whether I ought to say it during this feast.

PRECIOUS S.: A father's advice to his daughter is welcome at any time.

WANG: As your husband died in the Western Regions years ago, I, being your father, naturally am worried about you. I have a mind to choose, among the younger members of my Cabinet, a suitable husband for you. As I am getting old, I wish to have a son-in-law to live with me. What do you think of that, my child?

PRECIOUS S.: Oh, no, father. Even if my husband is dead, which I have good reason to believe is not the case, I should remain a widow and be faithful to his memory.

WANG: My dear child, you know nothing about life! The old proverb says: 'To remain a widow and be faithful to your husband's memory is easily said, but difficult to carry out to the end.' If you can't carry out your words loyally to the end you will become the laughing-stock of everyone!

PRECIOUS S.: I think the old proverb is as you say: 'To remain a widow and be faithful to your husband's memory is easily said, but difficult to carry out to the end.' If you can't carry it out to the end, that is none of your father's business.

WANG: Silence, you little wretch! I'd rather see you damned than the laughing-stock of everyone.

MADAM: Don't mind what your father says, dear.

WANG: You old baggage! You have utterly spoiled her.

MADAM: Do as you think best, and you'll have all my blessings.

GOLDEN S.: And my good wishes, too.

PRECIOUS S.: Thank you.

WANG: Now, my excellent sons-in-law, will you try to say something to her for me!

SU: No, my dear father-in-law, I don't think it would be any use.

WEI: Let me go to her, and before I have said half a dozen words, she is sure to consent to marry again.

I

[*Rises and crosses* D.C. *to audience.*]

I will give her one of my most charming smiles.

[*Pulls beard away from mouth and smiles at audience.*]

One hundred forms of ugliness is hidden by a smile.

[*Crosses to* L. *of* PRECIOUS STREAM.]

My dear sister-in-law, your father's suggestion that you should marry again is a very considerate one. I would like you to think it over carefully for your own sake.

[*Smile business to* PRECIOUS STREAM.]

PRECIOUS S.: Who is this man swaying to and fro before me?

WEI: Don't you recognize my musical voice and know that I am your brother-in-law Wei?

PRECIOUS S.: Have you the audacity to tell me you are Wei, the Tiger General?

WEI: Yes, your brother-in-law, the famous Tiger General.

PRECIOUS S.: What is your business here?

WEI: Eh – eh – –

PRECIOUS S.: Have you the insolence to try to persuade me to marry again?

WEI: Well . . .

PRECIOUS S.: How dare you speak of such a thing to me? The day you are under my thumb, you shall pay for this!

WEI: Nonsense and stuff.

[*Crosses* D.C. *to audience.*]

Stuff and nonsense.

[*Crosses back to his chair.*]

ALL: Well?

WEI: We–l–ll.

[*Sits.*]

SILVER S. [*Rises, crosses* R., *then back to* PRECIOUS STREAM]: Excuse me for a minute, please.

WEI: Where are you going with your mincing gait?

SILVER S.: To try and persuade my sister to re-marry.

WEI [*fiercely*]: Sit down!

[*Sweetly.*]

Dear.

    [*She curtsies and sits.*]

WANG: Precious Stream seems to be very self-possessed to-day. It may be true that her husband, Hsieh Ping-Kuei, is still alive.

SU: Yes, I think he is. I think he is.

GOLDEN S.: And I think so, too.

WANG: It would be a good thing to have him dead.

MADAM: No, better to have him alive.

WEI: Better to have him dead.

SILVER S.: Better to have him alive – dead.

SU and GOLDEN S.: No, better to have him alive.

WEI: No, better to have him dead, definitely dead.

    [*Gong.*]

VOICE [*off* R.]: Prepare yourselves to receive the Imperial Edict from His Majesty the Emperor of China.

    [*Gong. All rise, cross down, kneel on cushions placed in a row by* PROPERTY MEN. MAIDS *and* ATTENDANTS *in row behind.*]

His Imperial Majesty orders the Prime Minister Wang to welcome His Majesty, Hsieh Ping-Kuei, King of the Western Regions, to his court tomorrow, and bring Wei, the Tiger General, with him under arrest. Long live the Emperor!

    [*Gong.*]

ALL: We hear and we obey! Long live the Emperor!

    [*Gong.* ALL *rise looking at* PRECIOUS STREAM. PROPERTY MEN *collect cushions that* ALL *hold behind them.*]

Hsieh Ping-Kuei? King of the Western Regions?

    [ATTENDANTS *cross to* WEI *and take him prisoner.*]

WANG [*going* L.]: Good heavens! What shall I do? What shall I do?

MADAM [*following*]: You always know what to do.

WANG [*angrily*]: Of course I know. I am not speaking to you, I am addressing the audience.

[*Exeunt.* MAIDS *follow and exit.* SU *and* GOLDEN STREAM
follow and exit.]

WEI [*looking at* PRECIOUS STREAM]: I crave your pardon,
Your Majesty.

[PRECIOUS STREAM *laughs and exits.*]

WEI [*being escorted out by* ATTENDANTS]: I am a dead man! I
am a dead man!

SILVER S. [*crossing* D.C. *to audience*]: I am indeed as good
as a widow already. Very silly indeed! I don't like this act
at all.

[*Music starts.* SILVER STREAM *exits* L. *Music stops. Lights
fade. Gong No. 1 – Enter* READER L. *Spot on* READER.]

HONOURABLE READER: We have now the honour of being
present at the temporary court of His Majesty the King of
the Western Regions during his visit to China. It is one of
the most beautiful buildings in the Chinese Kingdom, and
is specially decorated to welcome its royal occupant. The
onlookers have to suppose that rich silk canopies hang over
their heads and soft carpets are under their feet, and that the
furniture is all of ebony, though what they actually see is
still the same old stage without any alteration.

The patient audience is requested not to be alarmed when
the author is compelled to bring in a new character at this
late hour of the evening [afternoon], because without him
the author himself would be forced to pay the penalty of
marrying a desirable yet undesirable Western lady. The
solution of this problem is in the person of His Excellency
the Minister of Foreign Affairs, a man of the world who
must have had many affairs in foreign countries. By this
arrangement the performance will speedily come to a satis-
factory conclusion, which will enable our patrons to get
home before [soon after] eleven [five], and will prove that
the Chinese play is no longer than a Western one, seldom
longer than *Hamlet*, and never longer than *Back to Methu-
selah*.

[*Exit* READER L. *Gong No. 2 – Lights up. Gong No. 3 –*
Music starts. Enter ATTENDANTS *followed by* HSIEH.
ATTENDANTS *go to* D.R. *and* D.L. HSIEH *to* D.C. *Music*
stops. PROPERTY MEN R. *place arm-chair* C.]

HSIEH: I left here no more than a beggar, and have returned
as a king. Let me sit on my throne.

[*Crosses* U.C., *sits.*]

As I came here from the Imperial Palace all the streets were
filled with people who kept on scattering flowers upon me.
If they had only shown me even the very slightest degree of
similar enthusiasm eighteen years ago when I was per-
forming my best feats of strength in those very streets, they
would have made me a much happier man! Their cheers
are now to me quite distasteful! My only happiness is the
company of my Queen!

[*He calls.*]

Attendants!

ATTENDANTS: Yes, Your Majesty.

HSIEH: Request Her Majesty the Queen to come to Court.

ATTENDANTS: Yes, Your Majesty.

[ATTENDANTS *both cross upstage and face* R.]

His Majesty requests the presence of Her Majesty the
Queen.

PRECIOUS S. [*offstage*]: To hear is to obey.

[*Music starts. She enters* R. *preceded by four* MAIDS, *who*
go R. *and* L. *She to* C.]

After wearing rags for eighteen years, I now have the joy
of being arrayed in royal robes.

[PROPERTY MAN L. *places chair for* LADY PRECIOUS
STREAM. *Up* C. *before* HSIEH.]

Your humble wife presents her respects to Your Majesty.

HSIEH [*standing*]: Thank you. Don't stand on ceremony.
Please be seated.

PRECIOUS S.: Thank you for your condescension.

[*She sits on his* L. MAIDS *upstage* R. *and* L. *behind* C. *chair.*]

May I ask how Your Majesty got on this morning at your reception at the Emperor's Court?

HSIEH: The reception was a great success. The Emperor has ordered the prisoner Wei to be placed at my disposal.

PRECIOUS S.: Splendid! What has Your Majesty done with him?

HSIEH: Nothing yet. I want you to decide for me.

PRECIOUS S.: Very good. Have him brought here.

HSIEH: Attendants! Order them to bring the prisoner Wei here at once!

ATTENDANTS: Yes, Your Majesty.

[*Both cross upstage and face* R.]

Bring the prisoner Wei here at once.

EXECUTIONER'S VOICE [*offstage*]: Without delay.

[PROPERTY MAN R. *puts cushion* C. *near footlights for* WEI *to kneel on.* WEI *enters* R. *with handcuffs on, comes down* C., *kneels, facing audience.* EXECUTIONER *is* R. *of him, with sword.*]

WEI: When I heard that I was wanted here, I became almost senseless. The prisoner Wei awaits Your Majesty's pleasure.

HSIEH: Who is kneeling before me?

WEI: The prisoner Wei.

HSIEH: Do you confess that you plotted to kill me during the Western Punitive Expedition?

WEI: I confess. I only crave your pardon, Your Majesty.

PRECIOUS S.: Do you confess that you have been swindling me out of what was due me in order to starve me to death?

WEI: I confess. I only crave your pardon, my dear sister – er – Your Majesty.

PRECIOUS S.: How can you be pardoned? No, you will not be pardoned.

HSIEH: No, you will not be pardoned. Therefore the penalty of your crime – –

PRECIOUS S.: Of your numerous crimes – –

HSIEH: Yes, the penalty of your numerous crimes is – –

[*Looks at his wife, who touches her throat with her sleeve.*]
is death.

WEI: Oh, no!

[*Bows down.*]

HSIEH: Executioner!

EXECUTIONER: Yes, Your Majesty!

HSIEH: Behead the prisoner!

EXECUTIONER: Yes, Your Majesty!

[EXECUTIONER *puts sword against* WEI'S *neck and starts to swing.*]

SILVER S. [*offstage*]: Please, Executioner, wait a moment.

[WEI *rises, goes* L., *followed by* EXECUTIONER. SILVER STREAM *enters and comes* C. *and addresses audience.*]

Oh, I am so glad I have come in time.

[*Curtsies.*]

I will ask my brother-in-law for his pardon. I have heard people say that many lives have been saved only through wives arriving in the nick of time.

[*Giggles to audience.*]

WEI [*kneeling at* L.]: Please don't waste your time in coquetting with the audience, but go in and ask for pardon at once.

[SILVER STREAM *goes* L. *of* WEI. PROPERTY MAN L. *puts cushion* C. *for* SILVER STREAM *to kneel on.*]

SILVER S.: You horrid wretch, you deserve death.

[*Up* C., *kneels before* HSIEH.]

My respects to Your Majesty, my dear brother-in-law.

HSIEH: Who is kneeling before me?

SILVER S.: Your Majesty's sister-in-law, Silver Stream.

HSIEH: What have you come here for?

SILVER S.: To ask for my husband's pardon.

[HSIEH *looks at his wife, who signs to him not to do so.*]

HSIEH: No, you have both behaved very badly to us. I cannot pardon him.

SILVER S. [*rises and hands cushion to* PROPERTY MAN L.]: Nothing can be done now.

WEI: You have come in time only to see me die.

SILVER S.: Let me call for help.

[*She goes up* L. *round stage and exits* R.]

EXECUTIONER [*sharpens sword on footlights*]: Let me finish my job. The sooner the better.

[*Starts to swing.*]

SILVER S. [*offstage*]: Executioner, pray wait a minute.

[SILVER STREAM *enters* R., *pushing* WANG *in front of her.*]

Quick, father. His Excellency the Prime Minister Wang is here.

[WANG *enters to* D.R.]

2nd ATTENDANT R.: I beg to report to Your Majesty that His Excellency the Prime Minister Wang is here.

[HSIEH *looks at his wife, who shakes her head.*]

HSIEH: Tell His Excellency that I can't grant him an audience at present, but if he will wait a few hours, I may give him a few seconds then.

ATTENDANT: Yes, Your Majesty.

SILVER S. [*down* C.]: This is no good. I must try again.

[*Goes up* L. *round back of stage and exits* R.]

ATTENDANT [*to* WANG]: His Majesty regrets that he can't grant you an audience at present, and says if you will wait a few hours His Majesty may be able to give you a few seconds then.

WANG: Oh, my God!

[*He faints in the arms of* PROPERTY MEN.]

EXECUTIONER: Now for it!

[*Starts to swing sword.*]

SILVER S. [*offstage*]: Executioner, do wait a second!

[*Enters to* D.R.]

Oh, quick, it's a matter of life and death. His Honour General Su and his wife are coming.

ATTENDANT: I beg to report to Your Majesty that His Honour General Su and his wife are coming.

[SU *and his* WIFE *enter to* D.R.]

HSIEH: Tell His Honour General Su and his wife that I shall be very glad to receive them if they promise not to refer in any way to the prisoner who is to be executed.

ATTENDANT: Yes, Your Majesty.

SILVER S. [C.]: Heaven have mercy on me. I have been running to and fro in vain. There is still one more chance.

[*Crosses upstage, round back of it – and exits* R.]

ATTENDANT [*to* SU]: His Majesty says he will be very glad to receive you if you mention nothing about the prisoner who is to be executed.

SU and GOLDEN S. [*cross to* WEI *and* EXECUTIONER]: That's very hard! We have come specially on his account.

[*They face* C.]

EXECUTIONER: I am sorry. I can't wait any longer.

[*Starts to swing.*]

SILVER S. [*offstage*]: Executioner, do wait a little.

[SILVER STREAM *enters to* D.R.]

Quick, mother! You are my last hope. Madam is coming.

[MADAM *enters to* R.C.]

ATTENDANT: I beg to report to Your Majesty that Madam your mother-in-law is coming.

HSIEH [*rising*]: All right. We must rise to welcome her.

[*Bows.*] My respects to you, my dear mother-in-law.

PRECIOUS S. [*curtsies*]: My respects, dear mother.

MADAM: Don't stand on ceremony, dear children.

[*Sees* WANG.]

What are you sitting there for, my dear?

WANG [*who has been on floor since his faint*]: I was told to wait here for a few hours before he could see me for a few seconds.

MADAM [*laughs*]: Serves you right.

[*Turns* L., *sees* SU *and* GOLDEN STREAM.]

What are you here for, my children?

[PROPERTY MEN *pick up* WANG.]

SU: We came to ask them to pardon Wei.

GOLDEN S.: But His Majesty forbade us to mention anything about the prisoner.

[PROPERTY MAN R. *puts chair* R. *of* HSIEH. PROPERTY MAN L. *puts two chairs* L. *of* PRECIOUS STREAM.]

MADAM: Oh, so that's it, is it?

[*Taps forehead with fingers.*]

Of course we mustn't mention the prisoner to His Majesty.

SILVER S.: But you – –

MADAM: Foolish child! Come with me, all of you.

[*All cross to in front of* HSIEH.]

HSIEH [*rising*]: Be seated.

[*All sit.*]

MADAM: And now let me have His Majesty's word of honour that he will not mention even the name of the prisoner Wei.

HSIEH: I gladly give you my word.

SILVER S.: But you said you would not mention about my husband to His Majesty.

MADAM: Certainly. I give him my word of honour, too.

[*To* HSIEH.]

Isn't that fair?

HSIEH: Oh, quite fair.

SILVER S.: Oh, mother, how can you!

MADAM: Silence! Don't let me hear you speak again.

PRECIOUS S.: Mother, darling, you are full of understanding.

MADAM: Am I? I want you to grant me a favour, and I hope you will show me how full you are of understanding.

PRECIOUS S.: Of course I will. Before you say the word, your request is granted.

MADAM: That is very kind of you.

[*Rises and curtsies before* PRECIOUS STREAM.]

And I must thank Your Majesty formally for your favour.

[*All rise.*]

PRECIOUS S.: Please don't, mother.

[*All sit.*]

What is it?

MADAM: I want you to pardon Wei.

PRECIOUS S.: But you have given your word of honour that you would never mention him.

MADAM: Yes, to His Majesty, not to Her Majesty.

HSIEH [*rising*]: But he deserves more than death.

[*All rise.*]

MADAM: No, remember your word and don't mention the prisoner to me, Your Majesty.

HSIEH [*sitting*]: Well, I'm . . .

[*All sit.*]

MADAM: Since Her Majesty has granted my request – –

PRECIOUS S.: No, I have not.

MADAM: Yes, you have. Everybody understood that you had granted it before I told you what it was, and I thanked you formally for your favour.

[*All nod.*]

PRECIOUS S.: Well, even if I promised you, I'm afraid my husband won't listen to me.

HSIEH: No, I won't.

MADAM: But you must; in this and every other kingdom all the best families are ruled by the wife. My husband here will tell you that he always listened to me and he will always have to listen to me. He will set you a good example, won't you, my dear?

WANG: Eh – ah – yes.

MADAM: And willingly?

WANG: Willingly.

PRECIOUS S.: Dear mother, you are indeed a darling. As I have already promised my mother, I'm afraid you will have to fulfil my promise.

HSIEH: I said it was for you to decide.

PRECIOUS S.: Splendid!

ALL: Splendid!

PRECIOUS S.: His life may be spared.

WEI [*looking up*]: Ah!

PRECIOUS S.: But he must be punished in some other way.

WEI [*bowing down*]: Oh!

PRECIOUS S.: I think a few strokes on his back might meet the case.

SILVER S.: Yes, I too think that he ought to be beaten, for he has behaved very badly to me.

PRECIOUS S.: Yes, he really deserves to be beaten severely.

WEI: Oh, no, I'd rather die; I'd rather die!

> [*He grabs sword and places it at his neck.* EXECUTIONER *swings, but* WEI *ducks just in time.*]

HSIEH: Attendants!

ATTENDANTS: Yes, Your Majesty.

HSIEH: Release the prisoner, and bring him here to be beaten.

ATTENDANTS: Yes, Your Majesty.

EXECUTIONER [*throws sword on the ground*]: Bad luck! I have been deprived of my diversion today.

> [*He exits* L. ATTENDANTS *come forward and bring* WEI C. *before* HSIEH. ATTENDANT L. *takes the handcuffs and gives them to* PROPERTY MAN L. PROPERTY MAN R. *places cushion* C. *for* WEI *to kneel,* PROPERTY MAN L. *picks up sword, takes it* L.]

HSIEH [*looks at his wife – she holds up four fingers*]: Give him four hundred strokes on the back.

ATTENDANTS: Yes, Your Majesty.

> [PROPERTY MAN L. *gives* ATTENDANT *stick.* PROPERTY MAN R. *ditto.* L. ATTENDANT *holds stick in front of* WEI'S *back.*]

WEI: I shall be a dead man long before they've finished.

HSIEH: Beat him!

PRECIOUS S.: Stop! Forty strokes will be enough.

HSIEH: All right, forty strokes.

ATTENDANTS [*together*]: Yes, Your Majesty.

[*Count aloud.*]

Five!

WEI [*yells*]: Ouch!

ATTENDANTS: Ten.

WEI: Ouch!

ATTENDANTS: Fifteen.

WEI: Ouch!

ATTENDANTS: Twenty.

WEI: Ouch!

ATTENDANTS: Twenty-five.

WEI: Ouch!

ATTENDANTS: Thirty.

WEI: Ouch!

ATTENDANTS: Thirty-five.

WEI: Ouch!

ATTENDANTS: Forty.

WEI: Ouch!

ATTENDANTS: We have given him forty strokes, Your Majesty.

HSIEH: You may leave him here.

ATTENDANTS: Yes, Your Majesty.

[*They hand sticks to* PROPERTY MEN *and retire to their places* D.R. *and* D.L.]

PRECIOUS S.: Now let bygones be bygones and take a seat beside your wife.

[WEI *rises.*]

SILVER S.: You must thank Their Majesties.

[PROPERTY MAN R. *puts chair* R. *for* WEI *and takes the cushion from the ground to put it on the chair.*]

WEI [*rising*]: Oh, thank you indeed! Ouch! Ouch!

[*Goes to chair* R., *tries to sit, finds it impossible to do so, rises and leans over back of chair.*]

SILVER S. [*rising*]: Why don't you sit down? Why do you stand in such a ridiculous position?

WEI: How can I sit down with wounds like mine?

SILVER S.: This will keep you from being naughty for a long time.

[*Sits.*]

MADAM: Yes, it will.

[*To* WANG.]

Don't be cross, dear. Aren't you delighted to see all our children happily united?

WANG: I am.

PRECIOUS S.: Oh, dear mother, there is a member who has lately joined our family. You mustn't go before meeting her.

ALL: Who is she?

PRECIOUS S.: My sister-in-law.

[*To* HSIEH.]

Isn't she your sister, dear?

HSIEH [*uncomfortably*]: Eh – eh – yes.

MADAM: But we never heard before that you had a sister.

PRECIOUS S.: Neither had he until recently. I haven't even seen her yet.

GOLDEN S.: Where is she?

PRECIOUS S.: I know that she is awaiting an audience here.

SILVER S.: Request her to come at once, please.

PRECIOUS S.: Yes, please.

HSIEH: Attendants!

ATTENDANTS: Yes, Your Majesty.

HSIEH: Request the presence of Her Highness . . .

PRECIOUS S.: His sister.

HSIEH: . . . immediately.

ATTENDANTS: Yes, Your Majesty.

[ATTENDANTS *cross upstage, turn* R. *and call.*]

His Majesty requests the presence of Her Highness, his sister.

PRINCESS [*offstage*]: To hear is to obey.

[*Music starts.* MA TA *and* KIANG HAI *enter* R. *Come down*
R.L. *and* L.C. PRINCESS *to* C. *Music stops.*]

MA TA: I beg to report to Your Highness that this is the
Court of His Majesty.

PRINCESS: Indeed!

[*She looks around.*]

What a queer place it is! China is indeed a queer land.
Everything is just the opposite to our country. To one who
has been born and bred in the Western Regions and accustomed to the freedom there, their punctilious etiquette and
strange customs are most trying.

[*She turns and looks at* HSIEH.]

Ma Ta and Kiang Hai!

MA TA *and* KIANG HAI: Yes, Your Highness.

PRINCESS: Who is the man sitting there like the King of
Heaven?

MA TA: He is His Majesty our King.

PRINCESS: How changed he is! I'm a little afraid of him, and
who is that little *goddess* sitting next to His Majesty?

KIANG HAI: The famous Precious Stream of the Wang
family. She is his wife.

PRINCESS [*starts* L.]: Oh, I can't abide this. Let us go back to
the Western Regions.

MA TA *and* KIANG HAI [*stopping her*]: Oh, no, we can't.

PRINCESS: What am I to do?

MA TA: You must go to her and salute her.

PRINCESS: I won't salute her.

KIANG HAI: If you don't, they will say that the women of the
Western Regions have very bad manners.

PRINCESS: Then I must do it for the reputation of our
women.

MA TA *and* KIANG HAI [*step* R. *and* L. *three steps*]: Yes, Your
Highness.

PRINCESS [*upstage* R.C.]: My respects to you, the famous
Precious Stream of the Wang family.

[*She gives her a military salute.* PRECIOUS STREAM *raises both hands. Down* C.]

Ma Ta and Kiang Hai!

MA TA and KIANG HAI [*cross in three steps*]: Yes, Your Highness?

PRINCESS: Why does she appear to try to fly when I salute her?

MA TA: She isn't flying, she's returning your salute.

PRINCESS: That is not a salute.

KIANG HAI [*saluting*]: She's never done this before. Their way of saluting is quite different from ours.

PRINCESS: What is the difference?

MA TA: Our way of saluting is like raising the hand to hit a dog.

[*Salutes.*]

KIANG HAI: Their mode of saluting is like churning cream.

[*Churns cream.*]

PRINCESS [*trying to churn cream*]: How ridiculous!

MA TA: They say that the hitting-a-dog salute is equally, if not more, ridiculous.

PRINCESS: Well, I must try to churn cream in her honour.

MA TA and KIANG HAI [*back three steps*]: Yes, Your Highness.

PRINCESS: Watch me, Ma Ta and Kiang Hai.

[*She goes up* R.C. *and churns invisible cream.*]

My respects to you!

[PRECIOUS STREAM *rises and curtsies.*]

PRECIOUS S.: Many thanks. Please don't stand on ceremony.

[*Down* C. *to audience.*]

How beautiful and charming the Princess is. I now quite see why my husband didn't return to me earlier. If I were a man, I should like to stay in the Western Regions for a few years, too. As I'm a woman I hate her! I do not wish to speak to such a bewitching little minx, but if I do not, she will say that the women of China are very impolite.

For the sake of preserving the reputation of the women in China, I will say a few kind words to her.

[*She goes up* R.C. *During this speech the* PRINCESS *has taken* PRECIOUS STREAM'S *chair next to* HSIEH. *She tries to make advances to him, he practically ignores her. She smiles at* SU, *who turns his back upon her. When* PRECIOUS STREAM *comes upstage, she rises and faces her.*]

I am indebted to you for having entertained my husband for me all these eighteen years.

PRINCESS [*aside*]: She is trying to be funny.

[*To* PRECIOUS STREAM.]

Oh, you needn't be, I was only too delighted to do so.

[*Churns cream.*]

PRECIOUS S. [*aside*]: The baggage! This is my father, and this is my mother.

[*They rise and the* PRINCESS *churns cream to them.*]

And these are my two sisters and two brothers-in-law.

[PRECIOUS STREAM *sits.* PRINCESS *moves over to* WEI.]

PRINCESS: But this man seems to have no face.

[*She touches* WEI'S *back. He turns.*]

WEI: Ouch! Ouch!

PRINCESS: Oh! Oh! I must go! I must go!

[*She retreats* L.]

PRECIOUS S.: Wait a moment, please.

[*Whispers to* HSIEH.]

So and So.

HSIEH: Oh, yes! Attendants! Request So and So to come here immediately.

ATTENDANTS: Yes, Your Majesty.

[ATTENDANTS *turn* R. *and call.*]

His Majesty requests the presence of So and So.

MINISTER [*off* L.]: Coming.

[*Music starts. He enters* R. *to down* C. *Music stops.*]

You most obedient humble servant, So and So, the Minister of Foreign Affairs.

[*Turns and bows to* HSIEH.]

My respects to Your Majesty.

HSIEH: Thank you. Don't stand on ceremony. I want to tell you that the Princess of the Western Regions has arrived here today, and hopes you will welcome her and see that she has everything she wants.

MINISTER: Yes, Your Majesty. Delighted, Your Majesty.

[*He takes the Princess's outstretched hand and kisses it.*]

My sincere welcome and respects to Your Highness.

[*As he kisses, all turn heads away.*]

PRINCESS: Oh, thank you.

MINISTER [*offering his right arm*]: Will Your Highness come with me?

PRINCESS [*taking his arm*]: With pleasure!

MINISTER: Excuse us, Your Majesty. Good morning, everybody.

[*They sweep round stage, then up* L.]

PRINCESS: Good-bye, everybody. Tell me, where did you learn your charming manners, Your Excellency?

MINISTER: In London.

[*Both exit* L.]

WANG [*rising.*]: Disgraceful!

MADAM [*rising*]: Scandalous!

SU and GOLDEN S. [*rising*]: Disgusting!

WEI and SILVER S. [*rising*]: Shameful!

WANG: This is too much. I think I shall retire.

[PROPERTY MEN R. *and* L. *remove chairs.* WANG *comes down* C., *bows to audience, exits* L. MADAM *follows him, curtsies, says 'Good-bye' to audience and follows him off.* SU *and* GOLDEN STREAM *come down* C., *bow and curtsy to audience.*]

SU and GOLDEN S.: Good-bye, we must go back.

[*Exit* L.]

WEI and SILVER S.: Good-bye. Thank you.

[*Exit* L. *followed by* TWO ATTENDANTS *and by* MAIDS.]

HSIEH [*rises*]: Let us retire.

PRECIOUS S. [*she rises*]: Do you always behave in the Western Regions as they two were doing? Why not give me a chance?

> [*She tries to take his arm.* PROPERTY MEN R. *and* L. *remove the two chairs.*]

HSIEH: For shame!

> [*He will not allow her to take his arm. She curtsies.*]

Our affection is for each other, and not for public entertainment.

PRECIOUS S. [*imitating the* MINISTER *and* PRINCESS]: My sincere welcome and respects to you, Your Highness.

> [HSIEH *commences to walk downstage, round and up* L.]

Oh, thank you.

> [*She offers her arm.*]

Will Your Highness come with me ? With pleasure!

> [*Kisses her hand to audience and exits after* HSIEH L.]

CURTAIN

GORDON DAVIOT

Richard of Bordeaux

A PLAY IN TWO ACTS

RICHARD OF BORDEAUX

Originally produced by the Arts Theatre Club at the New Theatre, London, on 26 June 1932. It was first publicly produced at the New Theatre, London, on 2 February 1933, with the cast given below.

FAIR PAGE, MAUDELYN	Richard Ainley
DARK PAGE	Gordon Glennon
RICHARD II	John Gielgud
ANNE OF BOHEMIA, *his Queen*	Gwen Ffrangçon-Davies
DUKE OF GLOUCESTER, *Thomas of Woodstock*	Eric Stanley
DUKE OF LANCASTER, *John of Gaunt*	Ben Webster
SIR SIMON BURLEY, *the King's tutor*	George Howe
DUKE OF YORK	Kinsey Peile
MICHAEL DE LA POLE, *Chancellor*	H. R. Hignett
EARL OF ARUNDEL	Frederick Lloyd
ROBERT DE VERE, *Earl of Oxford*	Francis Lister
MARY BOHUN, *Countess of Derby*	Margaret Webster
AGNES LAUNCEKRON	Barbara Dillon
HENRY, EARL OF DERBY, *Bolingbroke, son of Lancaster*	
	Henry Mollison
THOMAS MOWBRAY, *Earl of Nottingham*	Donald Wolfit
SIR JOHN MONTAGUE	Walter Hudd
JOHN MAUDELYN, *secretary*	Richard Ainley
EDWARD, EARL OF RUTLAND, *Aumerle, son of York*	
	Clement McCallin
A WAITING-WOMAN	Margot Macalaster
THOMAS ARUNDEL, *Archbishop of Canterbury*	Reyner Barton
A MAN IN THE STREET	Andrew Churchman
A SECOND	Alfred Harris
A THIRD	George Howe
WOMAN WITH LOAVES	Margery Phipps-Walker
WOMAN WITH VEGETABLES	Margaret Webster
FIRST PAGE	Gordon Glennon
SECOND PAGE	Bryan Coleman

LORD DERBY'S PAGE   Kenneth Ball
                          (*By arrangement with Miss Italia Conti*)
DOCTOR   Ralph Truman

The play produced by John Gielgud

ACT ONE

ACT TWO

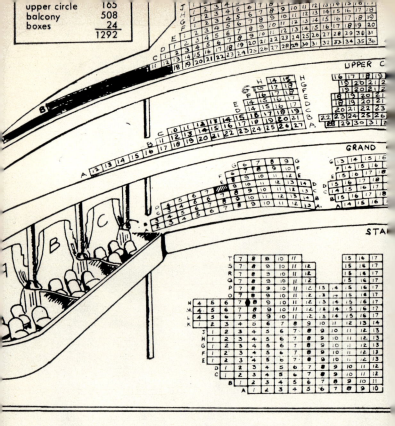

The three theatres involved in the dramatic side of the official Edinburgh Festival are the Lyceum, the Church Hill Theatre and the Assembly Hall. Even so, much of the excitement for a theatregoer at Festival time is, of course, nosing round the Fringe in search of rarities, curiosities and future hits, and there is a particular need for this sort of excitement in view of the rather dull nature of the official programme. On the Fringe, Oxford, Cambridge and Edinburgh are traditionally

strong contenders, much to go into he no self-respecting the work of the Tr of its activities is in

TICKET

For official prod Ticket Office is 21 burgh EH1 1BW, ne

Rose Marie.—Carlisle M.S., 4-9.
Student Prince.—Chester O.D.S., 11-16.
No, No, Nanette.—Colne & Nelson O.S., 11-16.
A Waltz Dream.—Coventry O.S., 18-23.
Gondoliers.—Cupar O.C., 14-16.
Lilac Domino.—Doncaster O.S., 4-9.
The Geisha.—East Grinstead O.S., 18-21.
Pirates of Penzance.—Exmouth O.S., Feb. 26-Mar. 2.
San Toy.—Falkirk O.S., Feb. 26-Mar. 2.
No, No, Nanette.—Falmouth Little Theatre Players, Feb. 26-Mar. 2.
Bitter Sweet.—Folkestone O.S., Feb. 25-Mar. 2.
Maid of the Mountains.—Galashiels O.S., Feb. 26-Mar. 2.
Princess Ida.—Gateshead O.D.S., 4-9.
Quaker Girl.—Glastonbury O.S., 4-9.
Yeomen of the Guard.—Grimsby O.S., Feb. 25-Mar. 2.
Sunny.—Halifax O.S., Feb. 25-Mar. 2.
Student Prince.—Harrogate O.P., Feb. 25-Mar. 2.
New Moon.—Keighley O.D.S., 11-16.
The Middle Watch.—Kendal D.S., 18-23.
Florodora.—Kidderminster O.S., 11-16.
Fresh Fields.—Kingsley Players, Totnes, 5, 7, 8, 9.
Lord Babs.—Kingsley Players, Totnes, 4, 6, 7, 9.
New Moon.—Lancaster D.O.S., 11-16.
No, No, Nanette.—Leatherhead and District O.D., Epsom, 19-23.
Madame Pompadour.—Leigh O.D.S., 11-16.
Show Boat.—Lincoln O.S., Feb. 25-Mar. 2.
Monsieur Beaucaire.—Llandudno O.S., 13-16.
Quaker Girl.—Matlock and District O.S., 12-16.
Maid of the Mountains.—Middleton O.D.S., 11-16.
Rebel Maid.—New Brighton O.S., 18-23.
Newport (I. of W.) O.S., 13-16.
Desert Song.—Peterborough O.S., 4-9.

ACT ONE

SCENE I

The corridor outside the council chamber in the King's Palace of Westminster, February 1385. In the middle are the double doors of the chamber. To the left of the door, in the rear wall, is a large mullioned window, through which a pale spring sun is shining. The corridor is wide, and deserted except for two PAGES *who, half-kneeling, half-sitting on the floor downstage, are throwing dice.*
One page is fair and slender, the other square and dark.

FAIR PAGE: That is the whole of last month's allowance gone.

DARK PAGE: There is always next month's.

FAIR PAGE: Very true. Your throw.

DARK PAGE [*playing with the dice and glancing at the door*]: How much longer do you think they will be! They have been two hours there at least. What can they find to do?

FAIR PAGE: Contradict each other. And when they are tired of contradicting each other, they contradict the King.

DARK PAGE: It seems a waste of time. I wish they would stop it. I'm hungry.

FAIR PAGE [*glancing at the door*]: So is the Duke of York, I expect. He will shepherd them out to dine presently.

DARK PAGE [*preparing to throw*]: At any rate, Robert de Vere will be funny about them at supper tonight, and I am on duty. That is a pleasant thought. [*Throws.*]

[*The door of the chamber is burst open impetuously, and* RICHARD *emerges, furious. The noise of the roughly opened door is drowned in the exclamations of the two pages as they read the* DARK PAGE'S *throw, and the door is shut quietly from inside, so that the pages are unaware of the King's appearance.* RICHARD *stands a moment raging silently. He is at this*] *time nineteen; a slender, delicately made youth with a finely cut, expressive face, and the fair colouring and red-gold hair which made his mother famous as the Fair Maid of Kent.*

His eye comes to rest on the two absorbed figures bent over the dice, and curiosity and interest gradually replace the anger in his face. He tiptoes over until he can lean over and watch.]

DARK PAGE: Beat that!

[*The* FAIR PAGE *throws and makes a movement of annoyance.*]

FAIR PAGE: Best of three?

DARK PAGE: Yes. [*He throws.*]

FAIR PAGE [*throwing a good one*]: Ah!

[*The* DARK PAGE *sees the King and tries to struggle to his feet, but* RICHARD *subdues him with a hand on his shoulder.*]

RICHARD: No, no. Go on with the game. Who is winning?

DARK PAGE: We are even, sir.

RICHARD: What! After a whole afternoon – –

FAIR PAGE: Oh, no sir. On this throw. Up till now I've been unlucky. In fact, I'm practically ruined, sir.

[*Enter, left,* ANNE, *the Queen. She is not beautiful, but she has great charm, with dignity breaking every now and then to discover a hidden mischief, and humour always in her eyes and at the corners of her mouth. She pauses to watch.*]

RICHARD [*flipping the boy's tunic with his finger*]: What! with your new coat still to play for? Poof!

[*The* FAIR PAGE *sees* ANNE, *and begins to rise, but* RICHARD *pushes him back.*]

FAIR PAGE: The Queen, sir.

RICHARD [*turning*]: Anne! [*To the pages, who have risen, he makes a good-humoured gesture of dismissal, as one shoos chickens, and they go out.*] Anne!

ANNE [*indicating her toilette with a slight, calm movement*]: Well, do you like my dress?

RICHARD: My dear, it's magnificent. Even that absurd thing is lovely on your head.

ANNE: You know you like it very well. You're jealous because I've made it the rage. You like to keep the prerogative of making things the rage to yourself, you and Robert. But your little barbarian wife is beating you at your own game. I came along to find out whether I could hear Uncle Gloucester thumping on the table, or if things were going quietly. But it's over, is it? Tell me, Richard, did they agree? Did they say yes?

RICHARD [*sulkily*]: It isn't over. As far as I can see they've only just begun.

ANNE: But – – Oh, Richard! Have you run away again! And you promised me that you would be patient, that you wouldn't – –

RICHARD: How can I be patient! I know I have a dreadful temper, but how can I be patient? They treat me like a child! They think my ideas are moonshine; idealistic nonsense. When I give my opinion they half-smile, a little pityingly; they pause a moment for politeness' sake, and then go on as if I had not spoken. Do you wonder that I go blind with rage?

ANNE: But, Richard, you are the King.

RICHARD: No, I am merely Edward's grandson. And my father's son. They compare me always in their minds with my father. They eye me and think: 'If the Prince had lived, there would be none of this pacifist nonsense.' War, war, war! It is all they ever think of. When there is no war they are bored. Tell me, what is shameful about peace?

ANNE: Shameful?

RICHARD: Yes, shameful. When they say it they avoid each other's eyes as if it were an indecency. When I plead that this armistice with France should be made into a permanent peace they look at me as if I were blaspheming. We waste men and money and material for generations on a futile struggle, and, when someone suggests that it would be sensible to stop the silly business, they talk about prestige, and are shocked and furious. It is like battering one's head against a wall. They will not listen and they will not try to understand. They are savages. They would rather hack a man in pieces than – than teach him to make velvet like that dress. [*He picks up a fold of her dress.*] Beautiful, isn't it, Anne? [*The touch of the cloth and the consciousness of her soothes him.*] Oh, we could make England so rich and so beautiful. The silversmith sent me something this morning. Something I had ordered for you. You shall have it tonight.

ANNE: My darling. It will be a celebration of our victory. [*She indicates the door.*] Yes, of course it will be a victory! You are not alone, you know. There is Michael de la Pole to back you. Your grandfather trusted him; surely they will trust him too?

RICHARD: They don't trust each other; how will they trust Michael? They suspect him of lining his pockets. They can never forget that his father was a merchant.

ANNE: And there's Robert. Surely Robert's tongue is an asset to any party? [*Even in her anxiety a dimple shows.*]

RICHARD [*sulkily*]: Robert just sits there and laughs.

ANNE: Laughs!

RICHARD: Oh, not openly, of course. But I know that he is laughing, and it makes me ten times more furious with the fools than I should otherwise be when I know that Robert is laughing at them and I am only able to rage.

ANNE: But you could learn to laugh too, Richard.

RICHARD: No, I can't. I've tried. Robert laughs because he doesn't care. It is all a play to Robert. But I care dreadfully. It matters to me. I want to kill them for their stupidity.

ANNE: Richard, you must go back. They can do nothing without you.

RICHARD [*with malicious satisfaction*]: That is why I came out. They think they are lords of England until it comes to signing a paper. For that they need me. [*With a sudden weariness*] And you have no idea how difficult it is sometimes not to sign, when my uncle Gloucester has been glowering, and my uncle Lancaster has been arguing, and my uncle York has been tactful and silly. My grandfather was distressingly prolific. If only I could trust them, Anne! If only I could trust everyone as I trusted when I was small. That was happiness: to take men as you found them, with no little flame of suspicion always shooting up in your mind to spoil things. I sometimes wish I could be – oh, I don't know; nobody in particular; just one of the people. I talked to the people once, in the rebellion; talked for hours to them; and they seemed quite happy in spite of being so poor. But how they stank, Anne! How they stank! It is an insult to God that a human being should smell like that.

ANNE: And that they should be hungry. Think of it, Richard. Not enough to eat. It is difficult to imagine, isn't it?

RICHARD: Even they are not to be trusted.

ANNE: Where thousands of men are brought together there will always be knaves. It was not the poor starving cottars who killed Sudbury. Don't be bitter, Richard, I shouldn't like you if you grew bitter.

RICHARD: That is serious. You disapprove of me often – –

ANNE: No, I don't.

RICHARD: – but if you began to dislike me – –

ANNE: What?

RICHARD: It would be the end of the world.

ANNE: I think the end of the world is a long way off. Now I must go or they will be coming to look for me. And you must go back. Richard, you and I have set our hearts on this peace. Because we both believe in it with all our souls we can make it come true. Perhaps, when I see you again, you will be able to tell me that they have been won over. Now, go.

RICHARD: Very well, I'll go back. They will attend to me now that I have been in a rage. Perhaps I can get my uncle

Gloucester to walk out in a rage, and then we shan't have to put up with him at dinner.

ANNE: Oh, Richard, be serious.

RICHARD: That's not fair. You tell me to take them lightly, and when I do you reprove me!

ANNE: You know what I mean. Don't offend them unnecessarily.

RICHARD: Very well. I shall do my best. We shall have such a happy evening, Anne, when the uncles have all gone. Robert is sprouting a new poem. [*He moves to the door.*]

ANNE: That will be lovely. [*Doubtfully*] I forgot to tell you that Henry is coming.

RICHARD [*stopping*]: Oh, my God! No, that is too much. What is the good of being a king if I have to put up with my cousin Henry for a whole evening!

ANNE: My dear, we can't help it. He and Mary – –

RICHARD: Mary too!

ANNE: – are staying in the Palace for the night, on the way to Hereford. We couldn't very well not ask them to supper.

RICHARD: I won't have it! I simply refuse.

ANNE: I don't very much like Mary.

RICHARD [*thawing after a moment to a grudging smile*]: Oh, very well. But I warn you that I shall be intolerable to him.

ANNE: You know that when the time comes you will be charming to him.

RICHARD: Possibly. I wonder if he will be thinking as unmentionable things about me as I am about him, all the time we are being polite to each other. A grim thought!

ANNE [*with a dazzling smile*]: Good-bye. I'm glad you liked my dress.

CURTAIN

SCENE 2

A council chamber, the Palace of Westminster, the hour being the same as in the previous scene. An informal conference is in progress, which has become momentarily more informal during the two hours of argument which have passed. The council are grouped round an oblong table.

The King's place at the head of the table is empty. There are present:

JOHN OF GAUNT, DUKE OF LANCASTER; *a good-looking man of middle age, who carries himself with the confidence of a practised diplomat.*

THOMAS OF WOODSTOCK, DUKE OF GLOUCESTER; *a soldier and less composed edition of his brother* LANCASTER. *He has the restlessness of all irritable men, and a perpetual air of being about to explode. An uncomfortable person.*

THE EARL OF ARUNDEL; *who is the prototype of all those retired soldiers who believe that the world is going to the dogs. A stupid-looking individual, with small suspicious eyes which seem always searching for slights.*

THE ARCHBISHOP OF CANTERBURY; ARUNDEL'S *brother; as bland as his brother is prickly.*

ROBERT DE VERE, EARL OF OXFORD; *a dark young man with a withdrawn air. He is even better-looking than* RICHARD, *but lacks that flame of spirit which illumines* RICHARD *to the most careless observer. If* ROBERT DE VERE *has vulnerable places, they are carefully hidden and protected by his good-humoured, cynical indifference.*

MICHAEL DE LA POLE, *Chancellor of England; elderly and white-haired, but shrewd; and, after many years of Courts and Governments, no more easily discomposed than* LANCASTER.

SIR SIMON BURLEY; *once the King's tutor and now Warden of Dover Castle; a ruddy, good-natured person with a smile always in his eye.*

K

EDMUND, DUKE OF YORK, *the King's third uncle; a pale, self-indulgent creature, deprecatory and devoid of resolution.*

GLOUCESTER [*in full spate*]: . . . disgraceful that we should be exposed to this. A ridiculous proposition to begin with, and hysteria to end with! You are far too lenient with him, Lancaster.

LANCASTER: My dear brother, I have neither jurisdiction nor influence over him. Our respective enemies have seen to that.

GLOUCESTER: Well, De la Pole, surely you can control him? Or you, Burley; you brought him up. And a fine mess you seem to have made of it.

BURLEY: If I might suggest it, your grace was hardly tactful in your methods. I have never had difficulty with Richard, except when my own judgement in dealing with him has been at fault.

YORK [*tentatively*]: It's getting late; nearly dinner-time. Do you think we should wait any longer?

DE LA POLE [*to* GLOUCESTER]: I think you are unfair in supposing that it is a matter of wanton bad temper, my lord. The King feels strongly on this subject. In his eyes it is something infinitely important, infinitely worth struggling for. Something constructive, as opposed to the policy of *laisser-faire* which – –

GLOUCESTER: Constructive! To let the French keep all they have taken from us! To kiss and make up and give them our blessing, just because Richard would rather stay at home and buy clothes than take an army into France like his father! The boy's a coward, I tell you. A lily-livered coward!

DE LA POLE: That, at least, is untrue. And we all know that it is. We have all of us fought in our time, my lords; but it has always been with the comfortable consciousness of the next man's elbow touching ours; as one of an army; as part of an adventure. Not one of us has walked alone into a hostile mob, and quelled it, as the King did three years ago. A mob which had just seen their leader killed before their eyes. Not one of us has done that, my lords – and I dare not say which one of us would have done it. That was a thing done without prompting, out of his own spirit. [*To* LANCASTER] You were in Scotland, my lord, the Duke of Gloucester was on the Welsh border, and the Duke of York in Portugal. The whole future of this country depended upon a boy of fifteen, and only his courage and initiative saved it from chaos. There is wonderful mettle there, my lords. It is for us merely to guide it, as Sir Simon Burley suggests, and not to thwart and deny it.

GLOUCESTER [*with an exclamation of derision*]: You are be-mused with him! You throw away the judgement that a man of your age and experience should have, for the favour of a graceless boy.

DE LA POLE: If I have committed myself to the anti-war policy, it is because I believe in the vision of youth, and in its capacity to evolve something which our hidebound practice and unsupple minds are incapable of conceiving; and not because of any love or favour that I hope for.

LANCASTER: Although as Chancellor it would please you more to see good gold in your own hands than spent on munitions.

DE LA POLE: I would rather see it thrown into the Channel than spent on munitions. At least it would be harmless there.

GLOUCESTER: The pirate turns preacher!

ARUNDEL: Visionary nonsense, that's what it is!

CANTERBURY: My dear brother, vision is not necessarily nonsensical. There have been occasions when it has proved heaven-sent. Even a crusade achieves something occasionally.

ARUNDEL: Oh, as a Churchman you feel bound to say things

like that. But I'm a soldier, and I want to know what good
– what practical good – anyone thinks it is going to do us
to go begging France for peace as if we were licked, making
ourselves the laughing-stock of Europe.

DE LA POLE: I can hardly expect Lord Arundel to understand
it, but what we are seeking is something new; some way
out of the stalemate; out of the everlasting alternation of
war and armistice and war again, which is all the history
this country has had within living memory. We want a
permanent peace in which we may be able to turn to things
better worth while than the eternal see-saw of conquest and
loss. It is in that hope that we are prepared to treat for a
peace with France.

ARUNDEL: Then I say that is treason! It is going back on
everything we have been taught to believe. It is betraying
the country and those who – –

[*Enter* RICHARD. *He walks to his seat rather as a child might
who knows that he has behaved badly but is still indignant
that anyone should think so.*]

RICHARD [*as they resume their seats*]: You were saying, Lord
Arundel – – ?

ARUNDEL: I was protesting yet once more, sir, against this
monstrous suggestion of – of – –

RICHARD: Of peace.

ARUNDEL [*unconscious of irony*]: Yes, of peace. England is not
beaten, sir, She has had reverses, of course, but so has France.
The spirit of the people is not broken, sir; the will to win is
still there and we have a first-rate army. Once this armistice
ends, there is nothing to hinder us from making a new
invasion which will result in unqualified victory, a complete vindication of our policy, and a still greater glory for
England.

RICHARD: And more cripples begging in the gutters, and
more taxes to cover the cost!

ARUNDEL: You can have no war without wastage, sir. As to

the cost, the captured provinces in France will more than repay the costs – –

RICHARD: When they are captured.

ARUNDEL: And I cannot help saying, sir, that it is a poor day for England when she has to count the cost before she takes her stand in a rightful war.

RICHARD: Oh, let us have done with humbug! My grand-father invaded France in a trumped-up cause which even he himself didn't believe in. My father helped him because he liked the game. They both lost practically all they had gained before they died; and now you suggest that I should lay waste France and kill forty thousand men because it is my sacred duty.

GLOUCESTER: I warn you that it is all very well to take this detached view of the war; you can say what you like here in conference and you can out-vote us here; but you will get short shrift in the Commons.

RICHARD: *I* will get short shrift! [*There is a horrified pause.*] You chose your words carelessly, my dear uncle.

LANCASTER [*pouring oil*]: Gloucester means that it will be difficult to persuade the Commons to give up claims to France which they have been taught to believe rightful and necessary.

RICHARD: It is for us to teach the Commons better. What the Commons are taught, they think; [*looking meaningly at* GLOUCESTER] as you very well know. Who are the Com-mons to decide the foreign policy of a country? A lot of little clerks and country knights, who know the price of hay and how to write a letter; how are they to judge? It is for us to see that they are neither misgoverned nor misled.

LANCASTER: But – supposing for a moment that this peace policy of yours is carried into effect, can you guarantee that France will be equally conscious of her high mission in European politics? Once our army is disbanded, how can you trust them to refrain from snapping up such a juicy morsel as England will be?

RICHARD: Because France wants peace, too, in her heart. There is no peace, because France too is plagued by people like you, like the Commons, like Arundel, like Gloucester, who say: 'It would be shameful to stop! We must go on.'

ARUNDEL: And we must! I am not ashamed to say it. We have interests in France which must be protected; we have colonists in Calais, if nothing else. The whole of France was ours once, and what we have done before we can do again.

DE LA POLE: That last sentence does more credit to Lord Arundel's sentiment than to his intelligence. When the late King and the Prince of Wales gained such spectacular victories in France they were opposed to a conscript and unwilling army. Today, France has learned her lesson and has a well-paid and well-supplied voluntary army, which will prove a very different proposition.

ARUNDEL: Maybe; but we have new artillery. Marvellous artillery!

RICHARD: Which Lord Arundel is dying to try on something more exciting than dummies.

YORK: We seem to be getting no nearer an agreement on the subject. Perhaps if we had dinner first – – What does anyone think?

GLOUCESTER: Does the Chancellor propose to tell the Commons that all the prospective wealth of France is to be given up for a will-of-the-wisp for an idea?

DE LA POLE: No, I propose to tell the Commons that, if we make this peace, they need no longer lose their trade with Flanders because of the French navy's depredations, and that the whole of France will be open for new trade instead of for annihilation. Your good Englishman has a very healthy respect for trade when fighting is not available.

GLOUCESTER: But you misjudge him if you think he can be

bribed by the prospect of trade into forgetting what is due to his country. We are not so far away from Crecy and Poitiers as all that!

RICHARD: Between now and Poitiers a starving army dragged itself beaten out of France. It is said that even my fire-eater of a father died disillusioned.

ARUNDEL: That is merely a matter of organizing supplies.

RICHARD: And when the organization breaks down, you and the other lords live on your stores, and the common soldier dies.

DE LA POLE: Parliament will, I have no doubt, be glad to be spared the cost of organization. I shall point that out too.

BURLEY: To say nothing of the relief of not having to keep up a few dozen useless and mouldering castles in France which no English nobleman will be induced to live in.

GLOUCESTER: Why shouldn't they live in France?

RICHARD: Because they are all afraid they will miss something in England if they do.

GLOUCESTER: Well, I warn you, England hasn't ceased to be patriotic because a few irresponsibles are willing to sell her to France. You will only succeed in making yourselves unpopular if you push such a proposition in Parliament. Already every public-house in London is seething with the gossip that the King is pro-French. The sound of it sours the ale on their tongues.

RICHARD: Your ear seems to be very close to the ground.

GLOUCESTER: I make it my business to study the temper of the people.

RICHARD [*in a tone which is a subtle insult*]: Yes.

GLOUCESTER [*angrily*]: And you would do well to study it, too! That is the thing which matters: the temper of the people; and not the high-falutin of a few unpractical idealists.

RICHARD [*mildly*]: You can hardly call the Chancellor unpractical; nor Sir Simon Burley. They are hardly men to be led away by – –

GLOUCESTER: And what about my lord of Oxford, who hasn't opened his mouth for the last hour? Youth, indeed! You talk about the vision of youth, and Lord Oxford spends his time in committee searching for a rhyme!

DE VERE [*who since the beginning of the scene has been studying a tablet*]: Having failed to find reason. [*Mock sententious*] It is a sobering thought for both of us, my lord, that my little song may still be sung when your glorious war is two little lines in the history books.

GLOUCESTER: What I am concerned with is not what I shall be in the history books, but what is to become of France in my lifetime. If this disgraceful peace were to become fact, what about Calais?

RICHARD: If necessary, we could do homage for Calais.

GLOUCESTER: Do homage for Calais! Are you mad? Are you crazy? Do homage for something that is ours by right of conquest! Have you no pride? What have you in your veins, water or sawdust? Whose son are you that you can suggest such a thing?

LANCASTER: My dear Gloucester – – !

GLOUCESTER: Your grandfather would turn in his grave to see you sitting in that chair and throwing away his conquests like empty eggshells.

RICHARD: Curious how everyone loses his head at the mention of Calais. We have no intention of throwing away Calais, my dear uncle. The best way to keep it is by mutual agreement.

GLOUCESTER: If you do homage for it you acknowledge that you hold it only by their goodwill, you – –

RICHARD: To hold it by goodwill is better than perpetually holding our breath about its military security.

GLOUCESTER: It is a contemptible suggestion, a degrading suggestion. I am ashamed that it should have come from a nephew of mine, and that a servant of Edward the Third [*glaring at* DE LA POLE] should aid and abet you in making it. If your father were only alive today – –

RICHARD: I wish to God he were! Then I should be hunting in Malvern – and you would be nagging the gardeners at Pleshy!

GLOUCESTER: This is too much! I sit on this council to give advice, not to be insulted. When you need my advice again you can send for me.

[*Exit angrily.*]

RICHARD [*recovering his temper abruptly*]: Well! [*The tone says:* 'That's that!'] I think that ends the conference for today, gentlemen. The papers I shall sign with the Chancellor this evening. The only other matter is Parliament's complaint of my extravagance, and that, being a more or less perpetual matter, can wait. [*Rising*] I expect you all to dinner.

LANCASTER [*as the others file out*]: May I have a word with you, if you are not too ravenous?

RICHARD: Ravenous! It takes me two days to recover my appetite after a conference. [*He props himself against the table.*] What is it that you wanted to say?

LANCASTER: You and I will never agree over this French business, Richard. We have quarrelled over it more than once. And it hurts my sense of fitness to quarrel the same quarrel more than three times. I have made up my mind to take my departure to Spain.

RICHARD: To Spain! But – –

LANCASTER: I know, I know! [*As one repeating a well-learned lesson*] Spain is France's ally, and France must not be offended. Hitherto I have had to let my military ambitions in Spain wilt because of your peace ambitions in France. But the end of the French armistice is coming, and if it ends, as I am sure it will, in the renewal of war, nothing is left in the way of my little Spanish expedition. I don't think that you can object to that. My claim to Spain, if not immaculate, is at least not greatly – 'trumped-up' was the word, I think? [*glancing slyly at Richard.*]

RICHARD [*smiling in spite of himself*]: No. I suppose you must go if you want to. But what about the Scots? If we fail in peace negotiations with the French, the Scots will be over the border like water.

LANCASTER: We can settle the Scots while my expedition is being fitted out.

RICHARD: The poor Scots! Well, you have the money and you have the men. What more do you want? My blessing?

LANCASTER: Yes. With your official sanction, and Parliament's unofficial hatred of the French, I can get them to vote a little gift towards my army's supplies. There is no need to beggar myself in Spain.

RICHARD: You know quite well that Parliament will vote anything against France. It is only the King's household accounts that they question. I am sorry that you are going.
[*In the tone of this last remark there is a suspicion of such naive wonder underlying its conventionality that* LANCASTER *is amused.*]

LANCASTER: And surprised to find yourself sorry?

RICHARD: Yes, a little.

LANCASTER: We have had small chance to learn to know each other, Richard. Each time that we have come within understanding distance of each other someone has told us of a plot that the other was hatching, 'm?

RICHARD [*thoughtfully*]: Yes.

LANCASTER: You always got incontrovertible proof, didn't you?

RICHARD: Yes.

LANCASTER: So did I! [RICHARD, *seeing the point, smiles, and there is a pause.*] You said just now of the Spanish project: 'You have the money and you have the men.'

RICHARD: Yes?

LANCASTER: With those men and that money I might, if I had cared, have done endless mischief in the last eight years. But, instead, I am taking them out of England. Think it over. I hope you are giving me pigeon-pie for dinner?

RICHARD: I think so. You go on. I'll follow. [*As* LANCASTER *goes out*] By the way, I suppose you weren't thinking of taking my uncle Gloucester with you to Spain?

LANCASTER [*smiling*]: No, you will have to deal with your own worries.

[*Exit* LANCASTER. RICHARD *moves to the window and stands there looking out, kicking disconsolately in a childish fashion with his toe. After a moment,* ROBERT DE VERE *comes in looking for him.*]

DE VERE [*crossing to him*]: Dinner, Richard.

RICHARD: I don't want dinner.

DE VERE: You will when you see it.

RICHARD [*in a burst*]: It is all coming to pieces, Robert! They won't try to understand, and Parliament will think as they do. It is going to fail.

DE VERE [*putting his arm across* RICHARD'S *shoulder in casual friendliness*]: Cheer up, Richard! It may fail this time. You can't expect them to absorb anything as repulsive as a new idea without some coaxing. But we are young, thank God; we have all our lives in front of us. We keep on coaxing, and presently they swallow the dose.

RICHARD: But you would think that we were trying to do something that would harm them, instead of something that would be to everyone's advantage!

DE VERE: Everyone's advantage is nobody's business. You should know that. Even we are not entirely guiltless of self-seeking.

RICHARD: What do you mean?

DE VERE: Analyse our noble desire for peace and it becomes strangely like a rather low desire for a quiet life.

RICHARD: How can you laugh, Robert?

DE VERE: How can I? A little natural aptitude, and some perseverance. Gloucester helps. Gloucester is very funny.

RICHARD: Gloucester! Funny! You know you don't mean that.

DE VERE: But I do mean it. Gloucester being righteous must make even the gods laugh.

RICHARD: Oh, Robert, I wish I had your Olympian view. I can only see Gloucester trampling to pieces everything we try to build. Don't you care about that?

DE VERE: You know I care.

RICHARD: You think I'm a fool to let them see. But I can't help it. Stupidity drives me crazy. Arundel and his 'will to win'! Does Arundel make you laugh, too?

DE VERE: Where Arundel is concerned it is a choice between laughter and being sick, and I find it more – convenient to laugh.

RICHARD [melting]: Robert, what should I do without you!

DE VERE: Struggle along, I dare say. Come, Anne will be waiting.

RICHARD [brightening]: Oh, yes; Anne. [Gloomy again] And I have nothing to tell her. I hoped I should be able to – and all I did was lose my temper again. [As they move out, brightening once more] But at least Gloucester will not be at dinner!

CURTAIN

SCENE 3

A room in the King's apartment, the Palace of Westminster, on the evening of the same day. In the back wall is, left, an embrasured window, and right, a small door. Down right is the fireplace. Centre is a table with the remains of supper. There is moonlight outside.

Supper is over. ANNE *is sitting by the fire with* MARY BOHUN, HENRY'S *wife, working at her embroidery. The others have pushed back their chairs a little, but are still lounging by the table.*

There are present: RICHARD; ROBERT DE VERE; THOMAS MOWBRAY, EARL OF NOTTINGHAM; HENRY, EARL OF DERBY; *and* AGNES LAUNCEKRON, *the Queen's waiting-woman.*

HENRY, LORD DERBY, *is the same age as* RICHARD, *but looks older owing to his sturdy build and solid manner.*

MOWBRAY *is also* RICHARD'S *age; a plain youth with a manner half-resentful, half-placatory.*

AGNES LAUNCEKRON *is slightly older than* ANNE; *a brilliant dark creature with an overflowing vitality. Her English is much more foreign than* ANNE'S.

MARY: I'm such a cold person. I'm never happy unless I have my toes to a fire.] *There is an outburst of laughter from the table, where* ROBERT *is talking.*] What are they laughing at?

ANNE: I don't know. I expect Robert is being outrageous.

MARY [*in a disbelieving tone*]: Lord Oxford is supposed to be very witty, isn't he?

ANNE: I certainly find him amusing.

AGNES [*noticing the moonlight*]: Oh, why do we stay and stifle in a little room on a night like this! [*She rises impetuously and crosses to the window.*]

HENRY: If you women wore looser dresses you wouldn't stifle so much.

AGNES [*opening part of the window and leaning out*]: It is like June tonight. You can almost smell the roses.

MARY [*to* ANNE]: I should like to wear fashionable things, you know, but my husband won't let me. He says he likes me best in my old things. He doesn't approve of shaved necks and plucked eyebrows.

[ROBERT DE VERE *joins* AGNES *in the window, and they stay there, laughing and talking in low voices.*]

ANNE: No? A harmless and amiable fashion, surely? One's neck looks so untidy in these new head-dresses if one doesn't shave it. Besides, it does great good to the Church.

MARY: To the Church!

ANNE: It gives the clergy something new to preach about.

HENRY [*demonstrating on the table to* RICHARD *and* MOWBRAY]: He was just about here when I noticed him. This is the far end of the ground, you see. He had just arrived as far as this when I noticed that he wasn't balanced properly. Curious how very few men know how to balance themselves properly. He was going at a great pace, but in that second or two I made up my mind. I marked a spot about two inches, or perhaps three inches – I should say three inches – to the right of the middle line, and about two hands'-breadths below the shoulder; marked it with my eye; and when he was within reach I swerved about half a foot, so as to get a screw effect, and let him have it. He lifted out of that saddle like a bird. I wish you had seen it. It was the neatest thing I ever did.

RICHARD: He isn't quite as heavy as you, is he?

HENRY [*slightly offended*]: He challenged me, so I suppose he considered himself up to my weight. [*Recovering his self-satisfaction*] He won't play for some time again, I think.

MOWBRAY: It must be quite two months since we had a tournament, Richard. You are not doing your duty as a provider of spectacles.

RICHARD: How can I provide spectacles with Parliament complaining for ever of my extravagance?

HENRY: That hasn't detained you so far!

MOWBRAY: They'll complain in any case.

RICHARD: I have more serious matters to attend to. Next month I shall be enduring the utter boredom of campaigning on the Scots border.

MOWBRAY: Confess, sir; that is sheer affectation. In your heart you love it.

RICHARD [*surprised*]: You're becoming quite acute, Thomas Mowbray!

MOWBRAY [*resenting the indulgent tone*]: Am I usually so dense?

RICHARD [*not listening*]: Yes, there are some things I like about it. I like wakening up in the morning, with the tent flapping, and Dibdin hissing while he takes the rust off the armour. And the smell of frying. And the footprints all black on the wet grass.

HENRY: Black! Footprints on dew aren't black, they're white.

RICHARD [*wearily*]: If you say so, Harry, they must be.

HENRY: I should think so! I may not know the latest fashions in clothes, nor how to write verse, but you can't tell me anything I don't know about campaigning.

DE VERE: The dust of battle is incense in Henry's nostrils.

HENRY: I think it wouldn't be a bad thing for this country if a few more people didn't mind the dust.

RICHARD: In fact, what this country needs is a really big war to redeem itself from the awful stigma of being at peace for more than two years!

HENRY: I wouldn't put it quite like that, but − −

RICHARD: But that's what you mean?

HENRY: There is such a thing as a righteous war.

RICHARD: My dear Henry, all wars are righteous! Even the bishops patronize them.

HENRY: When I was in the Holy Land once, we were in a very tight place. It was in a narrow valley like this [*demonstrating on the table*].

MARY [*looking meaningly at the couple in the window*]: Is it true, then, madam, what they say?

ANNE: It hardly ever is. But what do you mean particularly?

MARY: Well, it may be indiscreet of me, but they say that Lord Oxford finds your waiting-woman very attractive.

ANNE: Agnes is very attractive.

MARY: Her manners are very foreign.

ANNE: She has been brought up, like me, in a country where women do not wait until they are spoken to before they speak.

MARY: It must be so distressing for his poor wife when people tell her.

ANNE: Then why do they tell her?

MARY: It is only right that she should know what is going on.

ANNE: What is going on?

MARY: Oh, well, madam, you know best, of course.

ANNE: I see nothing wanton or strange in the fact that Robert should find Agnes amusing. Poor Lady Oxford is very dull.

MARY: Philippa Oxford is a good woman.

ANNE: I have no doubt of it.

MARY: And you yourself are so good, madam, that I am surprised that you take their – well, their friendship so lightly.

ANNE: It has never made me angry to see others happy. And if Lady Oxford has a grievance she probably enjoys it more than she does Robert's company.

HENRY: And there I had the whole five of them, and not a struggle left in the lot of them! [*He picks up his glass and drains it.*]

RICHARD: Marvellous. Do you approve of my malvoisie?

HENRY: Yes, not bad. Get it from Bramber?

MOWBRAY: Of course he does.

HENRY: You know what you're about, Richard! Keep in with these merchant princes, and take the perquisites, eh?

RICHARD [*coldly*]: I happen to have paid for that wine. Foolish of me, no doubt. Part of my lamented extravagance. [*Dropping to good-humoured abuse*] You are a clod, Henry. Is

Bramber's only charm in your eyes the fact that he is a wine merchant?

HENRY: Oh, well, I suppose it is good policy to keep in with the Lord Mayor, whatever he deals in.

RICHARD: Oh, have some more, for God's sake! Mowbray, pour him out some.

[DE VERE *sings in a low voice to* AGNES, *while* ANNE *and* MARY *talk.*]

ANNE: It is only that I think the Church has become too rich, and forgotten its mission. That is all. It has become a tyranny instead of a comfort, and I think something should be done to make it simpler and kindlier.

MARY: I should like to study these things, too, but the children take up most of my time, as you can imagine. And in a big household – – [*She sighs complacently.*]

ANNE: But don't you have a good housekeeper?

MARY: Oh, yes, she is fairly good. But I like to keep an eye on most things myself. Henry likes to see what he calls my touch in things. A wife takes so much more interest than a paid servant. Besides, don't you think men understand those matters of State better than we ever can?

RICHARD: Robert, if you must sing, sing openly and not in a corner.

DE VERE [*coming back to the table with* AGNES]: I can't sing at all. The song isn't finished yet. I was merely trying it out on Agnes, and now you've ruined my inspiration.

MOWBRAY [*with a glance at* AGNES]: Vere's inspirations are easily ruined, aren't they?

DE VERE [*surprised*]: Not as easily as Mowbray's digestion, apparently. Has your supper not agreed with you, Thomas?

MOWBRAY: My supper has agreed with me, thank you; but there are other things I find hard to stomach.

DE VERE [*refusing the lead*]: Such as my singing? Very well, I promise not to sing. Have you finished the wine, Henry?

RICHARD [*passing the wine*]: No, just in time.

DE VERE: Are you going campaigning in Spain with your father, Henry?

HENRY: No, I think this country might be interesting for a little. The Hereford estates need looking after.

DE VERE: If you imagine yourself as a country gentleman, Henry, you're wrong. You'll only get into trouble. England isn't big enough for you.

MOWBRAY: He has a family he wants to see something of, you know.

HENRY: Have you told the King your news, Mowbray?

RICHARD: News? What has old Thomas been doing?

MOWBRAY: I am going to be married.

RICHARD [*delighted*]: Married! Thomas, my dear friend! And I had no inkling of it! You are becoming a dark horse, Thomas. Who is the lady? Someone about the Court? Let us all guess. A silver girdle to the winner! I have first guess.

MOWBRAY: I don't think you know her, sir. It is Lord Arundel's daughter.

[*There is a moment of silent consternation, but* RICHARD *rises to the occasion.*]

RICHARD: *Arundel's* daughter! [*After a pause*] Well, my dear friend, I could have wished the alliance otherwise, but if you are happy I am bound to be content. Come, let us drink to Mowbray's happiness. [MOWBRAY *murmurs a half-shame-faced thanks, and they drink.*] And heaven grant him patience with his father-in-law!

[*There is a general laugh, rather hysterical and relieved.*]

Is the marriage to be soon?

MOWBRAY: Some time within the year.

AGNES: The lady must be very lovely to have tempted Lord Mowbray away from the Court beauties.

MOWBRAY: She is considered to be quite good-looking.

DE VERE: What admirable detachment!

HENRY [*into an awkward pause*]: I think it is time that I said good night.

RICHARD: What! With some malvoisie still in the flask?

HENRY: We are setting out very early in the morning. Mary!
[MARY *rises and takes her leave of* ANNE.]

RICHARD: Well, Simon Burley says it is going to be wet, so
put on an old coat for your ride tomorrow.

HENRY: I haven't any new ones. *My* coats are made for the
weather.

RICHARD [*taking leave of* LADY DERBY]: But not yours,
madam, I hope?

MARY: Indeed, yes, sir. In the country one lives as the country
people do, with rain for one's bath and russet for one's garb.

RICHARD: A little dull, surely. Good night. I hope you have
a safe journey.

MOWBRAY: If you don't mind, I think I shall take my leave
too. [*He looks half-defiant, half-shamefaced at* RICHARD'S
surprise.]

RICHARD [*making things easy for him*]: Thomas wants to write
love-letters! Very well, my friend. But don't try verse.
Your metre was always lame. Good night.

MOWBRAY: Good night, sir.
[*He takes his leave of* ANNE, *and follows the* DERBYS *out.
The four who are left stare after them.*]

RICHARD: With Henry! That is a new alliance, surely?

DE VERE: Perhaps he has been overcome by a longing for
beef and brawn.

RICHARD: It is a strange marriage – with Arundel's daughter.

DE VERE: Don't blame him too much; perhaps he is in love
with the girl. Which reminds me. [*To* ANNE] Have you
been shocking the Countess of Derby, madam? There was
a drawing aside of skirts, I thought.

AGNES [*with more scorn than she can utter*]: Skirts like that need
drawing aside! Has she no mirror, the woman!

ANNE: Lady Derby does not approve of us. I have been well
and truly snubbed all the evening. What one suffers in the
name of social duty!

RICHARD: But – Mowbray! After all those years, to go over to the Arundel camp. And to tell us when he had Henry here to back him! What has gone wrong?

ANNE: What is wrong is that he is jealous. I should have thought that was obvious.

RICHARD: Jealous of what?

ANNE: Of Robert. You and he and Robert have been together ever since you were small, and you never make any secret of your preference for Robert. You were never a good dissembler, Richard, and Mowbray is not a good second fiddle.

DE VERE: He won't be even second fiddle in the Arundel-Gloucester league.

AGNES: But it is much easier to play forty-fifth fiddle than second, you know.

ANNE: And he will feel that in some vague way he is getting even.

RICHARD: Getting even for what, in heaven's name! I have never been anything but friendly to him.

ANNE: That very thoughtless friendliness is a thorn to a jealous nature.

RICHARD: Then you think that he has deserted us? That this marriage is an ultimatum?

DE VERE: Perhaps he has merely a hankering to take part in one of Arundel's triumphant progresses after the next war.

RICHARD: Arundel makes me quite sick! He has never forgotten the shouts of the populace last time he rode through London after a victory, and to have that in his ears again he is ready to wade through blood.

DE VERE: And his grace of Gloucester is prepared to do likewise so that France may have the benefit of his administrative abilities.

ANNE: Don't laugh, Robert!

DE VERE [surprised]: Why not?

ANNE: None of us can afford to laugh at Gloucester.

DE VERE: Afford! Well, however expensive, I reserve the right to laugh when, where, and at whom I choose.

ANNE: You talk like a grammar!

RICHARD [*smiling at* ANNE]: Anne has never got over her first sight of Gloucester when he met her at Dover.

ANNE: I have certainly never changed my mind about him.

DE VERE: You must forgive her her prejudice. It was raining. Think of a wet day at Dover, all her baggage lost, and Gloucester to meet her! It's a marvel that she didn't go straight back to Bohemia.

RICHARD: Don't imagine such hells for me, Robert. I have had enough for one day. You really had finished that song, hadn't you?

DE VERE: Yes, but I wasn't going to waste it on Henry.

RICHARD: I thought so. Let us have it now. [*Sitting on the floor by* ANNE, *and leaning against her knee*] Oh, how tired I am! What a day! [*Musing, as* ROBERT *is preparing to sing*] You know, there are times when I quite like Lancaster.

DE VERE: When you have had an hour alone with Gloucester.

RICHARD: No, I mean it. He is the type of man one wouldn't mind having for a father.

DE VERE: Henry doesn't find him so congenial.

AGNES: You mean he doesn't find Henry so congenial. It must be dreadful, poor man, to have Lord Derby for a son! [*The others laugh at the passion of sympathy in her voice.*]

DE VERE: I know why you have discovered a liking for Lancaster.

RICHARD: Why?

DE VERE: Because he is going to Spain.

RICHARD: Tease if you like, but there are times when I very nearly trust Lancaster. Sing, Robert, and save your wits.

[DE VERE *begins to sing as the curtain falls.*]

CURTAIN

SCENE 4

A room in the King's Palace of Eltham, autumn, 1386.

There are present: RICHARD; ROBERT DE VERE; *and* MICHAEL DE LA POLE.

RICHARD [*to* DE LA POLE]: So you think I have been behaving badly?

DE LA POLE: With all due respect, sir, I think it was a mistake to create Lord Oxford Duke of Ireland at the present moment. In the circumstances it was – well, a slap in the face for Parliament.

RICHARD: That is why I did it.

DE VERE: And I had hoped it was for my graces, if not for my merits!

RICHARD: And my desertion of Parliament, do you think that a mistake too?

DE LA POLE: That was not so serious. In the present deadlock a certain amount of independence is good policy. It is when independence becomes wanton that it tends to alienate sympathy, and we cannot afford to alienate any sympathy just now.

RICHARD: Oh, you croak, Michael, you croak.

DE LA POLE: The situation is serious, sir. London is seething with rumours of a French invasion; the people have been worked into a state bordering on panic, and the invasion – mythical as far as I know – is being attributed to our supposed remissness.

DE VERE: But what connexion has this supposed raid with our policy? If we had been able to make peace there would have been no danger of a raid!

DE LA POLE: You can hardly expect the man in the street to examine the logic of a rumour. At the best of times he is not clear-thinking. When he is a little silly with terror it is enough to suggest to him that the King is responsible. He is angry and frightened, and only too willing to accept the scapegoat presented to him. There has been one thing wrong with our policy. [*Bitterly*] We have not sown the by-ways with lying rumour.

DE VERE: Yes, it is their deliberate policy. My squires have told me things.

DE LA POLE: A terribly effective policy.

RICHARD: Well, I refuse to go back to London until Parliament climbs down from its attitude of dictation. The responsibility of everything that happens in this country is laid on my shoulders, and that being so I must be free to direct it as I think fit. When Parliament is willing to share the responsibility, then it will have the right to dictate. All it has done so far in its history is to criticize.

DE VERE: And to pat themselves on the back when the King has pulled the chestnuts out of the fire.

DE LA POLE: The fact that they are willing to send a deputation down here augurs well for their reasonableness.

RICHARD: They are growing impatient, that is all. They want to get back to their wives, and their own much more important quarrels with their neighbours. At bottom the Commons care nothing what happens to the country. Even the Londoners, when they aren't worked up like this against the French, are less interested in foreign policy than in the fact that Stratford bakers make short-weight bread.

DE LA POLE: When do you expect the Commons?

RICHARD: I said that I would see a deputation of forty this afternoon.

DE LA POLE: Then they will be here presently. I have not paid my respects to the Queen. With your permission I shall do that before they come.

RICHARD: Very well. You will find her in the garden, I expect; she and Agnes are converting the flowers to Bohemian ways. [*Enter a* PAGE.] Well, is it the deputation?

PAGE: No, sir. The Duke of Gloucester and the Earl of Arundel have arrived, sir. They would be grateful if you would grant them an interview.

RICHARD: Either my uncle has bought himself a new tongue, or you lend him yours.

DE LA POLE: I think you had better see them, sir.

RICHARD: Of course I shall see them. I want very much to see both of them. Let them come in.

    [*Exit* PAGE.]

DE VERE: So they couldn't trust the Commons!

DE LA POLE: You'll be tactful, sir. It will not gain us anything to rouse more enmity.

RICHARD: Could there be more?

DE LA POLE: If you like, sir, I can conduct the interview on your behalf. I'm your Chancellor, don't forget.

RICHARD: I don't forget it, Michael. I shall never forget it. You have been a good friend to me. But I am going to see those two alone. Yes [*as the others protest*], you are to go, both of you. I am not frightened of Gloucester, and I will not have him think that I need support against him. Now go, quickly, before they come. [DE LA POLE *and* DE VERE *move reluctantly to a small door down left.*] And don't wait outside that door. If I want you I shall send for you. Go and advise the Queen about next year's roses.

    [*As they go out, the* PAGE *shows* GLOUCESTER *and* ARUNDEL *in.*]

Good day to you both. You wished to see me?

GLOUCESTER: I have come to see you as representative of the present Parliament.

RICHARD: I had expected a deputation of forty Commons.

GLOUCESTER: I am deputed to speak on their behalf.

RICHARD: Have the Commons been struck dumb, then? I wish I had seen so rare a sight!

GLOUCESTER: Since the deputation was entirely agreed as to

their point of view it was thought better that one man should present it to you.

RICHARD: And your – shield-bearer, what is he for?

GLOUCESTER: Lord Arundel is here to add weight to my message.

RICHARD: I see. A reinforcement.

ARUNDEL: No such thing! Our position requires no reinforcement, sir. I am here independently, in my own capacity.

RICHARD: I beg your pardon. But you have so many capacities: soldier, sailor, landowner, agitator, critic – – However, to business. I am prepared to listen to what you have to say.

GLOUCESTER: It will not take long in the telling. I am authorized by Parliament to say that no business will be transacted nor grants made until such time as you are willing to dismiss the Chancellor, and accept a Chancellor nominated by them.

RICHARD: By you, you mean. Is that all you have to say? I have already refused to dismiss De la Pole. Not only have they no right to demand such a thing, but they have produced not one excuse for such an outrageous request. Michael de la Pole has served this country well, both in my grandfather's time and mine – – But it is not for me to defend my Chancellor to you.

GLOUCESTER: He will have need of defence presently. If you refuse to consent to their demands Parliament will take other means of ensuring that their wishes are granted.

RICHARD: Their wishes! They are nothing but a hundred mouths for your own utterance! I would not dismiss a scullion at their bidding. Go back and tell them that. Tell them that the Duke of Gloucester may own Parliament, but Richard is still King of England.

GLOUCESTER: If you refuse to listen, sir, I am deputed to tell you that De la Pole will be impeached.

RICHARD: Impeached! There is nothing on which they could base an impeachment. You cannot try a man without accusing him of something.

ARUNDEL: There will be ample accusation.

RICHARD: You will see to that, you mean!

GLOUCESTER: And furthermore – –

RICHARD: Go on! Let us hear the whole of the enormity!

GLOUCESTER: Parliament considers that your present advisers are incompetent and a danger to the country.

RICHARD: I have heard that before. They have failed to show in what way they are incompetent or dangerous.

GLOUCESTER: And that from now on the King should be subject to a committee of advisers of greater worth and stability.

RICHARD: I should be subject to – – ! Are you mad? Do you know what you are saying? There is no such provision in the Constitution.

GLOUCESTER: In times of emergency new provisions must be made. It is suggested that the committee consist of Lord Arundel, the Duke of York, myself, two archbishops, and six other persons.

RICHARD [almost speechless with rage]: You are a brave man, Gloucester, to stand there and make a suggestion like that.

GLOUCESTER: I have excellent backing. My support does not end with the handful of men waiting for me in the courtyard.

RICHARD: You had better go before I forget even that handful of men in the courtyard. I could imagine things worth losing a crown for.

GLOUCESTER: Losing a crown may be easier and more immediate than you think, sir. There may not be precedent for a governing committee, but there is excellent precedent for deposing a king.

RICHARD: Is there no limit to your insolence?

GLOUCESTER: There is very little limit to our power. In the

present troubled state of the country the people will accept any measures which a strong Government choose to propose.

RICHARD: And who is responsible for the troubled state of the country? Not I! By God, not I! You have built this situation brick by brick; built it out of your own spite and contentiousness. You have hedged me round with lies until I am as much in prison as if you had built stone walls round me. You dare not murder me, so you murder my reputation. You have misrepresented every action of mine from the attempt to make peace with France to the gift of two marks to a page, until my name stands for everything that is wanton and contemptible. There is nothing that has not been used for your own ends. You have taken the prospect of a petty French raid and crazed the people with rumours of an invasion. You blame me for the raid, and when it comes to nothing you will claim that the defeat was due to your own foresight. There is nothing you will not stoop to in your campaign of lies, no slander so foul that you will not make use of it. You murder me by little bits, murder the thing that is me, and I have no redress. I cannot go out into the streets and shout: 'It is not so! I am not that! When I did such and such it was because of this and not because of that!' If my friends give the lie to your slander the people smile and say: 'You are his friends. We hardly expected you to say otherwise.' There is no stopping it! One cannot fight whispers any more than one can hold back Thames with one's hands. They laugh and run through one's fingers. And you have done this to me! You who come here in all your sanctity of self-righteousness to say what I shall or shall not do.

GLOUCESTER: I speak for the people.

RICHARD: The people! Poor little puppets who are cozened by this knave and that, until they do not know what they believe or why. I have never cozened them, nor will I truckle to them. The Constitution says that the King is the Law. It is for him to see that it is kept from being made a plaything by princes drunk with power and Commons rotten with bribery. Go back and tell them that, Gloucester! Tell them that!

GLOUCESTER: I warn you, Richard, that if you don't come back to London within the next two days, an end will be put to the situation by removing the stumbling-block. The situation is paralleled very closely in the case of your great-grandfather, Edward the Second; and I need hardly remind you of his fate.

RICHARD: You dare to hold that over my head! Get out of my sight. Get out of my sight, before it is too late. Do you hear me? Leave Eltham at once, you and your henchman. And be quick before it is too late.

ARUNDEL: We are going, sir. All that we came to say has been said.

GLOUCESTER: And all the answer we take back is that we left an hysterical boy, throwing the cushions about in his rage.

RICHARD: Oh, go, for God's sake go, and be thankful to your saints that you go at all.

[GLOUCESTER *and* ARUNDEL *go.*]

[RICHARD *snatches the dagger from his girdle as though he would follow them, but instead flings himself on the table, stabbing promiscuously and sobbing in incoherent rage.*]

Curse him! Oh, curse him! Oh, God, why do you let the fiend live!

[*Exhausted, he leaves the knife sticking in the table.*]

[*Enter* SIR SIMON BURLEY.]

Burley!

BURLEY: So you are glad to see old Burley?

RICHARD: I am always glad to see you, Simon. I don't have to be anything that I'm not with you. You've known the worst about me ever since I was five. And what is still better, I don't have to keep wondering what is in your mind.

BURLEY: Is it that I am so simple? Or because I have given you a piece of it so often?

RICHARD: Have you come to give me a piece of it now?

BURLEY: I have come with bad news, Richard. [*He removes the knife from the table.*] Carving one's initials is a plebeian pastime, my son.

RICHARD [*shamefaced*]: I lost my temper again. Gloucester has been here.

BURLEY: Yes, I thought it was Gloucester's men in the court-yard.

RICHARD [*in a low voice*]: He was unspeakable, Simon; unspeakable. [*Holding out his hand for the dagger*] You can give me that. I am quite better now. [BURLEY *hands over the dagger.*] They suggested the most outrageous things. They have elected themselves into a committee to rule me – Gloucester and Arundel and the rest, with my uncle York thrown in to be useful and say yes when they make proposals. Did you know about that? Was that what you came to tell me?

BURLEY: Yes, I heard about the commission. But it was a worse thing I had to tell.

RICHARD: That they threaten to depose me?

BURLEY [*shocked*]: No, not that! Did they threaten that?

RICHARD: Yes; if I don't go back to Town and do as they suggest they will treat me as Edward the Second was treated. If you didn't know that, what was your news?

BURLEY: That when you go back to London your five best friends are to be accused of treason and tried.

RICHARD: Burley! No! Even if I agree to their demands?

BURLEY: I don't think any concession you could make now will turn Gloucester from his purpose.

RICHARD: Who – who are the five?

BURLEY: Robert de Vere, Michael de la Pole, the Archbishop of York, Bramber, and – myself.

RICHARD: You, Burley! Why you? [*As* BURLEY *does not*

answer] Because you are my friend, is that it? That is offence
enough, isn't it? But what have any of them done but that?
It is not treason to obey one's King.

BURLEY: We have been leading you astray, apparently, and
that is accounted treason.

RICHARD: What is to be done? First of all we can raise the
London trained bands. [*As* BURLEY *shakes his head*] What
is wrong with that?

BURLEY: What is wrong is that they will not rise.

RICHARD: Not if Bramber is threatened? Bramber is the most
popular mayor that London has had for years.

BURLEY: Perhaps. But the rest of us are distinctly unpopular,
it seems. To be frank, sir, they say they have no intention
of getting their heads broken for Robert de Vere. [*As*
RICHARD *takes this mildly*] That Duke of Ireland business
was not very judicious.

RICHARD: I know. I do foolish things when I am furious.
And so our cause is unpopular?

BURLEY: Yes. But that is neither your fault nor Robert's.
Gloucester has used every underground channel in the
country to achieve that end. They pillory a fish-hawker for
slander, but you cannot pillory Gloucester and his friends.

[*Enter* ROBERT DE VERE.]

DE VERE: Richard, listen – – ! Oh, good day, Burley. [*To*
RICHARD] So you have heard the news?

RICHARD: That my friends are considered traitors? Yes.
Since when has obeying the King become treason?

DE VERE: My dear Richard! You hardly do justice to
Gloucester's inventive ability. Treason is merely the general
heading, so to speak. The charge takes two hours to read,
and is composed of thirty-seven sections. That we have
abused the King's tender age; that we have induced him to
waste the treasures of his realm (that is that last tournament
you gave, Richard; I told you it was a little gaudy); that we
have estranged him from loyal councillors and kinsfolk (the

excellent and loyal Duke himself, in fact); prompted him to murder Arundel and Gloucester (when I think how often I have restrained you from hitting Arundel over the head with a bottle!); and thirty-seventh, but by no means least, prompted you to betray Calais. You know, the one real mistake your poor councillors ever made, Richard, was to let you even mention the name of that misbegotten little French village. No Englishman is quite sane on the subject of Calais.

RICHARD: How do you know all this? Are you making it up?

DE VERE: You do me too much honour. I am quoting from Tressillian. He has just arrived with a copy of the charge. He is included among the traitors.

RICHARD: Tressillian too! What is to be done? Burley, bring De la Pole here, will you? He is in the garden, I think.

DE VERE: You will find him discussing roses with the Queen in the long alley. I left them there when I saw Tressillian arrive.

RICHARD: Don't let the Queen know yet that there is anything to worry about.

[*Exit* BURLEY.]

It is a dreadful thing to be my friend, isn't it, Robert?

DE VERE: I have not found it so.

RICHARD: If you and I had devoted our wits and the country's wealth to, let us say, annexing Scotland, the people would have blocked the streets to see us, and even the maimed soldiers would have thought us fine fellows. But because we pour most of our money into the pockets of London tradesmen, we are a despicable pair. It is a curious point of view.

DE VERE: We are young. There is still time for us to become the complete warriors. I think the occasion is about to be thrust on us. It is a comforting reflection that you showed very good form on that last Scottish campaign. You were a credit to your parentage, Richard.

RICHARD: Any man worthy of the name can fight when it is necessary. But it is so very seldom necessary, it seems to me.

DE VERE: This time it is going to be necessary.

[*Enter* BURLEY *with* DE LA POLE.]

RICHARD: This time? What do you mean?

DE VERE: Don't you know that Arundel has all his men mobilized at Reigate, and Mowbray and Henry are concentrating in the Midlands? I thought Burley told you that?

BURLEY: I didn't know! Are you sure that it is true?

DE VERE: Oh, yes. Tressillian has all the details. They are coming south to join Gloucester at Waltham.

RICHARD: And Mowbray is with them!

DE VERE: Mowbray is with them. I told you he hankered after military glory!

DE LA POLE: So it has come! I did not think Gloucester would have dared.

BURLEY: With a popular cause it requires little daring.

RICHARD: War, is it! Well, now we plan. Cheshire will be loyal, whatever the rest of England may be. I must go to London, that is obvious. But while I am keeping them quiet there by nibbling the cheese in the trap, you must gather what forces you can in Cheshire, Robert. De la Pole, you must get out of the country. No, don't argue. At your age you cannot fight, and you will not add to my popularity by staying with me. Oh, my dear old friend, don't argue. It will be so much off my mind if I know that you, at least, are safe. It is a pitiable reward for years of service, isn't it! To offer you *safety*, to consign you to exile. But it is all we can do for the moment. It shall not be for long, I promise you. I shall see you before you go. As for you, Burley, what about you?

BURLEY: I am coming back to London with you, sir.

RICHARD: No, no! That is foolish.

BURLEY: It is not foolish, sir. It is very good policy. If you and the Queen go back alone, immediate suspicion will be the result. But if we go back together, casually, they will not suspect that we know anything beyond the fact that Parliament has a word or two to say to us.

RICHARD: There is something in that. Robert, take the Chancellor away, and have horses saddled for both of you. Order a meal which you can eat before you go. You'll need men from the bodyguard. Warn the men you want, and let them eat while the others are preparing horses for them. When you go downstairs send Tressillian to me.

DE VERE: Yes, sir. [*Goes out with* DE LA POLE.]

RICHARD: What are you smiling at, Burley?

BURLEY: You sounded so like your father, sir.

RICHARD: Does that please you?

BURLEY: The Black Prince had his faults, but he was a very fine man.

RICHARD: Simon, I wish I was sure that I was letting you come with me because it is good policy, and not because I want the comfort of your presence.

BURLEY: There will be no danger, sir. You and the Queen can go to the Tower instead of Westminster. That is still the King's property, and the walls are conveniently thick.

[*Enter* ANNE, *radiant, with a bunch of roses.*]

ANNE: Look, Richard. In October! Smell, Simon. And all out of one border. What are you looking at me like that for, Richard?

RICHARD [*smiling*]: I was thinking that even if the heavens fell you would still be there.

ANNE: Of course I should. It hardly seems a fact worth remarking on.

[RICHARD *exchanges glances with* BURLEY, *who moves to the door, and* RICHARD *draws* ANNE *to a seat as the curtain falls.*]

CURTAIN

L

SCENE 5

A room in the Tower, a month later. It is evening and growing dusk.
RICHARD *is moving restlessly from the window, left, to the centre
of the room and back again. While he is at the window, enter*
MAUDELYN *softly at the door, right, and begins to light the
candles.*

RICHARD [*swinging round*]: Why do you creep about like
    that? What are you doing? What do you want?

MAUDELYN: I came to light the candles, sir.

RICHARD: I didn't say that the candles were to be lighted, did
    I? Leave them alone. It isn't time yet.

MAUDELYN: It is the usual time, sir.

RICHARD: Leave them alone, I tell you. It isn't evening yet.
    Has no one come with news?

MAUDELYN [*irresolutely*]: No, sir.
    [RICHARD *flings round to the window again and* MAUDELYN
    *begins to creep out, leaving the candles which he has lighted
    still burning.*]

RICHARD [*savagely*]: Put out those candles!
    [MAUDELYN *turns, and hesitates.*]

RICHARD: Well, what do you want!

MAUDELYN: I am sorry, sir. I did have a message when I
    came to light the candles. There is news, sir.

RICHARD: News! Well, tell me! Tell me quickly.

MAUDELYN: There's been a defeat, sir. They were cut off at
    Radcot Bridge. Because of the fog. It was – it was practically
    a rout, sir. Sir John Molyneux surrendered himself, and they
    – murdered him then and there, sir.

RICHARD: And Lord Oxford?

MAUDELYN: He – [*in his embarrassment and fear he cannot find
    a happier term*] he fled, sir.
    [RICHARD *strikes him across the face.*]

RICHARD [*in a furious whisper*]: How dare you! How dare you even think the word!

MAUDELYN: That is the message, sir.

RICHARD: Who brought it?

MAUDELYN: A man of Ratcliffe's, sir.

RICHARD: Where is he? Let me talk to him.

MAUDELYN: He has gone, sir. He wouldn't stay in London. He was making his escape.

RICHARD: When did this – this at Radcot – happen?

MAUDELYN: This morning, sir.

RICHARD: This morning! And it is only now I hear!

MAUDELYN: The message came some time ago, sir, but – –

RICHARD: And I was not told! Dear God! I was not told! Why not? Why not?

MAUDELYN: No one had the courage to tell you, sir.

RICHARD [*suddenly quiet*]: Only you. And I struck you. You say Lord Oxford – escaped?

MAUDELYN: Yes, sir.

RICHARD [*after a pause*]: You may leave the candles.

MAUDELYN [*pausing by the door*]: Is there anything I can do for you, sir?

RICHARD: No, you have done what you could. [*He slightly accentuates the first 'you'.*] Wait! Has anyone told the Queen of this message?

MAUDELYN: No, sir.

RICHARD: Then find her, and say that I should like to see her.

[*Exit* MAUDELYN. RICHARD *turns to the window again. The candles grow brighter as the daylight fades.*]

[*Enter, without warning,* ROBERT DE VERE, *pale, harassed, and dirty. He shuts the door and stands leaning against it.* RICHARD *turns as if not quite sure that someone has really entered.*]

[*In gladness*] Robert! [*In fear for him*] Robert, are you crazy when you come here!

DE VERE: I thought I should go crazy if I didn't.

RICHARD [*remembering and withdrawing a little*]: Well?

DE VERE [*after a pause*]: I'm sorry, Richard.

RICHARD [*bitterly*]: Are you by any chance *apologizing*?

DE VERE: When one has no excuse there is only apology.

RICHARD: And so you are *sorry* for throwing away the hopes of half England.

DE VERE: Richard, I am not excusing or explaining. But I must tell you how it happened. That is why I came here. I felt that I must tell you myself. I don't know why. I never did like other people's explanations of me, did I? It isn't that I want to minimize it. I just want to tell you myself.

RICHARD: Is there any more to tell than I have already been told?

DE VERE: They've told you we were defeated?

RICHARD: Routed was the word.

DE VERE: Yes, routed. The mist was so thick that one couldn't see more than three horses' length in any direction. The bridge looked deserted, and we went down to it. Then Henry appeared out of the fog without warning, and took us on the flank. It was not going to be a fight, it was going to be a massacre, hemmed in there between Henry and the bridge. If I could have believed in the possibility of winning, I might have led them. As it was, I could only see the futility of the slaughter. They were a fine lot to look at, Richard. They made a brave sight, all those days, marching down through the Midlands, four thousand of them. And now in ten minutes they would be masses of mangled flesh – all for nothing. We couldn't win, caught as we were. It was murder to let them fight.

RICHARD: And was the four thousand so perfect that you could not spare two as scouts to reconnoitre?

DE VERE: I may be a failure, but I'm not a fool. Of course we reconnoitred the bridge. The scouts came back to say that there was no one there. Time was important to us, and I thought we could risk it. I was wrong; that is all. I made a mistake in taking them to the bridge, but not in refusing to fight. If they were all dead tonight the situation would be the same.

RICHARD: So you advised them to surrender. Why didn't you surrender with them?

DE VERE: To Henry!

RICHARD: Molyneux did.

DE VERE: Yes, I have heard. They killed him. Would you have preferred me dead, Richard?

RICHARD [*in a burst*]: Yes! Oh, God, yes, a thousand times! I could have remembered you with pride then, dead with your honour safe.

DE VERE: My honour! Richard, you talk like your father. Do you expect me to fall on my sword because my troops had to surrender?

RICHARD: You ran away. 'Lord Oxford fled', says my page. A Vere bolting across the fields like a frightened rabbit! It is a sweet picture. The Duke of Ireland escaping. Troops in confusion may be noticed in the rear. You coward! You paltry coward!

DE VERE: I came to apologize for my bad generalship, but it seems that I must apologize for being alive.

RICHARD: You deserted your men when you had led them into a trap. You were trusted to rescue your friends in London, whose only hope was in you. And, when you failed, your only thought was your own skin. Robert de Vere! [*He turns away to the window.*]

DE VERE [*after a pause*]: Perhaps you are right, Richard. You had always a habit of being right when you were being most unreasonable. I know that I should have stayed there. But I couldn't do it. I wanted to live. And so I – ran away. Now I have confessed it.

RICHARD [*in a fury*]: Who wanted you to confess it? Curse

you, who wanted you to confess it? Do you think I like the
spectacle? Do you think it makes it more bearable for me
to see you humble yourself? Why come to me with your
excuses and abasement? Take them to those who find
interest in them!

DE VERE: Very well. I must go in any case, if I am even yet
to save my own skin. And, strange as it may seem, life is
still desirable. If I get away, it is unlikely that we shall meet
again. [*He pauses hopefully, his eyes on* RICHARD, *who has once
more turned to the window.*] Good-bye, Richard.

[RICHARD *does not answer, and* DE VERE *turns to the door.
Enter* ANNE, *and comes face to face with* DE VERE.]

ANNE: Robert! What is it? We thought you had escaped!

DE VERE: I had to see Richard first.

[*She looks past him to* RICHARD, *and understands that the
interview has been stormy.* RICHARD'S *back is eloquent.*]

ANNE: You aren't hurt?

DE VERE: Oh, don't.

ANNE: I didn't mean that. You know I didn't. What are you
going to do now? Where are you going?

DE VERE: I am getting a boat from the Essex coast. No one
will look for me in Gloucester's country. My unpopularity
will for once be a blessing. [*He tries to smile at her.*]

ANNE [*hurt by the smile, putting out her hand impulsively*]: Poor
Robert!

DE VERE [*simply, without the usual façade*]: My dear lady Anne.
I have to thank you for many kindnesses. Most of all, you
gave me Agnes, and made our marriage possible.

ANNE: Poor Agnes! What will she do?

DE VERE: She is coming with me.

ANNE: Be kind to her, Robert. It won't be easy for either of
you in these friendless times. But she has a gallant spirit.
And I know how happy one can be, in spite of all adversity.
Good-bye.

DE VERE: Good-bye. I wish I knew a blessing to say over you.

[*He hesitates, and looks back at* RICHARD, *still standing with his back to the room.*] Good-bye, Richard.

[RICHARD *does not answer, and* DE VERE *goes out.*]

RICHARD [*without turning*]: So you know?

ANNE: Yes; your page is crying his heart out on the stairs. He told me. Everything is lost, it seems.

RICHARD: Yes, everything is lost. And I have said dreadful things to Robert.

ANNE: He knows you didn't mean them, Richard.

RICHARD: I did mean them! Every word of them! He is a coward, a paltry feeble thing with no more courage than a child. He had four thousand men, and he was afraid to fight, afraid!

ANNE: No; his silly tender heart betrayed him. I know. That is the truth about Robert. What he saw when Henry and his men came out of the mist was not the glory of taking a risk, but the certainty of his men's deaths. His imagination betrayed him. You rail against him for the very thing that made him your friend.

RICHARD: And at a time like this he can think of Agnes!

ANNE: Oh, Richard, don't be ungenerous. Agnes is the one precious thing he can save from the wreck. The world is falling about his ears, and you grudge him Agnes. Think for a moment what the future is going to be for him. All his life he is going to remember that moment at Radcot Bridge. It is going to be a nightmare that he can never escape. Robert is not the man to forget, or forgive himself. You know that. You don't usually have to be told these things, Richard.

RICHARD: I know. I know what you say is true. I keep saying it to myself. But it doesn't rid me of the anger with him – the despair! It isn't because he lost us the battle; not altogether. It is because he was Robert, and he didn't fight!

ANNE: Your pedestal was too high, Richard. No one could have stayed on it. You must not blame Robert for that.

[*She moves to a chair and sits down with a small, sobbing sigh.*]

RICHARD: Where have you been all the afternoon? I wanted you.

ANNE: I have been to the Duke of Gloucester.

RICHARD: To Gloucester!

ANNE: To beg for Burley's life.

RICHARD: Anne! And did he – what did he say?

ANNE: It was no use. [*After a pause, as if living it over again*] I went on my knees to him.

RICHARD [*humbly*]: Anne! You make me ashamed of myself.

ANNE: Why? You are the King. You couldn't kneel to him. But I am a woman.

RICHARD: And he wouldn't listen?

ANNE: He said that it would be more suitable if I prayed for you and for myself.

RICHARD: That is all, then? There is nothing else we can do?

ANNE: Nothing.

RICHARD: How can they do it! In cold blood! A man who has never harmed them. Gloucester will take all Robert's lands. And the people throw up their caps at sight of him. 'Long live Gloucester, the man of action. He kills for his gains, instead of taxing us.' And, because I kill nobody, I am a fool. But I am being educated. They are teaching a willing pupil. To become an expert in murder cannot be so difficult.

ANNE: Richard, my dear – –

RICHARD: I swear to you, Anne, I swear to you now, that one day I shall be revenged on all of them. Before I die I shall pay my debt, and my friends' debt, to each single one of them. Gloucester, Arundel, Mowbray, Henry. Before I die I shall be King in deed as well as in name; I swear it. As for Gloucester – [*his passionate utterance sinks almost to a whisper*] he had better have spared Burley. He had better have spared him!

ANNE: It is difficult to understand just why the world has fallen on top of us like this, isn't it? We did so little wrong.

RICHARD: You forget our crimes. We wasted money on beauty instead of on war. We were extravagant – –

ANNE: I heard a piece of news when I was waiting to see Gloucester.

RICHARD: He kept you waiting?

ANNE: Oh, yes. He is that kind of man. That didn't make me angry.

RICHARD [*almost wistfully*]: Nothing makes you very angry, Anne.

ANNE: Some things do – terribly.

RICHARD: What was your news?

ANNE: Parliament have voted Gloucester and Arundel twenty thousand pounds.

RICHARD: What! [*There is a pause while he savours this in full. Then, in a quiet, amused tone*] How Robert would have laughed! [*As the situation overcomes him*] How Robert would have – –

[*He breaks down, covers his face, and falls sobbing into a chair.*]
[ANNE *comes to him and puts her arms round him.*]

CURTAIN

ACT TWO

SCENE I

An ante-room in the King's Palace of Sheen, three years later. On the right is the door to the inner chamber, to the left the door to the corridor; at the back a doorway to the courtyard.

There are present two people. One is the DUKE OF GLOUCESTER, *obviously waiting and obviously resentful. The other is* MAUDELYN, *the King's secretary, who is the page from the previous Act.* MAUDELYN, *now about twenty, has discarded his gay silks for a clerk's sober habit. He is seated unobtrusively at a table by the wall, busy with documents.*

GLOUCESTER [*calling to* MAUDELYN]: You! How much longer am I to be kept waiting?

MAUDELYN [*politely*]: Lord Arundel is with the King, sir.

GLOUCESTER: Arundel! What does the King want with Lord Arundel?

MAUDELYN: That is something outside my business, my lord. [*Resumes his writing.*]

GLOUCESTER [*muttering*]: Impudent young puppy! [*Looking again at* MAUDELYN] I remember you. [*Coming down to him, surprised*] You used to be Richard's page.

MAUDELYN: Yes, my lord.

GLOUCESTER: And a disgusting little fop of a page, too! [*Flicking the clerk's dress contemptuously*] And was your intended armour too harsh for your tender skin?

MAUDELYN [*more reminiscent than boastful*]: I used to beat the other pages in the lists.

GLOUCESTER: Then why the clerk's dress?

MAUDELYN: Because it keeps me near the King, my lord.

GLOUCESTER: That is a strange reason.

MAUDELYN: I had not hoped you would understand it, my lord.

[*Enter* ANNE, *on her way to the inner chamber. She sees* GLOUCESTER, *pauses, and bows coldly. She hesitates.*]

ANNE [*to* MAUDELYN]: Is the King not alone?

MAUDELYN: Lord Arundel is with the King, madam.

ANNE [*turning to go*]: I will come back.

GLOUCESTER: You are not looking well, madam. Does the hot weather not agree with you?

ANNE: I am not very well. It is nothing much. A little chill.

GLOUCESTER [*with more relish than solicitude*]: Have you seen a doctor, madam? Plague is very prevalent this summer.

ANNE [*coldly*]: It is nothing, thank you. [*More conciliating*] Please do not say to the King that I do not look well. I do not want him to be worried today.

GLOUCESTER: And why not today?

ANNE: Because today, I think, he is very nearly happy. [*Considering him*] Do you know what happiness is, my lord?

GLOUCESTER: I trust so.

ANNE: I have often wondered. You handle such a precious thing so carelessly. But it is a hardy plant, happiness. Joy – ah, no. When joy is killed it dies for ever. But happiness one can grow again. I will come back. [*Exit.*]

GLOUCESTER [*with a contemptuous shrug*]: Feverish!

[*Enter from the inner chamber the* EARL OF ARUNDEL. *While he is greeting* GLOUCESTER, MAUDELYN, *who since the first mention of the* QUEEN'S *looks has exhibited growing anxiety, follows the* QUEEN *out.*]

ARUNDEL: Gloucester! So you've been summoned to Sheen, too!

GLOUCESTER: I have. And I cool my heels for an hour while you have an audience. What did he want of you that took so long?

ARUNDEL: He wanted my *advice*! I don't like it. I don't like it at all!

GLOUCESTER: Don't like having your advice asked? You're unique.

ARUNDEL: I distrust meekness. And most of all I distrust the King's meekness. [*Warming at sight of* GLOUCESTER's *smile*] When Richard smiles I feel as if I were walking through long grass in a snake country. And today – – There is something wrong, Gloucester. He summons me from London, and then talks politely about ships and tonnage. And all the time they are smiling at something else, he and Rutland and Montague. Gloucester, do you think Richard can have something up his sleeve?

GLOUCESTER: That would be the only justification for the sleeves. Don't be ridiculous, Arundel! Richard is just where he was two years ago, and that is in our hands.

ARUNDEL: Things are not *exactly* as they were two years ago, my friend. [*Watching the advent of someone in the corridor*] Here is at least one weathercock which shows a change of wind!

GLOUCESTER [*following his glance, morosely*]: Mowbray. Yes, I'd forgotten him.

[*Enter* MOWBRAY, *very magnificent, on his way to the inner chamber.*]

So Mowbray comes to Court again!

MOWBRAY: I have that privilege.

GLOUCESTER: Is it the Plantagenet charm that blinds you, or those acres in Wales?

MOWBRAY: The King has been gracious enough to grant me the estates I claimed, and I am grateful. That is all.

ARUNDEL: And the King smiles, and you are pleased!

MOWBRAY: Why not? It is pleasant to be friendly again.

GLOUCESTER: You fool, Thomas Mowbray. Do you think Richard will ever forget that you helped to destroy Robert de Vere?

MOWBRAY: That is all past. If the King had not forgiven my part in that, he would not have supported me over those estates.

GLOUCESTER: You talk like a child. Because a bright toy is dangled before your eyes, you trust the hand that holds it. You make a mistake, my friend!

MOWBRAY [*slowly*]: It may not be I who makes the mistake. [*Abruptly*] I think I am quite capable of managing my own affairs, my lords. [*Exit to inner chamber.*]

GLOUCESTER: God, what clothes! How the fellow apes Richard!

ARUNDEL: I wish I could see behind the silk coat. Was it those Welsh fields that brought Mowbray to Court, or does he know something that we don't?

GLOUCESTER: In heaven's name, Arundel!

ARUNDEL: Has it ever occurred to you that Richard might be an enemy worthy of respect?

GLOUCESTER: That fool! That scented fop! A man who takes an hour to choose a pair of gloves! You must be ill, Arundel, that your knees fail before that silken packet of whims and fancies.

ARUNDEL [*angry*]: My knees don't fail! I hate the creature as I hate the – the French. I hate him all the more now that he gives me cause to wonder.

GLOUCESTER: What cause does he give you? Because he is meek? He had better be meek! Without backing he can do nothing. And where will he find backing in England?

ARUNDEL [*doubtfully*]: In England, no. [*With no great conviction*] There is Lancaster, of course.

GLOUCESTER: As long as there is a crown to be had in Spain, Lancaster will stay in Spain.

ARUNDEL: Yes, I know. I am only searching for reasons for the King's attitude. I don't like the way he calls me Admiral.

GLOUCESTER: You are the Admiral, aren't you?

ARUNDEL: I don't like the way he says it.

GLOUCESTER: My dear Arundel, you need a tonic – –

[*Enter from the inner chamber the* KING, *his hand on the arm of* EDWARD, EARL OF RUTLAND (*the Duke of York's son; a girlish youth, very pretty*), *and followed by* MOWBRAY *and* SIR JOHN MONTAGUE. MONTAGUE *is slightly older than the other three, and looks what he is: a poet, a scholar, and, on occasion, an efficient soldier.*]

RICHARD: Ah, my dear uncle! Discussing ships and tonnage with the Admiral? The Admiral is so interesting on ships and tonnage. I am sorry to have kept you waiting. Has the Queen not come?

GLOUCESTER: She was here a moment ago, but went away again when she found that I was waiting to see you.

RICHARD: I see. Edward, find the Queen and bring her here in five minutes. [*Exit* RUTLAND.] Mowbray, see that your father-in-law has some wine before he goes. You must have much to say to each other. [*As* ARUNDEL *and* MOWBRAY *are going out*] When next I see you, my lord, I shall have found a use for your ships, I hope.

[ARUNDEL *throws a puzzled glance at* GLOUCESTER, *which* GLOUCESTER *fails to return, and goes out with* MOWBRAY.]

GLOUCESTER [*indicating* MONTAGUE, *lingering by the court-yard entrance*]: Is Sir John Montague's presence necessary?

RICHARD: Not necessary, but pleasant. Sir John's presence sweetens the atmosphere when needful, like a bunch of herbs.

GLOUCESTER: Well? You sent for me?

RICHARD: I sent for you yesterday.

GLOUCESTER: Yes. I told your messenger that I was busy. I have the burden of this State on my shoulders.

RICHARD: I think there are ways of lightening that burden. I sent for you to ask you a question of some importance. How old am I?

GLOUCESTER: How old? Twenty-three, I suppose.

RICHARD: You acknowledge that I am twenty-three?

GLOUCESTER: Certainly.

RICHARD: In that case I am of age; and since I am not insane, I am fit, *by law*, to share in the government of the country and in the choosing of my ministers. Will you tell the Treasurer, Bishop Gilbert, and the Chancellor, Bishop Arundel, that I require their resignations?

GLOUCESTER: Resign! I don't know what good you think you are going to do by foisting a whim like this on the council. If you hope that the country will accept one of your own − −

RICHARD: In their places I have appointed Brantingham and Wykeham. You look disappointed? It *is* difficult to find objections to Brantingham and Wykeham, isn't it? I make no other changes for the moment, except [*he signs, unseen by* GLOUCESTER, *to* MONTAGUE, *who goes out*] to add one more to the council. A month ago I sent to ask an old acquaintance of mine to return from abroad.

GLOUCESTER [*quickly*]: Robert de Vere is dead − −

RICHARD: I don't forget it.

GLOUCESTER: And so is De la Pole. Who is there − −
    [*Enter the* DUKE OF LANCASTER.]

RICHARD: Oh, there you are. We were speaking of you.

GLOUCESTER [*astounded*]: Lancaster!

LANCASTER [*advancing smiling and quizzical to his brother*]: Well, Thomas, how are you?
    [*They shake hands.*]

GLOUCESTER: So you're back.

LANCASTER: Yesterday.

GLOUCESTER: Have you deserted your army, or have they deserted you?

LANCASTER: Still the same Thomas, as tactful as an angry wasp! My army is coming after me as soon as transport is arranged.

GLOUCESTER [*sourly*]: You had little luck in Spain, if all reports are true.

LANCASTER: No; too much fever. It played havoc with my troops. But I made myself so much of a nuisance that they have given me a fortune in return for my claim to the crown.

GLOUCESTER: So you have traded your royal ambitions for money.

LANCASTER: Yes, but I have also married my daughter Katherine to the heir.

[RICHARD *gives a small laugh.*]

GLOUCESTER: I fail to see the joke.

RICHARD: My condolences.

LANCASTER: Richard has asked me to be one of the council again, so we are to be colleagues.

RICHARD: It will give me much pleasure to have you both there.

LANCASTER [*perfectly understanding*]: I have no doubt of it. [*Looking at the* KING] You have grown up, Richard.

RICHARD [*not smiling*]: Yes, I have grown up.

LANCASTER [*hastily abandoning the subject*]: Another advantage which I plucked from my misfortunes in Spain is a peace treaty.

RICHARD: And in the next year or so we shall have peace with France, as well as with Scotland.

GLOUCESTER: With France! Is that maggot still alive in your brain?

RICHARD: More than alive. It breeds.

GLOUCESTER: And are you going to countenance a policy like that, Lancaster?

LANCASTER: I think, do you know, that I am. Richard has been good enough to suggest creating me Duke of Guienne. If I go to Guienne as Duke it will be enormously to my advantage to have a peaceful France round me.

GLOUCESTER: I see. I see. Well, it may suit the Duke of

Guienne to have peace with France, but it may not suit the people of England.

RICHARD: The people of England are less frightened by the idea than they used to be. They grow used to it. Presently they will adopt it quite happily, and imagine they fathered it. Some day they may even impeach you for suggesting war, Gloucester. What a heavenly thought!

[*Enter the* QUEEN, *with* RUTLAND, *followed by* MONTAGUE.]

ANNE [*to* LANCASTER]: My dear uncle! I am sorry that I missed you yesterday.

LANCASTER [*saluting her*]: You are lovelier than ever, madam. You seem to have lost your roses, but the lilies are very becoming.

ANNE: Lilies are more fashionable. Fleurs-de-lis are our token these days.

RICHARD: And this is your nephew Edward.

LANCASTER: York's son!

RICHARD: Yes, the Earl of Rutland.

LANCASTER: Why, you were just a baby four years ago.

RICHARD: He still is. [RUTLAND *protests.*] He likes better to play with my greyhound than attend to his duties.

LANCASTER: What are his duties?

RICHARD: To amuse me. Sir John I think you saw yesterday.

LANCASTER: Yes. But I had Sir John in Spain with me.

MONTAGUE [*puzzled*]: In Spain?

LANCASTER: In my pocket. I read your poems in Castile, John. They were water in a thirsty land.

GLOUCESTER [*to* RICHARD]: With your permission I shall take my leave. I presume that everything I was sent for to hear has been said?

RICHARD [*grinning unashamedly*]: Yes, I don't think I forgot anything. But won't you wait for dinner?

GLOUCESTER: No, I must get back to London.

RICHARD: It is going to be a very special dinner in Lancaster's honour. The cooks have been inventing stuffings all day.

GLOUCESTER: Eating is not one of my amusements.

RICHARD: No, I know. A hunk of cold beef on a bone is your meat. But that is a lack in you, not a virtue. Don't pride yourself on it. Good-bye. [GLOUCESTER *takes his leave.*] Edward, take the Duke of Gloucester to his horse.

LANCASTER: With the King's permission, I shall see you go. I want to hear all the news of your family. How is Humphrey?

[LANCASTER, GLOUCESTER, *and* RUTLAND *go out.*]

RICHARD [*flinging an arm exultantly round* MONTAGUE, *and appealing to* ANNE, *between laughter and triumph*]: Who says I am not a king?

ANNE: Are you happy, Richard?

RICHARD: I begin to know the taste of it again. But there is a feast of it coming. We shall be throwing happiness to the dogs presently, Anne, we shall have so much of it.

ANNE: You will have deserved it, Richard. You have been very patient, and patience comes hard for you, doesn't it?

RICHARD: It is a sweet sight to see Mowbray make his obeisance. Stumbling over the carpet, and not looking in my eyes. A few thousand acres of barren land – that is the price of Mowbray's allegiance.

ANNE: Perhaps he was glad to come back. He loved you once.

RICHARD: I remember. So much that he bit me like a jealous cur. [*Brightening*] And now that Lancaster is back, Henry will come to Court and bend his thick knee too. Anne, I've been thinking. Now that peace with France is coming, don't you think we might do something about Ireland?

ANNE: Isn't one always doing something about Ireland?

RICHARD: Yes – patching! I want to find out why the patches don't last. I want to know why the English settlers in Ireland always become more Irish than the Irish.

MONTAGUE: I think that is due less to the charm of Ireland than to the indifference of the English. We have a habit of raising our eyebrows, you know, at anyone who chooses to live out of England.

RICHARD: The indifference of the English? I think you are right, John. That *is* why we fail. [*To* ANNE] Now this morning I had a letter from an Irish chief who calls himself Art – Art – – [*He appeals to* MONTAGUE.]

MONTAGUE: Art Macmurrough.

RICHARD: Art Macmurrough. John, do go and find that letter; it was very amusing. [*To* ANNE, *as* MONTAGUE *goes out*] He wrote to me as one king to another – very sensibly on the whole. I should like to talk to that fellow, Anne. I should like to talk to all of them. Find out what they think and why. John is right, you know. We take no interest in them. How can the Irish be loyal to a King and Queen they never see? Anne, I've been thinking. Anne, wouldn't it be a fine idea to make pilgrimage to Ireland? You could teach the women to wear – – Anne, you're not listening!

ANNE: Yes, of course I am. [*She shivers*] It's cold, isn't it?

RICHARD: Cold! I'm on fire. I'm all blazing inside as if I were lit up. Think, Anne! Soon we – – [*He understands fully what she has said.*] Cold! In this weather? What is the matter with you?

ANNE: I don't know. I have shivers up and down my back, and I feel – strange.

RICHARD: Anne, are you ill?

ANNE: No, not ill. But I – my head feels so strange and light, and my feet feel as if they were shod like horses'.

RICHARD: Don't, Anne; you frighten me.

ANNE: There isn't anything to be frightened of. Besides, Richard of Bordeaux is frightened of nothing. Hasn't he faced his enemies for three years and outfaced them in the end!

RICHARD [*in a low voice*]: There are some things I – – [*Sitting down by her*] You aren't really ill, are you, Anne? (*He puts an arm round her.*] Shall I send for your women?

ANNE [*leaning against him and closing her eyes*]: No, stay there. It is so comfortable. [*Sniffing his coat*] Is that the new perfume? It is lovely. You always smell nice, Richard. The first time I saw you – do you remember? In the Abbey – I thought you looked like a flower. But I didn't know you had so many scents then! Darling Richard.

RICHARD: How long have you been feeling ill? Why didn't you tell me?

ANNE: I'm not ill. I got chilled at the pageant yesterday, that is all.

[*Enter* RUTLAND. ANNE *starts up at sound of the opening door.*]

RUTLAND: Richard, I'll go to Ireland, I'll go to hell for you, but don't ask me to be charming to Gloucester for you. There are limits to my – –

RICHARD: Send the Queen's waiting-woman here at once.

RUTLAND [*sobered by* RICHARD'S *look*]: Yes, sir. [*Exit.*]

ANNE: Why do you like Edward so much?

RICHARD: I don't know. He has great charm. Don't you think so?

ANNE: No.

RICHARD: You don't like Edward, do you? Jealous?

ANNE: I was never jealous of Robert. He was more worthy of you. It's funny how things are near one minute and miles away the next.

RICHARD: Shut your eyes and don't look at them. Oh, Anne!

ANNE: It is true about the peace with France, isn't it? Lancaster is going to help with that?

RICHARD: Yes, our dream is coming true. We'll have the most marvellous celebration that this country has ever seen, on the day that peace is signed.

ANNE [*childishly*]: Not a pageant. I get cold at pageants.

RICHARD: No, not a pageant. We'll think of something that

no one has thought of before. We'll search the world for beautiful things. We'll – –

[*Enter* RUTLAND *with a* WAITING-WOMAN.]

Anne, you must go to bed.

ANNE: Oh, not to bed. What about Lancaster's dinner?

RICHARD: To bed. And at once. In fifteen minutes I shall come along to see that you are there.

ANNE: You are a tyrant, Richard. Do you know it? You bully your most faithful and loving subject. Perhaps it would be wise to go to bed. You'll come soon, Richard?

RICHARD: In fifteen minutes.

[ANNE *attempts to rise, assisted by her* WAITING-WOMAN, *but collapses, and* MAUDELYN, *who has appeared with a* DOCTOR, *brings him forward.* RICHARD *moves away to let the* DOCTOR *come. As he comes to her again, the* DOCTOR, *having seen* ANNE, *prevents him.*]

DOCTOR: No, sir. You must keep away.

RICHARD [*surprised and indignant at the restraint*]: What do you mean? How dare you lay hands on me? Do you know who I am?

DOCTOR: It is because you are the King, sir, that you must keep away. You have a duty to your subjects, and the contagion is deadly.

RICHARD [*after a pause, in a horrified whisper*]: Oh, no! No!

[*The others –* RUTLAND, LANCASTER, MONTAGUE, *and others who have come crowding in at the news of the Queen's illness – move involuntarily away from her. Only the* WAITING-WOMAN, *after her first instinctive withdrawal, moves back to her with a cry of grief.*]

[*In sudden complete realization, desperate*] Anne! Anne!

[*He flings himself against the* DOCTOR'S *detaining arm.*]

CURTAIN

SCENE 2

The scene is the same. The time, two years later. MAUDELYN *is writing at the same little table.* SIR JOHN MONTAGUE *is lounging near by and occasionally casting an eye over* MAUDELYN'S *shoulder. The* DUKE OF YORK *and his son,* RUTLAND, *are chatting together; and the* DUKE OF GLOUCESTER *and the* EARL OF ARUNDEL, *a little apart, are listening to the conversation.*

RUTLAND [*concluding a tale, to* YORK]: Two of the kings didn't know what forks were for, and a third tried to eat his plate. Oh, you should have been there, father. Ireland was gorgeous! And there was another called – called – – [*To* GLOUCESTER] Uncle, what was the name of the king we gave the clothes to? You remember!

GLOUCESTER: No, I don't. I didn't come to Sheen to spend the time gossiping about Ireland. I came on business. And, now that the business is nearly finished, I must go. [*Looking disparagingly at the desolate-looking room*] A nice cheerful place to spend a winter afternoon!

RUTLAND: Oh, well, the name doesn't matter. [*Continues his gossiping to* YORK.]

MONTAGUE [*half to himself, half to* MAUDELYN]: It was cheerful enough two years ago.

MAUDELYN [*pausing in his writing and staring in front of him*]: Yes. She – she liked this room.

MONTAGUE: Because of the little tree in the courtyard.

MAUDELYN: And because you could see the river from the window.

YORK [*to* RUTLAND]: But the food, my dear Edward, the food must have been very – –

RUTLAND: Oh, no; we taught them how to cook, too. It was most amusing.

ARUNDEL: And did Gloucester find Ireland so amusing?

GLOUCESTER: Amusing! To see the King of England feasting barbarians and presenting them with gifts? Knighting traitors instead of quartering them? It turned my stomach.

MONTAGUE: At least we have achieved what no one has achieved for two hundred years: goodwill as well as peace in Ireland.

GLOUCESTER: The mistake you all make is to imagine that the Irish want peace. They are only waiting until our backs are turned.

ARUNDEL: London didn't like the sound of those banquets very much. The usual insane extravagance!

MONTAGUE: A military expedition would have cost ten times as much, including several hundred lives, and achieved nothing.

[*Enter* MOWBRAY, *with a paper, which he lays on the table for* MAUDELYN'S *use.*]

MOWBRAY: Has the King not come back?

GLOUCESTER: No, he hasn't. I had expected to be halfway back to London by now. It shows a distinct lack of consideration to leave us like this when – –

YORK: The message may have been important.

ARUNDEL: Yes, it may have been a message of love from the French which had to be answered without delay.

GLOUCESTER: Even that could surely have waited until we had decided the date of Parliament. That was all that remained to be done. They could have answered a dozen letters in this time.

ARUNDEL: I expect that he and Lancaster are deciding what time the sun should rise tomorrow.

MOWBRAY [*looking round, as if he had missed* LANCASTER *for the first time*]: Lancaster? Perhaps I had better go and find them. The King may have forgotten that the business wasn't finished. [*Exit.*]

ARUNDEL [*looking after him*]: Or been too long with Lancaster?

GLOUCESTER: Forgotten that the business wasn't finished!

YORK [*pacifically*]: This is the King's first visit to Sheen since the Queen's death. He is bound to find it a little upsetting.

GLOUCESTER: Pose, my dear brother, all pose! Richard likes his moods as becoming as his clothes.

RUTLAND: How dare you say that the King could pretend about a thing like that! You know quite well that all the time he was in Ireland he could never bear to – –

MONTAGUE: Rutland! My dear Edward, that gage is hardly worth picking up, surely?

RUTLAND: He shouldn't say such things. He knows they are lies. And to lie about a thing like that – something that – –! How can he!

[*Enter the* KING *with* LANCASTER *and* MOWBRAY *following.*]

RICHARD: I had not forgotten you, my lords, but I had other business.

GLOUCESTER: I should have thought that private business with Lancaster could have waited on public affairs. It is inconvenient enough for me to come all the way to Sheen for a council without wasting time at the end of it.

RICHARD: Be assured, my lord. You will never come to Sheen again.

GLOUCESTER: No?

RICHARD: I have given orders that the place shall be pulled down.

GLOUCESTER: Pull down the palace of Sheen? Are you crazy? What wantonness of destruction is this?

RICHARD: What I destroy is bricks and mortar. What is there in that to make *Gloucester* squeamish? About the date for assembling Parliament, my lords, would a fortnight hence be too soon?

ARUNDEL: The sooner the better. It is time that some attention was paid to England.

RICHARD: If all reports are true, England is well content. I may even yet become popular, it seems.

GLOUCESTER: With Calais just across the water? Let me tell you that 'God save Richard' still means 'God save Calais' to an Englishman.

RICHARD: To a Londoner, perhaps. But London is not England.

GLOUCESTER: In matters of policy it is.

RICHARD: Oh? Then why does my lord of Arundel waste his time in – Cheshire?

ARUNDEL [*disconcerted*]: In Cheshire! I have not been nearer Cheshire than the north of Wales.

RICHARD: Then rumour slanders you most foully, my lord. We must investigate the matter when Parliament meets. Shall we say the 25th? [*As the others agree*] The business will be mainly routine.

GLOUCESTER [*preparing to go*]: But not entirely routine, I hope. There will surely be the matter of a foreign alliance. The sooner you marry again the better.

[*There is a moment of complete silence.*]

RICHARD: You expect me to protest. I am going to disappoint you. I am going to marry again. At the earliest possible moment I shall marry the daughter of the King of France.

GLOUCESTER: A French alliance!

ARUNDEL: Marry a child! A child of eight!

YORK: My dear Richard – – ! You can't be serious.

RICHARD: After fifty years of war we have achieved peace with France. I am going to see to it that that peace is not broken in my lifetime.

YORK: And for that you are prepared to marry a child, too young to be either companion or wife to you? Is it wise, sir? There are other things to be considered. There is – there is the matter of an heir, for instance.

RICHARD [*savagely*]: Have my uncles not children enough!

[*Recovering*] There is no need for argument, my lords. The affair is practically settled.

GLOUCESTER: And what will the people say when you present them with a child as Queen, and a French brat at that?

MONTAGUE: They'll crowd the streets to see her, and tell each other how sweet she is. You forget the English passion for children, Gloucester. For once you miscalculate.

MOWBRAY [*with menace*]: It won't be the last time that Gloucester miscalculates.

LANCASTER: If you look at the matter without prejudice, my lords, I think you must see that the results of this alliance are likely to be very happy for England.

ARUNDEL [*beside himself*]: Happy! To have every scullion in France sniggering at us! To know that it is said everywhere that our King is so little a man that he must – –

MOWBRAY: Shut your mouth, Arundel, or I'll shut it for you!

ARUNDEL: Yes, Mowbray is famous for his strong-arm methods, isn't he? But I'm not afraid of you, Mowbray. I'm not afraid of any of you. I protest against this ridiculous marriage, and the alliance it is supposed to further. We are being made a plaything for France, and no one protests. The King and Lancaster are farming the country, and this council is a mockery.

YORK: My dear Lord Arundel – –

ARUNDEL: Be quiet! If you had stomach for anything but food, you would be protesting too. It is iniquitous that this council should be merely an echo for whatever the King and Lancaster choose to speak.

RICHARD: If that is how Lord Arundel feels about the council, the obvious course is resignation.

GLOUCESTER: Why should Arundel resign merely because he disapproves! You refuse free speech to anyone who disagrees with you.

RICHARD: I have always found you both marvellously free of speech.

RUTLAND: What the King objects to is not free speech, but bad manners.

ARUNDEL: Manners are being the ruin of this country. The mode is everything, and the method nothing. And now you think that free wine and coronation processions will blind the people to what you are doing. But I warn you, you make a mistake. The people will find a coronation little compensation for a French alliance. [*Taking his leave*] With your permission – – [*Exit.*]

YORK: Lord Arundel is hasty, sir. I trust you will treat anything he says as the utterance of his anger, and not of his considered judgement.

RICHARD [*dryly*]: I have great experience of Lord Arundel's considered judgement.

GLOUCESTER: Arundel has warned you, and I warn you! You propose to make us a joke for the whole of Europe, do you? You propose to sell us to France, in a marriage treaty, do you? Well, you can't do it. You can't do it, I tell you! You may be lords of Parliament, and sure of your majority in council, but you are not yet lords of what the common people think. I may be helpless here in council, but I am not yet helpless out of it. If you want me I shall be at Pleshy. [*Exit.*]

RICHARD [*wearily*]: Well, my dear Lancaster, we seem to have stirred a hornets' nest.

LANCASTER: More buzz than sting, I think.

RICHARD: The buzz is sufficiently distracting.

MONTAGUE: It has been a long day, sir. Gloucester will seem less tiresome after dinner, when you are less tired.

RICHARD [*bitterly*]: I am very tough, I find. It amazes me, sometimes, to find how much a human being is capable of surviving. Are those papers ready, Maudelyn?

MAUDELYN: They will be in a moment, sir.

RICHARD: I shall sign them now, then. Don't wait, my lords. Perhaps you can convert the Duke of York to our French alliance, Lancaster.

LANCASTER: I shall try. [*He goes out with* YORK, *followed by* MONTAGUE.]

[*The others,* MOWBRAY *and* RUTLAND, *who, since the* DUKE OF GLOUCESTER'S *exit, have been talking together, linger at a sign from the* KING.]

MOWBRAY: So Gloucester is bent on making trouble.

RUTLAND: Is he ever anything else? Has he not tried to wreck every idea we ever had as soon as we launched it?

MOWBRAY: We've been very patient, Richard. We should be fools to wait any longer. Say the word, and I shall see that he is quiet in future. I shall do the job myself.

RICHARD: You were always a bloodthirsty wretch, Mowbray.

MOWBRAY: I know how to kill an adder when I see one.

RICHARD: It is of Arundel that I want to speak to you. I think the time is ripe to deal with Arundel. I shall have him arrested tomorrow for treason. Five years ago he judged my friends traitors, on trumped-up charges. We shall not need to invent charges. He has had five years' rope to hang himself with. You two, with John Montague and two or three others, will be his accusers.

RUTLAND: Accuse Arundel! It would please me more than a dukedom.

RICHARD: You may get the dukedom too.

MOWBRAY: But what about Gloucester? Is he going free?

RICHARD [*almost caressingly*]: No, not free. No, I have been thinking. He has a great affection for Calais, it seems. He is besotted about it. Now, you are Captain of Calais, Thomas. And Gloucester is an old friend, not to say ally, of yours – –

MOWBRAY: Oh, Richard, I thought that was forgiven!

RICHARD: So perhaps it would be appropriate if you were to

show him Calais. Look after him well and show him the sights. Yes?

MOWBRAY: That is a good idea. Out of England. You are a genius, Richard.

RICHARD: His health has not been good lately, so look after him well. He might succumb unexpectedly.

RUTLAND: But will he go?

RICHARD: I shall go down to Pleshy and bring him back with me. Before we get to London you can join us, Mowbray, and persuade him to go to Calais with you. We can arrange the details at supper tonight.

[*Enter* LANCASTER.]

LANCASTER: Aren't you coming to dinner, Richard?

[*The conspirators melt away.*]

RICHARD: Coming, my good Lancaster, coming. Your impatience for the table does you credit at your age.

LANCASTER [*apprehensively*]: Richard, what are you plotting?

RICHARD [*arming* LANCASTER *to the door*]: Nothing but good, my dear uncle, nothing but good.

CURTAIN

SCENE 3

A street in London, evening, three weeks later. Two MEN *conversing. There are passers-by at frequent intervals, and, as they pass, the men pause in their conversation. They are very self-important and mysterious, and are greatly enjoying their solemnity.*

FIRST MAN: Well, I have it at first hand. My cousin knows the captain of the barge that took him off. He says one of Mowbray's men laughed and said, 'Take farewell of the Duke,

won't you? It may be a long time before you see him
again!'

SECOND MAN: I don't suppose there is any doubt that he
was – – [*He nods suggestively.*]

FIRST MAN: Well, as one man of the world to another, what
is there for us to think? And there is this other business – –
[*He pauses.*]

SECOND MAN: The treason affair, you mean?

FIRST MAN: That is what I mean. The two things hang
together, don't they?

SECOND MAN: Well, I must admit I don't approve of hole-
and-corner business, but I don't feel like shedding tears over
either of them. [*As they are joined by a third* MAN] Well,
Hobb?

THIRD MAN: Discussing the events of the day? What do *you*
think of them?

FIRST MAN: What is one to think? What *is* one to think?

THIRD MAN: It's pretty obvious, I should say, putting two
and two together.

FIRST MAN: That's what *I* say. My cousin knows the captain
of the barge that took them off, and he says that one of
Mowbray's men laughed and said: 'Take farewell of the
Duke, won't you? It will be a long time before you see
him again.' What are you to make of that?

SECOND MAN: Well, I can't help thinking that neither of
them was any loss. If everything that You Know Who
had done in his time was as sensible as this, he would get
more people to cry, 'God save him'.

THIRD MAN: Yes, the old man was a bad lot. And so was the
other, in a way. But that doesn't alter the fact that –
well – –

FIRST MAN: Did you hear that a certain Person went to
Pleshy himself, and led Someone into an ambush?

THIRD MAN: No! Is that true? Did you hear anything
definite as to what happened at Calais?

FIRST MAN: No, no; nobody knows that, of course. We can only put two and two together. But, as men of the world, I don't think it is difficult to – –

[*Enter, from opposite ends of the street, two* WOMEN. *One carries a sack of loaves slung over her shoulder, the other is carrying a basket of vegetables in front of her. As they pass on opposite sides of the street they notice each other, but are both too much burdened to stop.*]

WOMAN WITH LOAVES [*calling cheerfully as they pass*]: Hullo, Meg! All well? So they've murdered the Duke of Gloucester at last!

WOMAN WITH VEGETABLES: That they have! And good riddance, I say. Did they cut his throat?

WOMAN WITH LOAVES [*her voice rising to still more power as they draw apart*]: No, hit him over the head, they do say. Heard about Lord Arundel?

WOMAN WITH VEGETABLES: Who hasn't? I don't give much for his chances.

WOMAN WITH LOAVES: Nor me! What times! And flour gone up a halfpenny!

[*They go out at opposite sides. The three* MEN *stare after them in silence.*]

FIRST MAN [*after a pause*]: I always said that women had no discretion.

SECOND MAN: *Nor* accuracy.

THIRD MAN: *Nor* a sense of proportion.

[*They turn to their gossiping again.*]

CURTAIN

SCENE 4

A balcony in the King's Palace of Westminster, overlooking the hall; three years later. Night. Music from below and the sounds of a social gathering. Two PAGES *leaning by the railings and watching the scene in the hall.*

FIRST PAGE: I hate parties. The palace is never one's own until they are over. And then there is the clearing up.

SECOND PAGE: Did you see the King's face when I spilt the sauce over that fat old boy in the leather coat?

FIRST PAGE: Talking of fat, Henry is putting on weight, isn't he? He must do himself well on those crusades.

SECOND PAGE: He does himself well always. Hadn't he seven children before he was thirty?

FIRST PAGE: I think I can hear his voice booming from here. [*Peering in an effort to locate Henry*] Between his voice and the children I don't wonder his wife died.

SECOND PAGE: It's fun up here. You can see what everyone is doing. Now they're going to dance. Why do you think the De Courcy woman wears purple?

FIRST PAGE [*still peering into a different corner of the hall*]: Look! They're quarrelling!

SECOND PAGE: Who? Where?

FIRST PAGE [*pointing*]: Henry. He's quarrelling with Mowbray.

SECOND PAGE: So they are. Goodness! *Really* quarrelling.
 [*As the sound of the quarrel grows, the expressions of the faces of the* PAGES *change from excited interest to dismay.*]

FIRST PAGE: They're coming up here! [*They back away a little from the railing.*] Let's go. Quick!
 [*They go out as* MOWBRAY *and* HENRY, *flushed and furious, come up from the hall, followed immediately by*

LANCASTER *and* RUTLAND, *who are endeavouring to keep them apart.*]

MOWBRAY: Call me a traitor, would you! Liar that you are! What are you trying to do? Spoil my standing with the King? You can't do it, let me tell you. The King is my friend.

HENRY: You'll find out how much your friend he is if I tell a tale or two.

MOWBRAY: Do you think he'd believe your lies? When did he ever trust you, Henry? If you weren't Lancaster's son he wouldn't even tolerate you.

HENRY: And you think he trusts you, you turncoat? Well, try him. Just try him.

LANCASTER: Are you crazy, Henry, to stir up trouble in this way?

HENRY: It was Mowbray who stirred it, not I!

[*Enter the* KING.]

RICHARD: What is the meaning of this? You may not love each other as old allies should, but must you brawl in public, and under my roof?

LANCASTER [*in great anxiety*]: Take no notice, sir. They have both drunk more than is good for them. They don't know what — —

MOWBRAY: Do you suggest that I am drunk? I am sober enough to know that your son has accused me of plotting against the King. Is Henry going to take refuge behind the excuse that he is drunk, or is he going to answer my challenge and fight like a gentleman?

HENRY: Of course I am going to fight! When and where you please. You cannot call me a liar and go unharmed for it.

RICHARD: Will someone explain?

HENRY: Yes, sir. I'll explain. We were riding up from Brentford together about a month ago, and your faithful servant Mowbray tried to persuade me that you had never for-

M

given either of us, and that our best course was to band together for our common protection.

MOWBRAY: You lie! It was you who made that suggestion. Why should I say a thing like that? I am Earl Marshal of England and the King is my friend. You are a liar, Henry.

[*He strikes him deliberately across the face with his glove.*]

HENRY: And you are both a liar and a hypocrite.

[*He picks up the glove.*]

LANCASTER: Henry, for God's sake, don't! You are digging your own grave.

RICHARD: A charming scene! And so you fight, do you?

LANCASTER: Forbid them, sir. There is no need to take an evening quarrel so seriously.

RICHARD: You think not? But it was not tonight that the conversation they speak of took place. They both admit that there was such a conversation. Their quarrel is merely who said what. If they choose to fight, let them. Why should I prevent it?

LANCASTER: For your own fair name, sir.

RICHARD: For my name! How does it concern me?

LANCASTER: It concerns you because such a fight can have but one result. You, and I, and everyone else, know that Mowbray can beat my son. If you let this matter be decided by a duel, it will be said that you arranged the affair.

RICHARD: All my life rumour has flayed me; my skin has grown hardened.

HENRY [*to* LANCASTER]: How dare you say that I cannot beat Mowbray!

LANCASTER: You know very well that you have never beaten Mowbray in the lists since you grew up.

RICHARD: It is some time since they were matched.

LANCASTER: You are determined to have this fight?

RICHARD: If they do not fight, what is the alternative?

LANCASTER: The alternative is to overlook what is merely

an evening quarrel occasioned by too much wine and the consciousness of old enmity.

RICHARD: Old alliance, you mean, surely? Come, Lancaster, you know that these two are as sober as you or I. They are quite seriously accusing each other of a grave offence against peace and honour. If they want to fight, I shall do nothing to prevent it. This thing must have an issue. You must see that. I will have neither my Court nor my country turned into a bear-garden when it seems good to my subjects. There must be an end to this bickering. That is all, my lords.

[MOWBRAY *and* HENRY *go out, but* LANCASTER *lingers.*]

Well, old friend and enemy? What is it now?

LANCASTER: You know very well, Richard. I forgave you for what you did to Gloucester, because it was, in a way, a just retribution; although it was iniquitous that you should have been the means of it. But this is wanton. Henry may have harmed you once – –

RICHARD: You think he would not harm me again? Well, perhaps not. But do you seriously think that I set Mowbray on to this?

LANCASTER: I know you didn't. Chance has delivered them both into your hands.

[RICHARD *looks suddenly and intently at* LANCASTER.]

RICHARD [*after a pause*]: You are a clever man, Lancaster.

LANCASTER: It doesn't matter to me what you intend to do with Mowbray. All that concerns me is that he will kill my son if they are allowed to fight.

RICHARD: You don't flatter Henry. It was tactless of you to decry his fighting powers. He is very vain of his talent in that respect.

LANCASTER: You never liked Henry much, did you, Richard?

RICHARD: No, he was such a show-off when he was small, and he never grew out of it.

LANCASTER: Yes. He is not very lovable. A solid person;

stupid, a little – but dependable. It is a type that the English-man admires and understands, though, Richard. You would do well to be careful.

RICHARD: Is this a threat?

LANCASTER: My dear Richard, have I ever threatened you, even when I was in a position to do so? And just now I am a suppliant, not an overlord. I am merely warning you of what the consequences may be; a little because there are many things in you that I like and admire, but mostly because my son is in danger. I neither like nor admire my son particularly, but he is my *son*. Richard, if I have ever served you well in times when you needed service greatly, remember it now and forbid this duel.

RICHARD: You have certainly served me well, and I have always acknowledged it.

LANCASTER: Your gifts have been princely, I know. I have been well recompensed. You do not have to remind me. But I have never *begged* for anything before.

RICHARD [*after a pause*]: The alternative is exile. Ten years' exile.

LANCASTER: Ten years! It is a reprieve for Henry, but not for me. I am not as young as I was, and my health – – Ten years – – [*He considers.*]

RICHARD [*conversationally*]: Mowbray goes for life.

LANCASTER [*astounded*]: For life! [*A pause.*] I see. You have a long memory, Richard.

RICHARD: An excellent memory.

LANCASTER: But ten years' exile for Henry punishes me more than Henry.

RICHARD: Very well, we shall make it six. That will be no hardship for anyone that I can see. Henry is more often out of England than in it.

LANCASTER: Thank you. That may be still too long for me, but I cannot complain. Henry has put himself in the wrong, and you have taken your chance. I wish you could have found it in your heart to be generous over this, Richard; to have overlooked the whole thing.

RICHARD: There is no question of either generosity or the reverse when one pays debts.

LANCASTER: Anne might have counselled generosity.

RICHARD [*furious*]: Be quiet! How dare you, Lancaster? Even you cannot say that to me.

LANCASTER: I beg your pardon.

[*Enter a* PAGE.]

PAGE: The Earl of Derby and the Earl of Nottingham wish the King's approval of the day they have chosen for the contest.

RICHARD: Are Lord Derby and Lord Nottingham still in the palace?

PAGE: They are in the ante-room, sir.

RICHARD: Ask them to come here.

[*Exit* PAGE.]

LANCASTER: I am sorry, Richard. I shouldn't have said that.

RICHARD [*still in pain*]: No.

[*Enter* MOWBRAY *and* HENRY.]

I have decided that such a duel as you contemplate will have a bad effect both in London and in the country generally. I forbid it.

BOTH: But, sir – – !

RICHARD: That is enough. I forbid it. But do not imagine that I am going to put up with your factiousness. There will be no peace for anyone while either of you is still in this country. I am sending you both abroad. You, Henry, will leave England for six years. And you, Mowbray [MOWBRAY *allows a faintly conspiratorial smile to appear*], will leave England and never come back. [MOWBRAY'S *smile vanishes in puzzlement.*]

[HENRY *is about to burst into protest, but* LANCASTER *restrains him.*]

Nothing but my generosity restrains me from arraigning

you both before a court of law, when your fates would probably be inconceivably harsher. You may go now. I shall expect you both to take formal leave of me before you depart from England. Lancaster, you will be responsible for your son's acceptance of his punishment.

LANCASTER: I will. If you will permit me, sir, I too will take leave of you now.

RICHARD: Take leave? Where are you going?

LANCASTER: At my age the life of Courts is upsetting. I think a quiet existence at one of my manors will be more greatly to my mind in future.

RICHARD: Very well. Let it be as you please. When you want to come to Court you know that you will be welcome.

[LANCASTER *takes his leave and goes out with* HENRY, *but* MOWBRAY *lingers.*]

Well, my dear Thomas, have you grown roots?

MOWBRAY: Richard, you were bluffing, weren't you? What do you really mean me to do?

RICHARD: I thought that I had made that perfectly plain. As soon as you have settled your estates to your satisfaction, you leave England for good.

MOWBRAY: But you can't mean that, Richard! You can't! What have I done? Because Henry and I quarrelled is surely no reason to punish me? I've been your friend for years now. You can't believe the things he said. You can't believe that I plotted against you. Haven't I been your right hand? Didn't I help you with Gloucester? Didn't I?

RICHARD: And who more appropriate?

MOWBRAY: What do you mean? I don't understand you, Richard. Is a sentence of exile to be my reward? Indefinite exile! Think of it! To leave everything I have in England, and not know whether I shall ever see it again! It's unthinkable.

RICHARD: You thought it a very happy fate for Robert de Vere.

MOWBRAY: Robert de Vere! [*A pause.*] Oh! [*There is in the half-whispered exclamation a whole world of understanding and despair.*]

RICHARD: There are surely worse fates than exile, my friend. Simon Burley – you remember him? a charming old man – died on Tower Hill, an ugly death. And Archbishop Neville, you knew him; he starved to death in a country parish. And there was Bramber, and Tressillian – – But why go on? It is a depressing subject. Beside such fates as these, a well-to-do exile seems almost happy, doesn't it? You have your fortune, and the world is yours to choose from; you have little to complain of, it seems to me. [*As* MOWBRAY *says nothing*] Well, are you dumb as well as rooted?

MOWBRAY: You take my breath away.

RICHARD: No, no. That is just what I am pointing out. You may breathe until you die of old age, in any country in the world but England. Give thanks to God, Thomas Mowbray, and take your luck as it comes. You have never known what it was to suffer misfortune. All your life you have been friends with the party in power. You could hardly expect such luck to last for ever!

MOWBRAY: So you never trusted me, Richard.

RICHARD [*preparing to go*]: My dear Thomas, the only persons I trust are two thousand archers, paid regularly every Friday. [*Exit.*]

CURTAIN

SCENE 5

A room in the lodgings of the EARL OF DERBY, *in Paris, three years later.*

The table is strewn with small pieces of armour which HENRY, *humming tunelessly, is engaged in polishing. Among the armour is a flask of wine.*

At the moment he is burnishing a gauntlet, con amore.

Enter a PAGE.

HENRY: Well? [*Exhibiting the gauntlet*] There's what I call a polish. That's what my gauntlets should look like, you young sluggard! [*Dabbing a forefinger at the joints*] No rust in the hinges and [*flexing his fingers*] a shine on the fingers that blinds the other fellow when your hand moves. See? Well, what do you want?

PAGE: A kind of priest person has arrived in Paris to see Lord Derby. He says he comes from England.

HENRY: From England, eh? Let him come in.

PAGE: He is very shabby, sir. Had I better ask him his business?

[ARUNDEL, ARCHBISHOP OF CANTERBURY, *appears behind the* PAGE.]

CANTERBURY: Forgive my intrusion, my lord. I feared to entrust my credentials to your page, and my habit is not – reassuring.

HENRY [*peering at him*]: Well, I'm – – ! [*He motions to the* PAGE, *who goes out.*] Canterbury! My dear Archbishop! 'A sort of priest person!' [*He laughs.*] What are you doing in France, and in that get-up? Are *you* on pilgrimage?

CANTERBURY: Only to you, my lord.

HENRY: Since when has Henry Derby been a saint!

CANTERBURY: I am not so much a pilgrim as an ambassador.

HENRY: Ambassadors are sent to princes, my lord, not to poor exiles.

CANTERBURY [*glancing round*]: Your exile, I am delighted to observe, appears not too greatly uncomfortable.

HENRY: Not bad, not bad. It would have been more comfortable if I could have married the Duke of Berry's daughter. Richard was a dog in the manger to object to that.

CANTERBURY: When the King sent you into exile it was no part of his plan that you should make yourself popular in France.

HENRY: What did he expect me to do? Die of the sulks like Thomas Mowbray? They give you very good hunting in France.

CANTERBURY: The King has always looked upon France as his own preserve.

HENRY: Yes, I suppose he would have had me turned out of France too, if my father didn't happen to be Duke of Lancaster.

CANTERBURY [*after a pause*]: My lord, you – are the Duke of Lancaster.

HENRY: Do you – – Is my father dead?

CANTERBURY: That is what I came to tell you.

HENRY [*after a pause*]: We didn't always see eye to eye, you know. [*Another pause.*] He had a fine seat on a horse. So you *are* an ambassador! But why did Richard choose you?

CANTERBURY: I do not come from the King, my lord. I represent all those persons with whom you have been corresponding in England. [*As* HENRY *moves abruptly*] Don't be alarmed, my lord. Your cause is mine.

HENRY [*heartily and quite without irony, as one sufferer to another*]: Yes, I heard that he had dismissed you.

CANTERBURY: You do not rate my motives very highly.

HENRY: I'm a practical man, my lord.

CANTERBURY [*with a little bow*]: I shall endeavour to keep the conversation at a practical level. The King says that you shall stay in exile. I am here to suggest that you return to England.

HENRY [*playing with a gauntlet*]: It is a very kind suggestion, but the King has ten thousand excellent reasons against it.

CANTERBURY: The King is going to Ireland.

HENRY: Oh? More feasts to the charming Irish?

CANTERBURY: No. This time it is a visit of retribution.

HENRY: Oh, have the Irish been misbehaving again?

CANTERBURY: Very gravely. They have killed Roger Mortimer.

[*The hand which is playing with the gauntlet is suddenly still.*]

HENRY [*after a pause*]: It was tactless of them to kill the King's heir. So Richard is going to Ireland?

CANTERBURY [*watching the hand*]: Yes. He is taking all the available troops with him.

HENRY [*with an effort at lightness*]: An expensive expedition!

CANTERBURY: Very. But the Lancaster estates are to provide the expenses.

HENRY [*throwing down the gauntlet*]: No! No! After his promises to my father? He wouldn't dare. What excuse has he?

CANTERBURY: His excuse is that he promised for Lancaster's peace of mind. And that, he says, is now assured.

HENRY: I always despised Richard, but I didn't think him capable of *this* iniquity.

CANTERBURY: Say, rather, of this folly.

HENRY: Folly?

CANTERBURY: To make you from a mere exile into a martyr. No wrong rouses your Englishman to such sympathy as disinheritance. The King has committed in his time many follies, but this is – stupidity!

HENRY [*slowly*]: Yes, it *is* – stupidity. [*Puzzled, almost inquiring*] He used not to be stupid.

CANTERBURY [*thoughtlessly*]: So even you see that?

HENRY: Even I?

CANTERBURY [*amending*]: After some years of exile. You realize the change. What is destroying Richard, my lord, is something more potent than his enemies. Success. Remember this, Henry Lancaster, in days to come: it is not the possession of power that offends the multitude but the flaunting of it. You may have all earth for your footstool if you refrain from – prodding it with your toe.

HENRY: So Richard has overreached himself.

CANTERBURY: Yes, the people look askance. He takes no one's life, but everyone's peace of mind. He holds England in his two hands and laughs like a wicked child, and men pause and hold their breath, not knowing what he may do with his toy. They hope that someone may rescue it before it is too late. Do you come back to England, my lord?

HENRY: I should like to be sure of my welcome.

CANTERBURY: I bring you the promise of two thousand men at the moment you land, and ten thousand volunteers will be yours in a week.

HENRY: Promises are cheap.

CANTERBURY [*producing a document*]: Promises, as you say, are – easy. But what a man puts his hand to he is usually ready to fulfil.

HENRY [*glancing down the list of signatures*]: But I have never written to – – Some of these are Richard's friends.

CANTERBURY: He owes money to all of them, and they begin to lose hope. They think that you may collect for them – with interest.

HENRY: For services rendered. I see.

CANTERBURY [*as HENRY appears lost in thought*]: Well, my lord?

HENRY: My father – did he send me any message?

CANTERBURY: The messengers from your father are half a day behind me.

HENRY: We didn't always see eye to eye, you know. It's a

funny world, isn't it! We belonged to the wrong fathers, Richard and I. In his heart, you know, Lancaster always liked Richard better than he did me. (*Ignoring* CANTERBURY'S *protest*] They talked the same language.

CANTERBURY: You certainly should have been the Black Prince's son; a soldier, a man to stir the nation's sleeping pride. But it is not yet too late for you to save England's prestige. If you come back with me now, my lord, there is a great future in front of you.

HENRY: If I come back with you now, it is to claim my estates.

CANTERBURY: Yes, yes. That is understood. And whatever greatness the future may hold for you, you will owe to the fact that your cause was just.

HENRY: To the fact that Richard was foolish, you mean. [*He pours out two glasses of wine.*]

CANTERBURY [*as* HENRY *pushes a glass across to him*]: Well, my lord?

HENRY [*giving him a toast*]: To the folly of princes!

CURTAIN

SCENE 6

A room in Conway Castle, six months later. SIR JOHN MONTAGUE, *alone.*

[*Enter* MAUDELYN, *as if from a journey.*]

MAUDELYN: Sir John! He's here, sir. Aren't you coming down? [MONTAGUE *takes no notice. He appears to be sunk in a stupor.*] Sir John!

MONTAGUE: Oh, God, I wish I were dead!

MAUDELYN: But it's the King, sir.

MONTAGUE: I know, I know.

MAUDELYN: But there's no one here to welcome him but you, sir. You must come down! Please, sir! We've been travelling since dawn, and he is tired and hungry.

[*Enter* RICHARD, *alone.*]

RICHARD [*amiably*]: Well, my friend, are things so bad that you haven't even a greeting for me?

[*Exit* MAUDELYN.]

MONTAGUE: Oh, God, I wish I were dead. I've failed, Richard.

RICHARD: So it would seem. I have come all the way north through Wales without seeing a single man wearing the White Hart. All the more reason that I should see at least one on the doorstep of Conway. Come, John, pull yourself together and tell me. What has become of the Cheshire men I sent you from Ireland to raise?

MONTAGUE: I did raise them – quite a likely looking lot. And because Henry was coming north fast, I took them into Wales, to march south through the mountains to meet you and the Irish army. Bristol way, somewhere. But Chester surrendered to Henry, and when my Cheshire lot heard that they just melted away. Deserted in bands of twenty and thirty at a time. I am left with only my own men.

RICHARD: Poor John! And so you have been holding your head for a week, wondering how you were going to tell me. Cheer up, you've told me, and I haven't exploded. Things aren't hopeless yet, you know. There is still the Irish army. I left it with Edward at Bristol. I thought that I should be happier with my own Cheshire men. We shall go south and join them as soon as you have given me the meal which you haven't yet offered me.

MONTAGUE: But – there isn't any Irish army.

RICHARD: What do you mean?

MONTAGUE: They've gone over to Henry.

RICHARD: The men I had in Ireland! But Rutland! Edward? He had twenty thousand men when I left him.

MONTAGUE: He sent a messenger to say that there was nothing for it but surrender. It would have been useless to fight, he said; the men had no heart for it.

RICHARD: Yes; that has a familiar sound. It is a fatal thing to be my friend, isn't it?

MONTAGUE [*with more generosity than conviction*]: You can't blame Edward altogether. York had been forced to give way, and he just followed his father's example.

RICHARD: I don't blame him. Why should I? And so we have no army?

MONTAGUE: No. I have scoured all the Welsh fortresses – Flint, and Holt, and Beaumaris – but there is no help there.

RICHARD: No help anywhere, it seems. There is one thing you haven't done, John.

MONTAGUE: What!

RICHARD: You haven't said: 'I told you so.' It was a mistake to twist Henry's tail any further.

MONTAGUE: Why did you, Richard?

RICHARD: Oh, I don't know. What does it matter now? This looks like the end.

MONTAGUE: You take it very calmly.

RICHARD: I am so tired. My life has lost direction, John; and I have no longer anything for compass. We had a vision once – Anne and I. We made it come true, too; as near as visions may be true. And then Anne – – But for me there was still a purpose; a debt to pay. The prospect of that payment filled the years for me. And in the end I paid it. [*Under his breath*] Gloucester, Arundel, Mowbray, Henry. It is intoxicating to achieve one's purpose, John. There were times when I wanted to stop the very passer-by and say: 'I have done it! I have done what I set out to do!' It was so heady a draught that I may have drunk too deep, perhaps. [*Coming to the surface*] Sweet reason has not been my ruling characteristic these last months, has it? Oh, well. The only question that remains to us now is whether I go and surrender myself with all the dignity of our combined forces, or whether I sit at Conway like a snake-scared bird waiting to be taken. While we are discussing the momentous question, perhaps you will give me something to eat and drink? Wales may be picturesque, but it is a sorry – –

[*There is a noise of arrival outside. Enter* MAUDELYN.]

MAUDELYN: It's the Archbishop of Canterbury, sir.

RICHARD: Alone?

MAUDELYN: With only two followers.

RICHARD: A deputation from Henry! Let him come in.

[*Exit* MAUDELYN.]

I seem fated not to eat today. Oh, smile, John, smile, for God's sake. Is the approach of the Archbishop not sufficient gloom?

MONTAGUE: What do you think – – [*He has not sufficient courage to finish 'he has come to say'.*]

RICHARD: I think that it *would* be Arundel's brother who came on a mission like this.

[*Enter* MAUDELYN *with the* ARCHBISHOP, *and two followers.*]

Good day, my lord.

CANTERBURY: Good day, sir. I come on rather an unhappy mission, and since I am an ambassador I trust that you will treat all that I have to say as the utterance of another, made through my mouth. I come, in fact, from your cousin Henry.

RICHARD: I fail to see that you should apologize for that. Being ambassador *for* Henry is not worse than being ambassador *to* him. You were the person who went into France to invite him to England, weren't you?

CANTERBURY: I was, sir, I was. But there again I went as the ambassador of the English people, and not in any personal capacity.

RICHARD: My poor Archbishop! It must be a sad fate never to have the chance of speaking for oneself. But speak for

Henry, and we shall take care to blame Henry for all the impertinences.

CANTERBURY: The Duke of Lancaster, sir – –

RICHARD: Who! Oh, yes – Henry. Go on.

CANTERBURY: The Duke of Lancaster, sir, would have you know that he has come into England, not wantonly, to stir up trouble, but at the request of influential nobles and with the consent and approbation of the common people and of all law-abiding citizens, to ensure that this country shall be better governed than it has been for the last twenty years.

[MONTAGUE *moves impulsively, but* RICHARD *restrains him.*]

RICHARD: Go on, my lord.

CANTERBURY: The Duke of Lancaster has no desire for war, and if you, sir, are willing to surrender your person to him he undertakes that no harm shall befall you while in his care.

MONTAGUE: What guarantee have we of that?

CANTERBURY: The Duke of Lancaster suggests that the King should accompany me and my two servants, along with his own household and retainers, to Flint, and from there ride with the Duke and the other nobles, honourably and openly to London.

MONTAGUE [*whose attention has been called by* MAUDELYN *to something beyond the window*]: You say you came here alone from Flint with only two followers?

CANTERBURY: With only the two who await me now.

MONTAGUE [*pointing out of the window*]: And what are these, then, may I ask? What are these?

CANTERBURY: These what? [*At* MONTAGUE'S *tone*] Really, Montague!

MONTAGUE: These points of light among the trees?

CANTERBURY: I really don't know. The sun is shining on something bright, I expect.

MONTAGUE: Yes, on something bright! Do you think we are

fools? That is the sun shining on helmets and spear-points. You and your two followers!

RICHARD: Come, come, Montague. Let us not be hasty. We can hardly accuse the Archbishop, who is not only an ambassador, but a holy man of God, of deliberately concealing the truth. We must accept his word for it that the points of light are merely – points of light, my lord?

MAUDELYN: Don't, sir, don't! You are walking into a trap.

RICHARD: Fie on you both! Have we not the ambassador's word that we ride honourably and openly to London?

CANTERBURY [*uneasily*]: I am merely delivering the message with which I was entrusted, sir.

RICHARD: You have made that amply clear. Am I allowed to make conditions?

CANTERBURY: I am to use my own discretion.

RICHARD: What! So much licence to a mere mouthpiece! Well, let us be thankful for it. My only condition in giving myself up to my cousin is that safe conduct will be granted to my friend, Sir John Montague, and my secretary, John Maudelyn. That they shall be free to come and go as they will. No rides to London, honourable or otherwise, for them.

[*The others protest that they are going with him in any case, but he motions them to silence.*]

Well, my lord?

CANTERBURY: I think I may say that that will be granted.

RICHARD [*sharply*]: Don't think! I want an answer to that. It is to be your word for their safety.

CANTERBURY: Then I give you my word, sir.

RICHARD: There is one other matter. I want a promise that the Queen's household at Windsor will remain unchanged for the moment. That the attendants and friends that she knows may be allowed to remain with her, and that she shall be in no way disturbed or frightened.

CANTERBURY: Sir, we should never dream – –

RICHARD: Will you give me an answer? Is the Queen to be left unmolested? Do you promise that?

CANTERBURY: Certainly, sir, with all my heart.

RICHARD: Then we shall ride with you to meet Henry. But first I hope you will join us in a meal.

CANTERBURY: I'm afraid there will not be time for a meal.

RICHARD: Time!

CANTERBURY: It is advisable that we travel by daylight.

RICHARD: What are you afraid of? [*Bitterly*] My armies? [*As* CANTERBURY *does not answer*] Be assured, my lord. I shall ride with you to meet my cousin. But I have no mind to go fasting.

CANTERBURY: I very much regret – – Perhaps you can eat as you go. We must set out at once.

RICHARD [*indignantly*]: Must! [*Recovering*] I see. May the King invite his grace of Canterbury to drink with him? Maudelyn, bring some wine. [*Exit* MAUDELYN.] Perhaps, after all, you are right, my lord, in so firmly refusing our hospitality. Judging entirely by appearances I suspect that Sir John's larder will not come up to Lambeth standards. But his cellar is always good. That was a good wine you gave us last year. A little light, perhaps, but very fragrant. Italian, was it?

CANTERBURY: I – I don't remember.

RICHARD: But you shouldn't have served it in those goblets, you know. Delightful cups they were – a benediction to the eye – but so bad for the wine! Your small talk is not as good as usual, my lord.

[*Enter* MAUDELYN *with three cups of wine. He offers the tray to the King.*]

[RICHARD *is automatically about to take his cup when he pauses.*]

RICHARD: Let the Archbishop choose his.

CANTERBURY [*stiffly*]: I hope you don't think, sir, that – –

RICHARD: You are still my guest, my lord, and as a good

host it would pain me to force upon you something which all your life you have so signally avoided.

CANTERBURY: What is that, sir?

RICHARD: A risk. What shall we drink to? Let me give you – My cousin, your master.

[CANTERBURY, *after a moment's surprise, drinks.* MAUDE-LYN *puts down his cup, untouched.*]

CANTERBURY: It was not a fortunate toast, sir.

RICHARD: Why not?

CANTERBURY: Canterbury has no master who is not king. Shall we go?

RICHARD: Tell them to saddle the horses again, Maudelyn.

[*Exit* MAUDELYN.]

CANTERBURY [*as* RICHARD *makes no movement*]: Will you make ready, sir?

RICHARD: I have lost my wardrobe. You will not have to wait even for that.

[*He turns to the door.*]

CURTAIN

SCENE 7

A room in the Tower of London, a month later. RICHARD, *alone, with a tray of food, untouched, beside him.*

[*Enter* MAUDELYN.]

MAUDELYN: You haven't touched your food, sir.

RICHARD [*amiably*]: I'm not hungry, Maudelyn. And it is hardly the kind of food to stimulate appetite, is it?

MAUDELYN: No, it isn't very pleasant, sir. I'm sorry. I did protest when they gave it to me, but – –

RICHARD: Don't protest. Maudelyn, for heaven's sake. I don't want you to get into trouble. It would be dreadful if they took my last friend from me. How does it feel to be butler, body-servant, nursemaid, and bottle-washer, as well as secretary?

MAUDELYN: I like it, sir. If the circumstances were happier, there is no fate I should like better.

RICHARD: You may even have to mend my clothes, presently. Look at these shoes. To lose one's kingdom may be humbling, but to be down at heel is utter humiliation. I had no idea that when you had only one set of clothes they wore out so quickly. [*Rising*] Ah, I'm stiff yet. Riding that awful little pony was as bad as riding a fence. It was like Henry to think of that pony. Even his revenges lack vision. A tradesman, Henry. Did you see him as we came through London? He ducked his head to each blessing like a street singer catching coins in a hat. I got no blessing. Did you hear what they called me? Traitor! It was a strange word to choose, surely?

MAUDELYN: Does it matter, sir, what the mob shouts?

RICHARD: It shouldn't, but it hurts. They counted me a friend once. But I lost their friendship when I gave my other hand to France. They never quite forgave me that.

MAUDELYN: It made me sick at heart to look at them, and know that grown men should make such a rabble.

RICHARD: They are children, Maudelyn, such children; the sport of every knave with a glib tongue. They will go on being gulled; and beauty will go on being at their mercy. [*His eye lighting again on his shoes*] I might set a new fashion, of course; shoes with no toes. Would it be effective, do you think?

MAUDELYN: If you please, sir – –

RICHARD: Well, Maudelyn, what is it that requires so much effort to say? Do you want to leave me? Is that it?

MAUDELYN: Oh, no, sir! God forbid! It's just that – well, I

noticed your shoes, sir. And I thought, sir – – I have a spare pair that look a little better than these. If you would care – – [*He pauses.*]

RICHARD: If I should care! But don't be rash, Maudelyn. You don't know where your next pair of shoes is coming from.

MAUDELYN: They are not very beautiful, of course. If you would rather not – – I just thought – –

RICHARD: Maudelyn, I love you. Go and get the shoes before Henry comes.

MAUDELYN: I have them outside, sir. [*Picking up the tray, and carrying it to the door*] I brought them – well, just to be ready, in case – –

RICHARD [*gently*]: It was almost as difficult to tell me about the shoes as it was to tell me the news of Radcot Bridge, wasn't it?

MAUDELYN: Well, they're not very beautiful shoes, sir.

RICHARD: At any rate, I didn't hit you this time.

[MAUDELYN *puts the tray outside and comes back with the shoes.*]

MAUDELYN: You see, sir; they're very plain.

RICHARD: They are ravishing. You should get a principality for this, my friend.

[MAUDELYN *takes off the worn shoes and puts on the new ones.*]

Are you crying, Maudelyn?

MAUDELYN: No, sir, I have a cold.

RICHARD [*patting his shoulder*]: Get rid of it. [*Surveying the shoes*] Now you can tell them that I am ready to receive Henry, if it is convenient for him.

MAUDELYN: The Duke of Lancaster is not staying in the Tower, sir. He has gone to the Palace at Westminster.

RICHARD: So Henry has settled at Westminster? I'm afraid the decorations will be wasted on him.

MAUDELYN: They are expecting the Duke at any moment,

though, sir. At least, that is what it looked like. There was
a – –

RICHARD: An atmosphere. I know.

[*The door is flung open without warning and* HENRY *comes in,
followed by the* ARCHBISHOP OF CANTERBURY *and the*
DUKE OF YORK.]

I know that I am your prisoner, Henry. But it might have
been a little more graceful to announce your arrival. You
should learn from the Archbishop how to do an evil thing
gracefully. [*To* CANTERBURY] Good day, my lord. Are
you ambassador today, or do you for once represent the
Archbishop of Canterbury? [*To* YORK] Good day, my lord,
I am glad that your son is safe. Will you tell him so from
me?

YORK: You must believe me, Richard, when I say that all
this is inexpressibly painful for me.

RICHARD [*soothing*]: Yes, yes. It is a little painful for me, too.

YORK: In unprecedentedly difficult times I have done as it
seemed to me best for all. I hope that you will not blame
Edward, or me, for the course we have felt impelled to take.

RICHARD: I have said already that I am glad your son is safe,
and I mean what I say. It occurs to me to be glad, too, that
your son is safe, Henry. Rumour has never been kind to
me, but I shudder to think what it would have said if Lancaster's heir had not come safely back from Ireland.

HENRY: All this is beside the point.

RICHARD [*with an echo of* HENRY'S *manner*]: Yes, yes, let us
not waste time. To business, to business.

CANTERBURY: We have come, sir, bringing a formal deed
of abdication which, if you are still willing, we require you
to sign.

RICHARD: And if I am not willing? What then? Don't be
distressed, my lord; I shall sign. The cares of government I
shall turn over to my cousin with thankfulness. As to the
kingdom and the glory, I have had enough of them. [*He*

nods to HENRY, *as if he had spoken.*] Too much, perhaps, as you say. I may have been extravagant in my own household. But when they are financing your next war, Henry, they may remember my tournaments with regret. Well, let me see the deed.

[*The* ARCHBISHOP *lays the paper before him, and* RICHARD *scans it.*]

[*Slowly*] 'Insufficient and useless.' 'Unworthy to reign.' It is not a generous document, is it? 'Tyranny.' Have I been a tyrant? Curious I never thought of myself as a tyrant. At least no tyrant has shed less blood. Nor been so tolerant of others' modes and minds. I have never persecuted anyone for their own good. I leave that to you, Henry. What the towns will save in feasts to the King, they will spend on the burning of heretics. Have you a pen, Maudelyn?

MAUDELYN [*in a strangled voice*]: No, sir.

[RICHARD *looks up, surprised. His expression softens at sight of his servant's face.*]

CANTERBURY: I have one here, sir.

RICHARD: You have forgotten nothing, have you, my lord? [*He muses over the paper again.*] Henry, when I gave myself up to you in Wales, I made conditions which you accepted but saw fit not to keep.

HENRY: I have explained already that your guard was as much for your own safety against the people as from any motive of imprisonment.

RICHARD [*pityingly*]: You were never very ingenious, Henry. [*In his normal tones*] Before I sign this abdication I want to be reassured in the presence of these witnesses that the conditions will be carried out. That I shall be set free – strange as it may seem, life is still desirable [*he smiles faintly at that, as at a memory*] – that the Queen will not be further molested, and that I shall be granted an adequate livelihood. You agree to these three things on condition that I sign this paper?

HENRY: I agree.

RICHARD: And you, my lords?

YORK and CANTERBURY: We agree.

[RICHARD *signs the deed. The* ARCHBISHOP *takes the document into his keeping.*]

HENRY: I think it will be for your own safety if – –

RICHARD: What! More measures for my safety! What now?

HENRY: If you leave London for a time. I suggest that you go, with a suitable escort, to the north. Let us say to Pomfret Castle.

RICHARD [*in sudden fear*]: No!

CANTERBURY: I think you will find it more judicious to take the Duke of Lancaster's advice, sir.

RICHARD: No, I tell you! I shall leave London, yes. Do you think I want to experience again the hatred in the streets, the sneers, the lying accusations flung at me like mud? Yes, I shall leave London, but I will not leave it a prisoner. I know your suitable escorts, Henry. I suffered one all the way from Wales. I shall leave London with my friends, freely, as you promised.

HENRY: It does not suit us that you should join your friends in London.

CANTERBURY: You must see, sir, that trouble before the coronation is to be avoided at all costs.

RICHARD: I have no wish to make trouble. The best way to prevent it is to let me join my friends as soon as possible, otherwise they may plot to secure me a crown which I have freely given up.

HENRY: They may plot, but without your physical presence they will have no following. You would be well advised to go to the north for some time.

RICHARD: I shall go north in any case, but not under your escort. Why should I?

HENRY: Because you have no choice.

RICHARD [*after a long pause*]: I see. And you, my dear uncle, you agree to this?

YORK: I think you can trust Lancaster to do what is best, Richard. The situation is awkward, very awkward.

RICHARD: Very. [*Looking* HENRY *in the eyes*] But Lancaster will get rid of the awkwardness in due course, I have no doubt.

HENRY [*uneasy under the scrutiny*]: It will only be a matter of a few weeks, until things have settled down.

RICHARD: Would Maudelyn's presence in Pomfret be dangerous for me?

HENRY: I think it better that none of your friends should be with you just now.

MAUDELYN: But I must, I must! I go everywhere with the King.

HENRY: You can still go everywhere with the King. There is a place for you in my household.

MAUDELYN: I'd rather die. [*To* YORK] My lord, you know that I have been all my life with the King. Speak for me, please. Don't separate me from the King. Please! Speak for me!

RICHARD: Hush, Maudelyn. I don't want you to come. You can look after the Queen for me, now that they have taken her other friends from her. [*To* HENRY] Or would that perhaps be dangerous for someone?

HENRY: No, I see nothing against that.

MAUDELYN: But I want to be with you, sir. I must come with you.

RICHARD: Maudelyn, you are the only person left to whom I can say: 'I want this', and know that I shall have what I want. I want you to stay with the Queen at Windsor until – until I come back. I know that you would prefer to come with me, but I ask you to do this for me instead.

MAUDELYN: I can't, sir, I can't! If I let you go I may never see you again.

RICHARD: Even if you didn't you would know that you had done me a great service. That is something. You could do me no service at Pomfret.

MAUDELYN: I could be with you, sir.

RICHARD: I would rather that you were with the Queen.

CANTERBURY: I think, since our business is finished, and time presses – –

HENRY: Yes, we must take our leave. I shall ask Sir Thomas Swynford to escort you north tomorrow. If you like, I shall take Maudelyn with me now, and see that he is sent safely to Windsor tonight.

RICHARD: With a suitable escort?

HENRY: Safely.

RICHARD: Very well. You had better go, Maudelyn. [*Seeing* MAUDELYN'S *mutinous and despairing face*] Give us a moment, my lords. [*To* CANTERBURY *and* YORK] Good-bye, my lords.

YORK: We shall have you back very soon, Richard, very soon.

RICHARD: Do I see you again, Henry? No? That is a pity. I should have liked to see how a crown became you. Take care that your son does not steal it from you!

[*All go out but* RICHARD *and* MAUDELYN.]

MAUDELYN: How can you ask it of me, sir?

RICHARD: Is this mutiny?

MAUDELYN: You know that I can do nothing for the Queen! You think that I shall be safe at Windsor. That is why you want me to stay. And you will be all alone up there – all alone! I can't bear it, sir.

RICHARD: But you are wrong, quite wrong. I want you to be a companion to the Queen. She must be very lost among all the strange faces. Think of it, Maudelyn. Poor little foreigner! But tomorrow morning you go to see her, tell her that I am coming soon, and make her happy. You can do that for me, can't you?

MAUDELYN [*with difficulty*]: Yes, sir.

RICHARD: Good-bye, Maudelyn. I shall remember the shoes; and the night you came to light the candles. You have been a good friend to me. [*Someone calls outside.*] They are very impatient, with all time in front of them.

MAUDELYN [*trying to talk of ordinary things*]: Yes, they have to meet a committee of the Commons. One of the guard told me.

RICHARD [*also making conversation*]: Oh? Are the Commons going to vote Henry a fortune in consideration of his services to the country?

MAUDELYN: No, sir. The gifts he made to his followers were out of all reason, they say. They are complaining of his extravagance.

[*A radiant smile breaks on* RICHARD'*s tired face.*]

RICHARD: Extravagance! Isn't life amusing? [*There is an impatient knocking.*] Good-bye, Maudelyn. [MAUDELYN *kisses his hand fervently and almost runs out.* RICHARD *stares after him, stares at the empty room, and then slowly the amusement comes back to his face.*] Extravagance! [*He savours it.*] How Robert would have laughed!

CURTAIN

*The Penguin Shakespeare and
the Penguin Poets are described in the
next two pages*

THE PENGUIN SHAKESPEARE

Each of the thirty-four volumes of the Penguin Shakespeare includes a list of Shakespeare's works, a short biography of the poet, and an essay on the Elizabethan theatre, as well as an introduction to the play.

THE PENGUIN POETS

Each of these volumes of the Penguin Poets includes an introduction to the work of the poet concerned.

★ NOT FOR SALE IN THE U.S.A.
† NOT FOR SALE IN THE U.S.A. OR CANADA